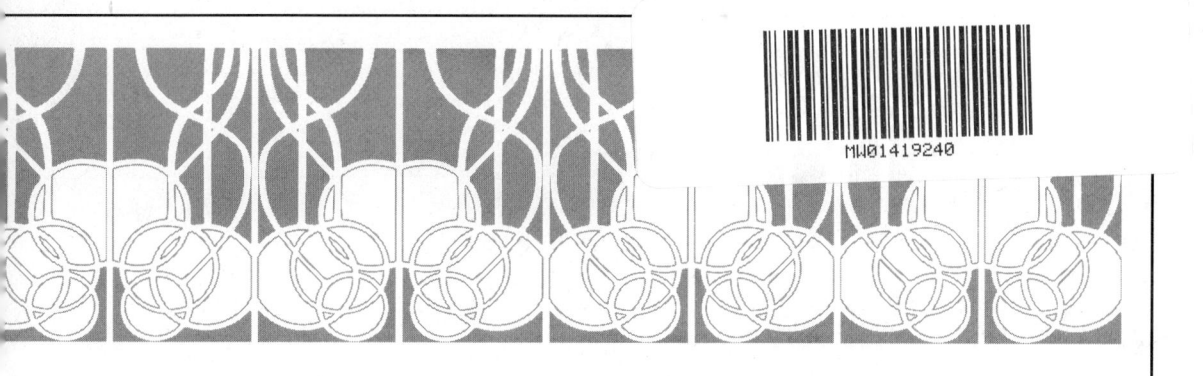

READING FIRST
BUILDING READING COMPETENCE

SUZANNE D. ROBERTSHAW • ROBERTA E. HAMBLEN • RICHARD FELDMAN
University of Central Florida   *Cornell University*

MAXWELL MACMILLAN
International Publishing Group

READING FIRST
BUILDING READING COMPETENCE

SECOND EDITION

Associate Director: Mary Jane Peluso
Editor: Maggie Barbieri
Production Supervision: Publication Services, Inc.
Text Design: William E. Frost Associates, Ltd.
Cover Design: Blake Logan
Cover illustration: Janie Paul

This book was set in 11/13 Else Light by Publication Services, Inc.
and printed and bound by Halliday Lithograph Corporation
The cover was printed by Phoenix Color Corp.

Library of Congress Cataloging-in-Publication Data

Robertshaw, Suzanne D.
  Reading first: building reading competence / Suzanne D. Robertshaw,
Roberta E. Hamblen, Richard Feldman.—2nd ed.
    p.   cm.
  ISBN 0-02-402111-3
  Includes index
  1. College readers. 2. English Language–Textbooks for foreign
speakers. I. Hamblen, Roberta E. II. Feldman, Richard
III. Title.
PE1417.R57 1990
428.6'4–dc20   89-27100
                                                                                                   CIP

Copyright © 1990 by Maxwell Macmillan International Publishing Group

All rights reserved. No part of this book may be reproduced or transmitted in any form or by any means,
electronic or mechanical, including photocopying, recording, or any information storage and retrieval
system, without permission in writing from the Publisher.

Earlier edition copyright © 1984 by Macmillan Publishing Company, a division of Macmillan, Inc.

Collier Macmillan Canada, Inc.

Printing: 1 2 3 4 5 6 7 Year: 0 1 2 3 4 5 6

Maxwell Macmillan International Publishing Group
866 Third Avenue
New York, NY 10022

Printed in the U.S.A.

ISBN 0-02-402111-3

The authors are indebted to the following persons and companies
for permission to reprint materials appearing in this text:

(Chapter 1) Reprinted by permission of Rollins College.
(Chapter 5) Adaption of outline, "Emotional Stress: Its Causes,
Effects and Resulting Behavior" from Chapter 10, in *Psychology,*
Third Edition, by Spencer A. Rathus, copyright © 1987 by Holt,
Rinehart and Winston, Inc., reprinted by permission of the publisher;
Copyright, Aug. 17, 1987, *U.S. News & World Report.*
(Chapter 6) From "Acid Rain," *Editorial Research Reports,* Vol. I,
No. 9, pp. 174–175; reprinted by permission of the publisher;
From *Editorial Research Reports Subject-Title Index,* January
1977–December 1987, p.1, reprinted by permission of the publisher.
(STRATEGIES: MINI-UNIT 1) From *Readers' Guide to Periodical
Literature,* September 1983, copyright ©1983 by the H.W. Wilson
Company; From *The American Tradition: A History of the United States,*
by R. Green, L. Becker, and R. Coviello, Copyright 1984, Merrill
Publishing Company, text reprinted by permission of the publisher.
(STRATEGIES: MINI-UNIT 2) From *The Wall Street Journal Index,* 1986,
reprinted by permission of the publisher; Copyright 1988 by The
New York Times Company, reprinted by permission; Copyright
1986 by The New York Times Company, reprinted by permission.

PHOTO CREDITS

Page 0–1: Photographs reprinted by permission of Cornell University.
Page 7: © Cornell University.
Page 16: Photograph reprinted by permission of Cornell University.
Page 22–23: Courtesy of Chris Schwartz.
Page 35: Photograph reprinted by permission of Cornell University.
Page 42–43: Photographs reprinted by permission of Cornell University.
Page 58: Photograph reprinted by permission of Cornell University.
Page 60: Photograph reprinted by permission of Cornell University.
Page 64–65: Photograph reprinted by permission of Cornell University.
Page 81: Courtesy of Chris Schwartz.
Page 90–91: Photographs reprinted by permission of Cornell University.
Page 96: Photograph reprinted by permission of Cornell University.
Page 118–119: © Cornell University.
Page 142–143: Courtesy of Eric Liebowitz.
Page 149: Courtesy of Eric Liebowitz.
Page 162–163: Courtesy of Maggie Barbieri (top photo on p. 162),
             Courtesy of Sona Doran (middle photo on p. 162),
             Courtesy of Eric Liebowitz (bottom photo on p. 163).
Page 180–181: Courtesy of Bettmann Archives.
Page 202–203: Photograph reprinted by permission of Cornell University.
Page 218–219: Courtesy of Sona Doran.
Page 225: Photograph reprinted by permission of Cornell University.
Page 242: S. Barnard, *View Along East Battery,* Courtesy of Yale University
         Art Gallery, Mabel Brady Garvan Collection.
      Courtesy of the Granger Collection, New York.
Page 243: Courtesy of U.S. Naval Academy Museum.

PREFACE

Reading First builds academic skills and cultural knowledge, two of the most urgent needs of students at the intermediate level in their study of English as a second language (ESL). First, this text systematically develops those reading and vocabulary skills that make academic ESL students independent, efficient readers. Second, it provides extensive structured pre-reading activities and readings that acquaint students with academic life at American universities. The readings also help students perform the everyday tasks that challenge nonnatives in a new environment.

Academic reading is varied and copious. If international students are to successfully complete course assignments in their academic field, they must have command of as many reading strategies as a native in order to compensate for lack of proficiency in other areas of language. To ease the transition from low-intermediate to advanced ESL student (and ultimately to matriculated student), we emphasize the following reading skills: predicting, both before and while reading; reading for the main idea and implications; distinguishing between fact and opinion; scanning for specific details; and skimming for the general idea.

Since the publication of the first edition of this textbook, there have appeared several intermediate-level textbooks that adequately deal with these reading strategies. Unfortunately, there has been no low-intermediate textbook that develops both knowledge of American culture and academic skills as this text now does. If advanced ESL students are to be expected to research and write term papers, it is important that **intermediate** students be introduced to reading longer texts, such as readings from college textbooks, as well as researching topics in a university library. Thus we have added the **Strategies** section, a reading component that systematically introduces and reinforces both surveying (skimming longer reading selections) and research skills.

Success in reading depends on the level of the reader's background knowledge. *Reading First* builds up this knowledge both through extensive pre-reading activities and through the numerous readings themselves. Questionnaires and surveys ask students to reflect on the cultural habits of everyone in the classroom, building a network of information about the topic from a global perspective. Photographs and drawings help students predict the content and vocabulary of the upcoming readings. The readings themselves are rich in information about the specific culture of an American university. Narrative readings revolve around an ongoing cast of characters who function as native models. Informative expository readings provide vital information for anyone embarking on an American college career in a wide range of prose styles.

Our major goal, to develop independent and efficient readers, is furthered by our emphasis on using the appropriate reading strategies for each particular reading task. Guessing the meaning of unknown words from context is one such strategy. Students using English for academic purposes will need to understand many words that they will rarely use otherwise. Accordingly, after the brainstorming discussion at the beginning of each chapter, students spend most of their time reading. As such, this text is ideally suited for a multiskill English program where the reading instructor is free to focus almost exclusively on the all-important reading task.

The eleven chapters, which are in order of increasing difficulty, are organized similarly: Each is composed of an extensive pre-reading discussion, one long reading, and three or more thematically related short readings. Applications of the reading skills to authentic academic texts are provided in the **Strategies** sections, which follow Chapters 1–6, and in two mini-units at the end of the book. All chapter readings, except those reviewing vocabulary, are preceded by **vocabulary in context** exercises, and followed by **comprehension questions**. Additional vocabulary exercises follow long readings and some short ones. Exercises designed to reinforce the various reading skills are provided both when the skill is introduced and in subsequent chapters.

Reading First has been tested in classrooms at the Intensive English Programs at both Cornell University and the University of Central Florida. Students' entry TOEFL scores ranged from 375 to 475, the majority of them falling between 400 and 450.

S. D. R.
R. E. M.
R. F.

READING SKILLS

College-bound ESL students must be prepared to read efficiently, yet we have found that they either avoid reading long, complicated selections or spend hours deciphering them with a dictionary, often inaccurately. Instead, students can and must be taught to bring appropriate "tools" to every task. We have therefore taught and exercised these reading skills in *Reading First*.

Predicting from titles, subtitles, illustrations, abstracts, and so forth, is an essential skill. Each chapter begins with an extensive pre-reading activity designed to cultivate this skill. Students investigate cultural perceptions of such topics as housing, time, money, and transportation through questionnaires and attitudinal surveys; photographs and drawings give students yet another tool to investigate cross-cultural differences. By paying attention to these differences, students learn to orient themselves to readings and avoid the gross mistakes in vocabulary interpretation sometimes made when they have no idea what a reading is about.

Scanning, or locating specific information quickly, is also an essential skill when the reader's goal is to find the answers to certain questions in the reading, without having to read every word, sentence, and paragraph. Students very often have such goals, and scanning is exercised in the text in real-life academic and practical contexts. Time is of the essence here, and the teacher must help the students approximate the speed at which successful American students work. Abundant practice in scanning throughout the text eventually culminates in scanning and then evaluating entries from a periodical index in the **Research Mini-Unit** at the end of the book.

Another common reading goal is identifying the **main idea** of a passage. Main idea questions are included with many of the expository readings in the text. This gives students ongoing practice in distinguishing the main idea from its supporting points, be they major or minor details.

Finding the main idea is often the goal of a student evaluating a text to determine its relevance and whether or not it should be read carefully. Because **skimming** is frequently used to find the main idea, these two skills are introduced together in Chapter 5. Students must learn as quickly as possible that reading is not a process of building up from nothing, letter by letter and word by word. By becoming aware of what they already know, and by understanding and using the structure of texts in American English, they become efficient readers. Six skimming activities culminate in the extended exercise in the **Surveying Mini-Unit**. Here students will find they can understand an entire chapter by using extensions of practiced skimming skills.

Distinguishing between **fact and opinion** is vital for critical reading. Opinion interpreted as fact can lead to the blind acceptance of ideas, while a more critical approach enables readers to disagree when relevant. *Reading First* also asks students to search out **implications** in more than twenty-five readings, starting in Chapter 4. The aim is to get students into the habit of making explicit that which is implicit in a text.

It should be noted that in Chapters 1, 2, and 3 students are asked to state which line in which paragraph justifies their answers. This greatly enhances the students' ability to discuss their choices and compare them with those of other students. Once the habit is formed (after Chapter 3), we no longer ask them to write down this information, although teachers are urged to continue the practice.

VOCABULARY SKILLS

Reading First offers a variety of vocabulary exercises, including both traditional and more innovative formats. Most exercises ask students to choose the correct answer from a list of choices (multiple choice), thus taking advantage of the students' greater receptive or passive knowledge of English and providing further reading practice. Traditional exercises using **fill-ins** and **synonyms** are most likely familiar to the students from their native language reading and vocabulary textbooks. They are also useful as practice for the type of exercises used in standardized texts in the United States. Each chapter includes one or more **word form** exercises, which concentrate on word families, thus greatly enlarging the students' repertoires as well as reinforcing basic grammatical constraints.

Reading First features several types of innovative vocabulary exercises as well. In order to develop the readers' independence, the text relies heavily on **vocabulary in context** exercises to teach important words before each of the long and short readings. The students learn to guess the meaning of a word from its context in a story or other reading format.

Psycholinguistic research has shown that word recall is enhanced by acquiring vocabulary items in their natural environments, thus building up associative networks to speed up and ensure correct recall. Using this principle, we have included **word association** exercises that involve reading vocabulary words in real-life situations and determining how to apply them in new situations.

Finally, *Reading First* offers several explanations and exercises that deal with the effects certain aspects of the English language have on reading, notably **prefixes, suffixes** and **homonyms**.

STRATEGIES: READING SKILLS APPLIED TO ACADEMIC MATERIALS

The purpose of the **Strategies** sections is twofold: to give students practice in surveying, and in beginning research for term papers in the university library. Many ESL students in Amercan universities are enrolled either full-time or part-time in credit courses by the time they have obtained a 500 on the TOEFL exam, without necessarily having had any experience with reading long, academic texts or doing research with periodicals in the library. The reading activities in this section provide students with a solid foundation in these two areas.

Surveying a reading text is similar to skimming because it gives an overview. It is what good readers do automatically when examining something they are considering reading. In a long article, for example, they look at the title, subtitle, introduction, paragraph headings, any charts or graphs, and other visuals such as photographs. As a result, they have an outline of the author's ideas before reading carefully. They can use this structure to make predictions and then read to confirm what the major or minor details are. This information gives students control over what could otherwise be an intimidating reading selection.

Surveying skills are taught and exercised in the Strategies sections located at the end of each of the first six chapters, and culminate in the **Surveying Mini-Unit** at the end of the book. We have selected readings from three authentic textbooks (personal finance, psychology, and American history), as well as a university housing brochure, a syllabus, and an academic calendar. Students learn to use the organizational tools that the authors have devised (tables of contents, headings, outlines, charts, and graphs); they then go on to read certain sections from each of the three college textbooks intensively.

Doing research in the library can be both an exciting and intimidating task. Most college-bound ESL students are quite motivated by the prospect of using a university library. In fact, after being isolated in the ESL program, they often see it as a way of integrating themselves into regular university life before actually starting in a credit program. On the other hand, many students may have never used the type of reference materials found in American universities. The volume of materials available to them may be overwhelming. In **Strategies**, *Reading First* features three extensive research activities to both introduce students to the research process and motivate them in their studies. The two sections following Chapters 3 and 6 deal with finding information in the university library and using reference books to select a topic for a term paper. The **research mini-unit** takes the process further as students scan periodical and newspaper indexes to find relevant articles for their term papers.

HOMEWORK

Reading First offers sufficient reading tasks for both classroom and assignments. At first, the long readings with accompanying **vocabulary in context** exercises should be done in class. Since students are usually familiar with objective, gamelike exercises such as **fill-ins, word forms,** and **word associations,** all of these are appropriate for homework assignments from the beginning of the term. As skills develop, students can be assigned long readings as homework. Short readings and accompanying **vocabulary in context** exercises and **comprehension** exercises can be done in class or as homework assignments. It is recommended that **scanning, skimming**, and **vocabulary in context** exercises be done in class to ensure that students are using their heads instead of their dictionaries, and are not using more time than they should. In general, the teacher will want to introduce new types of reading skills and vocabulary exercises in class. The *Strategies* sections should be done mostly in class because of the importance of timing and sequencing.

ACKNOWLEDGMENTS

We would like to thank the following for their invaluable help in preparing this text: Elliot Judd of the University of Illinois in Chicago; Amy Sonka of Boston University; Benne Willerman of the University of Texas; Mary Ruetten of the University of New Orleans; Tim Robinson of St. Edwards University; Barry Taylor of the University of Pennsylvania; Richard Bier of Indiana University; Susan Anker of St. Martin's Press; Joel Brauser, Maggie Barbieri, and Betty Mirando of Macmillan Publishing Company; as well as Wayles Browne, Charles Rock, Walter Popp, Beth Feldman, and Marjean Stear (our illustrator), all from (or formerly from) Ithaca, New York. We would also like to thank Erik Beukenkamp of Cornell University, Consuelo Stebbins of the University of Central Florida, and the staff at the Grand Marais (Minnesota) Public Library for their institutional support in the development of this textbook.

CONTENTS

CONTENTS

1 Housing	**1**
Moving In	7
The Apartment	11
The House	13
The Sorority	16
STRATEGIES: A Brochure from a University Housing Office	19
2 Money	**22**
At the Bank	29
Cashing a Check	34
Working	35
STRATEGIES: A College Personal Finance Textbook	38
3 Studying	**42**
Advice to Freshmen	50
Problems With Chemistry	56
Take My Advice	57
STRATEGIES: Library Research for the Term Paper	60
4 Time	**64**
Time for Dinner	69
It's Earlier Than You Think!	80
Clocks and Watches	81
STRATEGIES: Academic Schedules, Calendars, and Course Syllabi	83

5   Health — 90

At the Clinic	95
A Medicine Bottle Label	103
A Seminar Report	104
The High Cost of Health Care in the United States	106
Safety-Sealed Packaging	109
STRATEGIES: A College Psychology Textbook	111

6   Weather — 118

The Thunderstorm	123
A Weather Forecast	128
A Hard Job	131
Temperate Climates	133
Weather Forecasting	135
STRATEGIES: Preliminary Steps in Researching a Topic	136

7   Shopping — 142

At the Mall	149
Marketing Research	157
A Supermarket Special	159

8   Transportation — 162

Getting Home	168
Public Transportation	176
Getting to Gordon's House	178

9   Police — 180

Call the Police!	185
Parking	190
Furnell's Finest	194
The Crime Beat	200

10   Restaurants — 202

Don's Birthday Dinner	207
A Quick Lunch	213
Changing American Eating Habits	216

11   Driving — 218

Going Home	224
Traveling by Car	231
Cost-Saving Suggestions for Vacation Driving	233
Population Changes and Their Effects	236

STRATEGIES: MINI-UNIT 1: SURVEYING — 239

A History Textbook Chapter (Antebellum America) — 239

    Review of Surveying Skills — 239
    Surveying: Table of Contents — 242
            Complete Chapter — 244
    Chart Reading: Pie Chart Immigration, 1821–1860 — 248
            Bar Graph Slave owners — 249
    Careful Reading: Section Seven, *The Slave South* — 250

STRATEGIES: MINI-UNIT 2: RESEARCH — 253

Periodical and Newspaper Indexes in the Library — 253

    Reader's Guide to Periodical Literature — 253
    Wall Street Journal Index — 255
    New York Times Index — 256

A *New York Times* Article on Acid Rain — 259

    Surveying to Determine Relevance:
      "Sugar Maple Faces Extinction" — 260

VOCABULARY INDEX — 261

SUBJECT INDEX — 267

READING FIRST
BUILDING READING COMPETENCE

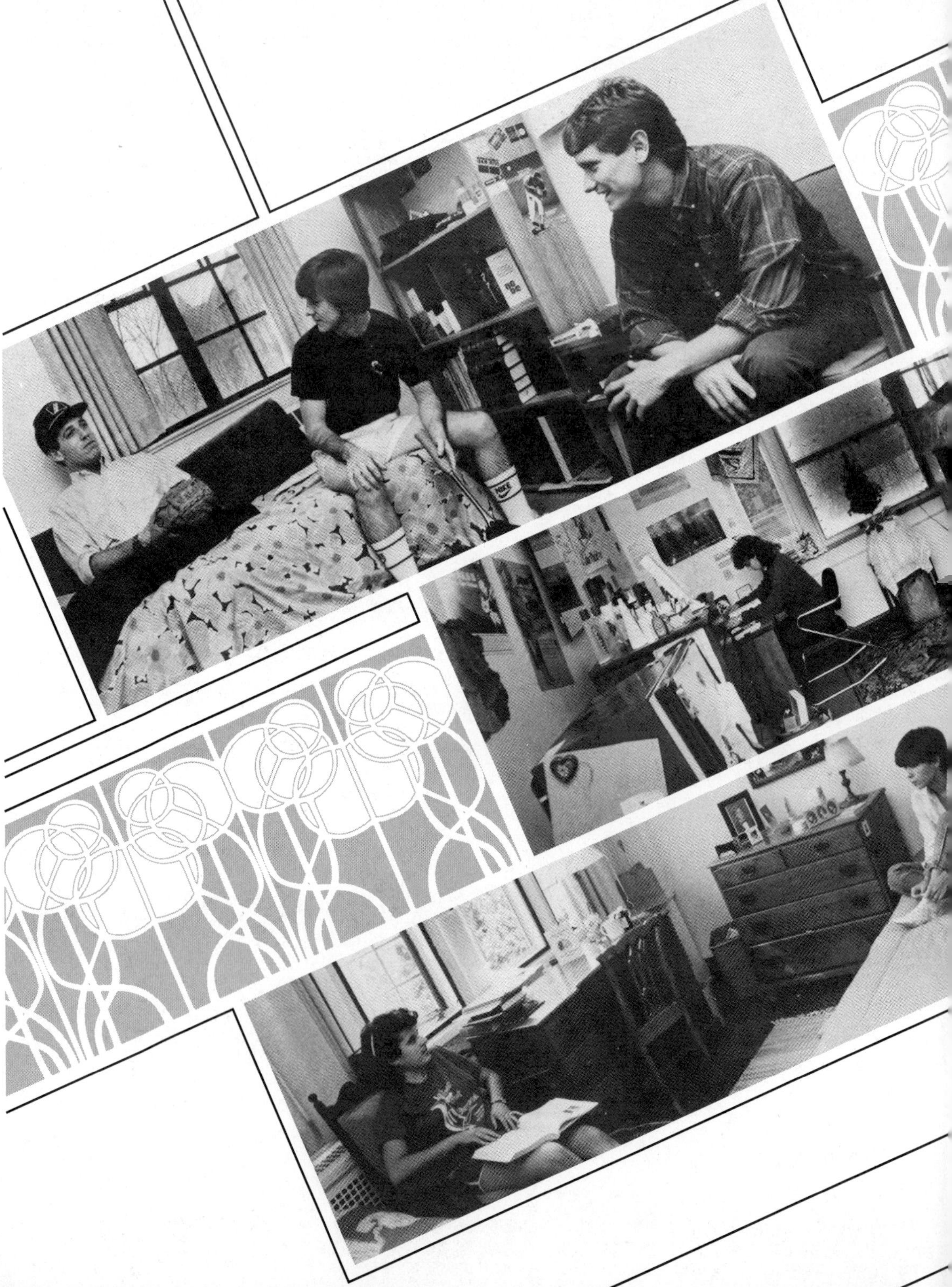
NIKE

CHAPTER ONE

HOUSING

HOUSING 3

PRE-READING EXERCISE

This chapter is about **housing**—where people live. Before reading the chapter, answer these questions about housing in your country and in the United States. Work with another person (a partner), and discuss the answers with your classmates.

1. Where do university students usually live in your country?

   _____ near from shool
   _____
   _____

2. How is student housing in your country different from the type of housing that is shown in these photographs of university dormitories? (ký túc xá)

   _____
   _____

3. What other types of housing do you know about for American university students?

   _____
   _____

4. Write down the advantages (good things) and disadvantages (bad things) about each type of housing below.

TYPE OF HOUSING	ADVANTAGES (có lợi)	DISADVANTAGES (≠ có lợi)
university dormitory		
apartment		
house with other students		
parents' or relatives' house		
another type of housing		

4   Chapter 1

5. Write down the advantages and disadvantages of living with Americans, and not people from your own country.

   Advantages ___ study more langugne ___

   Disadvantages ___ Disfferent culture, custome loud music ___

6. In your university, where can you go to get information about student housing? ___

7. Put a check (✔) by the topics below that will probably be in Chapter 1.

   ___ dormitories   ___ buses   ___ houses
   ___ cars   ___ police   ___ restaurants
   ___ apartments   ___ doctors   ___ moving
   ___ friends   ___ professors ___ music

A. VOCABULARY IN CONTEXT

When you are reading and you see a new word that you don't know, don't stop. Go on to the next sentence. Try to guess the meaning of the new word from the *context*. Context means all the words before and after the new word.

Read this short paragraph and the question after it, as an example.

The two women in this room are freshmen. It is their first year in college. The two men on the floor below were freshmen last year.

Look at the underlined word in the preceding paragraph. The word is used in the following example. Three sentences are wrong and one is right. Circle the correct meaning. For example:

A freshman is

a. a student who is a man.
b. a first-year college or university student.
c. a student who is a woman.
d. an American student.

Can (a), a student who is a man, be the answer? Why?
Can (b), a first-year college or university student, be the answer? Why?
Can (c), a student who is a woman, be the answer? Why?
Can (d), an American student, be the answer? Why?

HOUSING 5

A <u>freshman</u> is

a. a student who is a man.
b. a first-year college or university student. *(circled)*
c. a student who is a woman.
d. an American student.

What other words in the sentences helped you choose the correct answer?

Line ___1___   *their first year in college*

Now do the following exercises, circling the correct meaning or the best way to end the sentence.

1. Eric lives in a <u>double room</u>. Walter lives in the same room. They like their room.

   A <u>double room</u> is

   a. a room with two windows, each on a different wall.
   b. a very large room
   c. a room with two doors.
   d. a room where two people can live. *(circled)*

   What other words in the sentences about Eric and Walter helped you choose the correct answer?
   Line ___2___

2. Lee and Daphne live together in a double room. They are <u>roommates</u>.

   <u>Roommates</u> are

   a. friends.
   b. parents.
   c. people who live in the same room. *(circled)*
   d. people who clean a room.

   What other words helped you choose the correct answer?
   Line _____

3. Eric <u>moved in</u> last week. He carried all his things into his room. He also carried in his stereo. Then he put his things where he wanted them.

   To <u>move in</u> is to

   a. come in out of the rain.
   b. transport your things to a new home and start to live there. *(circled)*
   c. carry people's things for them.
   d. have friends in the right places.

   What other words helped you choose the correct answer?
   Line _____

6   Chapter 1

4. When Lee went away to college, her parents were worried. "She's very young. I'm afraid she'll have problems so far away," they said. Her brother was not worried. "She's smart; she'll be all right," he said.

Lee's parents are worried because

a. something bad might happen to Lee in the future.
b. everything has already gone very badly for Lee.
c. everything is all right.
d. she's smart.

What other words helped you choose the correct answer?
Line _____ _____

5. Gordon's room is next to the front door of his house. His room is on the first floor. Another student from the same department lives in the room on the second floor right above Gordon's room.

If a building has many floors, it is

a. old.
b. long.
c. high.
d. departmental. cỡ quan

What other words helped you choose the correct answer?
Line _____ _____

6. The student who lives on the second floor often comes downstairs to Gordon's room on the first floor.

When you go downstairs, you go

a. from the first floor to the second floor.
b. from a lower floor to a higher floor.
c. upstairs.
d. from a higher floor to a lower floor.

What other words helped you choose the correct answer?
Line _____ _____

B. LONG READING

Now read "Moving In." If there is a word you do not know, try to guess it from the context. (van)

MOVING IN

It is early September. Classes at the university will begin in two days. Nobody is studying yet. Everybody is moving in.

Eric lives in a double room in a dormitory. He likes his room because it is warm and has big windows. He has a stereo record player and a lot of records. He likes loud music.

This year Eric has a new roommate. His name is Walter. Walter likes the room because it is sunny. He thinks that it will be noisy, but he isn't worried. He has brought a tape recorder and cassettes. He likes the same kind of music that Eric does.

On the floor above them two young women are moving in. They are both freshmen. Lee is a little worried, because it is the first time she has been away from her parents. They live in California. Daphne has traveled a lot, both with her parents and alone. Lee is glad that there are big windows, because she likes a lot of sun. Daphne hopes the room will stay warm in the winter.

Last year Sarah Anne lived in the dormitory. She didn't like it because it was very noisy. Also, the dormitory was expensive. She is moving out of the dormitory into an apartment where she will have two roommates. The apartment is quiet, so they will be able to study. There is a small kitchen. They will buy food at the supermarket and cook for themselves.

Daphne and Lee wanted to talk and get to know each other, but they couldn't hear each other because of the loud music coming from the floor below. When Daphne went downstairs, the door was open. "Hey," she said, "please don't play the music so loud."

"Aw, don't tell me you're studying already," said Eric.

"No, we are trying to talk," Daphne answered. "Why don't you come up and join us if you feel like it?"

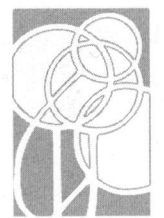

C. COMPREHENSION QUESTIONS

The following questions are about the reading that you have just finished. Finding the correct answer to the questions is not enough. You should also be able to *support* your answer or show why it is correct. You should be able to find the words in the text of the reading that helped you choose the correct answer. You should be able to say which *paragraph* and which *line(s)* helped you choose the answer.

Circle the best way to complete each sentence. You may look back at the reading to help you answer the question.

A room with big windows is usually

(a.) sunny.
b. warm.
c. noisy.
d. a double.

Paragraph __4__   Line __4 + 5__

The correct answer is (a). You will find the answer in *paragraph 4*. (Each new paragraph begins with an *indented* line to the right of the margin.)

> xxx xxxxxxx x xxxx xxxxx xxx xxxxxxx xxxxxx xx xxxxxxxx xxx xxxx xxxxx xx xxx xxxx xxxxxx x xxx xxxxxx xxxxxxx xxxxx xxx xxxxx xx xxx xxxxxxxx xxx x xxxxxx xxx xxxx xxxxxx xxxx
>   x xxx xxxxx xxxxxx xx xxx xxxxxx xxxxx xxx xx xxxxx xxxx x xxxx xxxxxx xxxxx xxxxxxx xx xxx xxxxx xxx x xxxxxx xxx xxxx xxxxxx xxxx xxx xxxxx xx xxxx xxx xx xxxxx xxxx x xxxx xxxxxx xxxxx xxxxxxx

Finally, you will find the answer in *lines 4 and 5*.

> Lee is glad that there are big windows, because she likes a lot of sun.

When you answer the comprehension questions, circle the correct answer. Then write the number of the paragraph and line where the correct answer is located in the text, as in the example given.

1. Nobody is studying today because

   a. everyone is lazy.
   b. classes have not started yet.
   c. everyone is tired.
   d. the dormitory is very noisy.

   Paragraph _____ Line _____

The correct answer to 1 is (b), classes have not started yet. You will find the answer in paragraph 1, lines 1 and 2.

Now answer the following comprehension questions and write down the paragraph and line where you found the answer.

2. Eric and Walter both like

   a. quiet rooms.
   b. quiet music.
   c. cold weather.
   d. loud music.

   Paragraph _____ Line _____

3. Before Daphne came to Furnell, she had already spent some time

   a. here.
   b. away from her parents.
   c. in a dorm.
   d. in a place with a lot of sun.

   Paragraph _____ Line _____

4. Sarah Anne lived in the dormitory last year. This means that she was a student last year. We know that she is not

   a. a freshman.
   b. a woman.
   c. a musician.
   d. a good student.

   Paragraph _____ Line _____

5. Lee and Daphne could not talk to each other because

   a. they were busy moving in.
   b. it was very noisy.
   c. they were worried.
   d. they wanted to listen to music.

   Paragraph _____ Line _____

6. Daphne and Lee wanted Eric and Walter to be quieter, but they did not want them to be angry. Therefore, the women

   a. told the men to turn off the stereo.
   b. started studying right away.
   c. didn't know what to do.
   d. invited the men to talk with them.

   Paragraph _____ Line _____

D. VOCABULARY IN CONTEXT

Read the following short paragraphs. Look at the underlined word. Then choose the meaning of the word or the best way to end the sentence. For example:

The university is made up of many buildings. Some have rooms for classes in them. Others are dormitories.

A building is

a. smaller than a house.
(b.) divided into rooms or groups of rooms.
c. large and noisy.
d. not very expensive.

1. Furnell University has a large campus. Nearly all the university buildings are on this campus. There are trees and grass around the buildings.

    A campus is an area where

    a. there are several towns.
    b. there is a school or university.
    c. there is a town.
    d. there is a building.

    What other words helped you choose the correct answer?
    Line _____ _____

2. Eric went into his room. It was very cold. Then he noticed that the window was open and understood why it was cold.

    Eric noticed the open window. In other words,

    a. he had never seen it before.
    b. someone had told him about it.
    c. he read about it.
    d. he saw it and thought about it for the first time.

    What other words helped you choose the correct answer?
    Line _____ _____

3. Walter has six younger brothers and sisters. He knows how to take care of children. He is used to children.

   When you are used to something

   a. you like it.
   b. you are tired of it.
   c. you are accustomed to it.
   d. you want it very much.

   What other words helped you choose the correct answer?
   Line _____ _____

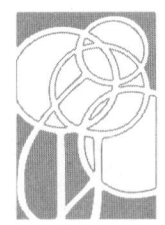

E. SHORT READING

THE APARTMENT

Yesterday Luis and Martha moved into an apartment building for married students. They like it because it doesn't cost very much and it is near the campus.

When they carried their things from the truck into their new apartment, they noticed that there were a lot of children playing behind the building. It was very noisy. Luis and Martha were not very worried about this, because they both come from New York City. They are used to noise.

F. COMPREHENSION QUESTIONS

Choose the best way to complete each sentence. You may look at the reading to help you find the correct answer.

1. Luis and Martha are

   a. freshmen.
   b. married.
   c. children.
   d. builders.

   Paragraph _____ Line _____

12   Chapter 1

2. Luis and Martha

   a. like noise.
   b. do not like noise.
   c. worry about noise.
   d. are accustomed to noise.

   Paragraph _____ Line _____

3. Luis and Martha saw children playing behind their building. The children's parents were probably

   a. freshmen.
   b. students.
   c. from New York City.
   d. worried people.

   Paragraph _____ Line _____

G. MORE THAN ONE WAY TO SAY IT

Sometimes you can say the same thing in different ways. Two words that mean almost the same thing are called *synonyms*. *Choose the word or sentence that is most like the underlined word. For example:*

The apartment building is big. It is

a. new.
b. noisy.
c. large.
d. for children.

1. Does that apartment cost much? Yes, it is

   a. expensive.
   b. quiet.
   c. big.
   d. warm.

2. Loud music is

   a. noisy music.
   b. quiet music.
   c. California music.
   d. New York music.

H. SHORT READING

THE HOUSE

Don lives at home with his parents in the country, but he is in town today. He has come with his pickup truck to help Gordon move. Last year Gordon lived in a small room near campus. It was dark, cold in the winter, and very noisy. Now he and seven other graduate students are renting a house together. It will be cold in the new house, too, but it will be quiet. They are all going to study hard.

Don and Gordon quickly unloaded the boxes of books and clothing from the back of the pickup truck. After all his things were put away, Gordon sat down, picked up his guitar, and started to sing. He did it quietly, so that he wouldn't bother his housemates.

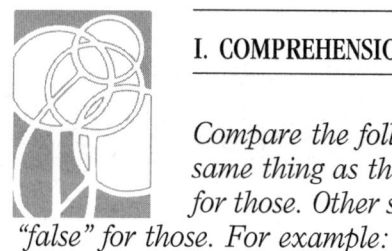

I. COMPREHENSION QUESTIONS

Compare the following sentences to the reading. Some say the same thing as the reading but in different words. Circle "true" for those. Other sentences do not agree with the reading. Circle "false" for those. For example:

True   (False)   Don lives in New York City.

Paragraph __1__   Line __1__

1. True   False   Don is moving in today.
Paragraph _____ Line _____

2. True   False   Gordon's room last year was not big.
Paragraph _____ Line _____

3. True   False   Gordon will live alone this year.
Paragraph _____ Line _____

4. True   False   Gordon's things were in boxes.
Paragraph _____ Line _____

5. True   False   Gordon finished moving in in one day.
Paragraph _____ Line _____

14 Chapter 1

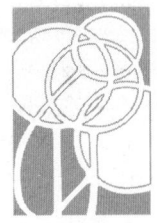

J. WORD FORMS

1. **Nouns** are words that name things, people, places, or ideas. Some nouns from the preceding short reading are:

Things: truck   He has come with his pickup <u>truck</u> to help. . . .
         boxes   Don and Gordon quickly unloaded the <u>boxes</u> of
         books   <u>books</u> and clothing. . . .

clothing

Can you find the missing nouns in the rest of this exercise? Write them in the blanks at the left.

People: ___Don___   <u>Don</u> lives at home with his parents in the country. . . .

         _____   He has come with his pickup truck to help Gordon move.

2. **Some verbs** are words that tell what nouns do. Here are some of the verbs in the short reading. Write the missing verbs in the blanks at the left.

has come   He <u>has come</u> with his pickup truck to <u>help</u> Gordon
help move   <u>move</u>.
are renting   Now he and seven other graduate students
                 <u>are renting</u> a house together.
are going   They <u>are</u> all <u>going to study</u> hard.
to study
unloaded   Don and Gordon quickly <u>unloaded</u> the boxes of books
                 and clothing from the back of the pickup truck.
_____   Gordon sat down, picked up his guitar, and started
_____   to sing.
did   He <u>did</u> it quietly, so that he wouldn't <u>bother</u> his
bother   housemates.

Other verbs tell how things are. Here are some of these verbs in the reading. Write the missing verb in the blank at the left.

is   Don lives at home with his parents in the country, but
                 he <u>is</u> in town today.
was   It <u>was</u> dark, cold in the winter, and very noisy.
will . . . be   The new house <u>will</u> still <u>be</u> cold, but it will be quiet.
_____   When all his things were put away, Gordon sat
                 down. . . .

3. **Some adjectives** describe nouns. Many adjectives come just in front of nouns. Write the missing adjective in the blank at the left.

small   Last year Gordon lived in a <u>small</u> room on campus.

_____   Don and Gordon quickly unloaded the boxes of books in the new house.

    Other adjectives come after a verb. Find the missing adjectives and write them in the blank.

dark   It was <u>dark</u>, and <u>cold</u> in the winter, and very noisy.

_____

_____

4. **Adverbs** modify verbs, telling how, when, or where things happen. Fill in the missing adverb.

today   But he is in town <u>today</u>.
hard   They are all going to study <u>hard</u>.
quickly   Don and Gordon <u>quickly</u> unloaded the boxes of books and clothing. . . .

_____   He did it quietly, so that he wouldn't bother his housemates.

Adverbs can also modify adjectives or other adverbs. They are used in front of the word they modify.

very   It was dark, and cold in the winter, and <u>very</u> noisy.

K. VOCABULARY IN CONTEXT

Read the following short paragraph. Look at the underlined word. Then choose the meaning of the word or the best way to end the sentence.

1. Some students want to live with other similar people. If they are men, they join a club called a <u>fraternity</u>. The <u>fraternity</u> buys or rents a house where they live, eat, and give parties.

    A <u>fraternity</u> is

    a. a club where men students live.
    b. a dormitory.
    c. a family home.
    d. an ideal society.

    What other words helped you find the correct answer?
    Line _____ _____

16   Chapter 1

2. Women students have the same kind of clubs, but they are called <u>sororities</u>.

A <u>sorority</u> is

a. a club where women students live.
b. a fraternity.
c. a dormitory.
d. an ideal society.

What other words helped you find the correct answer?
Line _____ _____

L. SHORT READING

THE SORORITY *(club for women)*

Don is also helping Ellen today. Last year she lived in a dormitory, but now she is moving into a sorority house. There she will be one of a large group of women who have chosen to live together and eat meals together. They are planning to give parties and invite the men from the fraternity across the street. Don does not belong to a fraternity, but Ellen is going to invite him to the first party.

M. COMPREHENSION QUESTIONS

Choose the best way to complete each sentence.

1. Ellen is moving into a
   a. dormitory.
   b. fraternity house.
   c. sorority house.
   d. party.

   Paragraph _____ Line _____

2. Don is
   a. Ellen's friend.
   b. a sorority member.
   c. a fraternity member.
   d. Ellen's student.

   Paragraph _____ Line _____

STRATEGIES

READING A UNIVERSITY HOUSING BROCHURE

PRE-READING EXERCISES

*Working in groups of two or three, try to remember **where** each person from Chapter 1 lives (dorm, apartment, etc.) and **with whom** each person lives. If you cannot remember any of them, or if you disagree about certain answers, go back to the four readings in this chapter to check:*

	Where He/She Lives	With Whom He/She Lives
Eric		
Walter		
Lee		
Daphne		
Sarah Anne		
Luis		
Martha		
Don		
Gordon		
Ellen		

Now answer the following questions and discuss them with your classmates.

1. What type of housing do you live in?
2. Is it on a university campus?
3. Do you have roommates?
4. How many roommates do you have? (A **double** room is for two people, a **triple** is for three people, and a **single** is for one person.)
5. Did the university send you some information about campus housing?
6. If so, what types of information were included?
7. Which things were the most important to you in deciding where to live?

WORD FORMS AND WORD FAMILIES

The words **residence, resident**, and **residential hall** are words that are related to university housing. They all come from the verb **to reside**, meaning "to live."

Resident and **residence** are both *nouns*, but one means a place (**residence**) and the other means a person (**resident**). **Residential** is an adjective that describes the hall; **residential hall** is another way to say "dormitory." In a dormitory there is usually a **resident aide** or **resident assistant (R.A.)** on each floor. He or she is a student who works for the university by giving out information or helping with problems. The **residential hall** or dormitory has a **head resident**, also a student, who is in charge of all the **R.A.s**.

While reading the following passage about student housing at Furnell University, look at how these words are used.

STRATEGIES 19

READING A BROCHURE FROM A UNIVERSITY HOUSING OFFICE

The housing office at a university includes a lot of information in the brochure that they send to future students. Here is a list of the different topics that are explained in the Furnell University Housing brochure.

Residential Life at Furnell University:

a. Residential Life Staff
b. Dining Services
c. Room Application Procedures
d. On-Campus Housing
e. Fraternity and Sorority Residence Halls
f. Residence Halls Information Chart
g. 1990–91 Room Charges
h. Graduate Student and Family Housing
i. Off-Campus Housing

Residential Living at Furnell

1990 – 1991

Furnell University Housing Office
200 Barnes Hall
Greenville, NY 14850
(607) 255-2700

QUESTIONS

1. Which section will tell you about the resident aides who live on each floor of the dormitories? _____

2. Which section gives information about all the residence halls on campus? _____

3. Where should you look if you want to know whether cats are allowed in the dormitories? _____

4. If you already know that you want to live in student housing, where can you find out how to apply? _____

5. If you want to compare the cost of student housing and private housing, which section(s) of this brochure can help you? _____

READING A UNIVERSITY HOUSING CHART

The following is a chart listing all the dormitories and residences at Furnell according to:

1. *type of residence* (larger, smaller building; special-interest)
2. *number (#) of beds*
3. *size of rooms* (single = sg; double = db; triple = trp)
4. *percentage (%) of freshmen* and other new students
5. whether it is *on or off campus*

Make sure that you understand these five categories of information before you read the chart, then answer the questions that follow.

RESIDENCE HALL INFORMATION CHART

Type of Residence	# of beds	size of rooms	% of fresh.	on/off campus
LARGE BUILDING				
Elizabeth Hall	163	db trp	60	on
Grange Hall	180	db trp	72	on
Lamuertrie Hall	245	sg db trp	56	on
Brewer Hall	217	sg db	45	on
Fitzhammer Hall	125	db trp	68	on
SMALLER BUILDING				
Beach Hall	43	sg db	30	on
Crummer Hall	76	sg db	34	on
Hancock Hall	84	sg db	36	on
Jones Hall	55	sg db trp	64	on
SPECIAL-INTEREST HOUSING				
Matthews House	22	sg db	15	off
Fine Arts House	31	sg db	10	on
Furnell Outdoor Club	48	sg db trp	13	on
French House	22	sg db	0	off
Ujamaa House	38	sg db	18	on

For more information about FU housing, Contact this office:

Furnell University Housing Office
200 Barnes Hall
Furnell University
Greenville, NY 14850
Tel. (607) 555-2700

COMPREHENSION QUESTIONS

Answer the following questions by referring to the residence hall chart.

1. Which group of residence halls has some halls off campus?

2. Which type of residence has the *highest* percentage (%) of freshmen?

3. Which type of housing has the *lowest* percentage (%) of freshmen? Why?

4. What group of dorms has triple rooms?

5. Look at the following names of special-interest houses. See if you can predict what the special interest of each residence is.

   a. Matthews House *Environmental Studies students; organic gardening ecology*
   b. Ujamaa House
   c. Fine Arts House
   d. FU Outdoor Club
   e. French House

6. Look at the chart. What else do these special-interest houses have in common?

7. Does your college or university have any special-interest housing? If so, describe some of the houses.

8. Why do you think that four out of five special-interest houses do not have any triple rooms?

9. If you live in a dormitory or special-interest housing at your university, where does it fit into this chart? Add it to the chart, including as much information about it as you can.

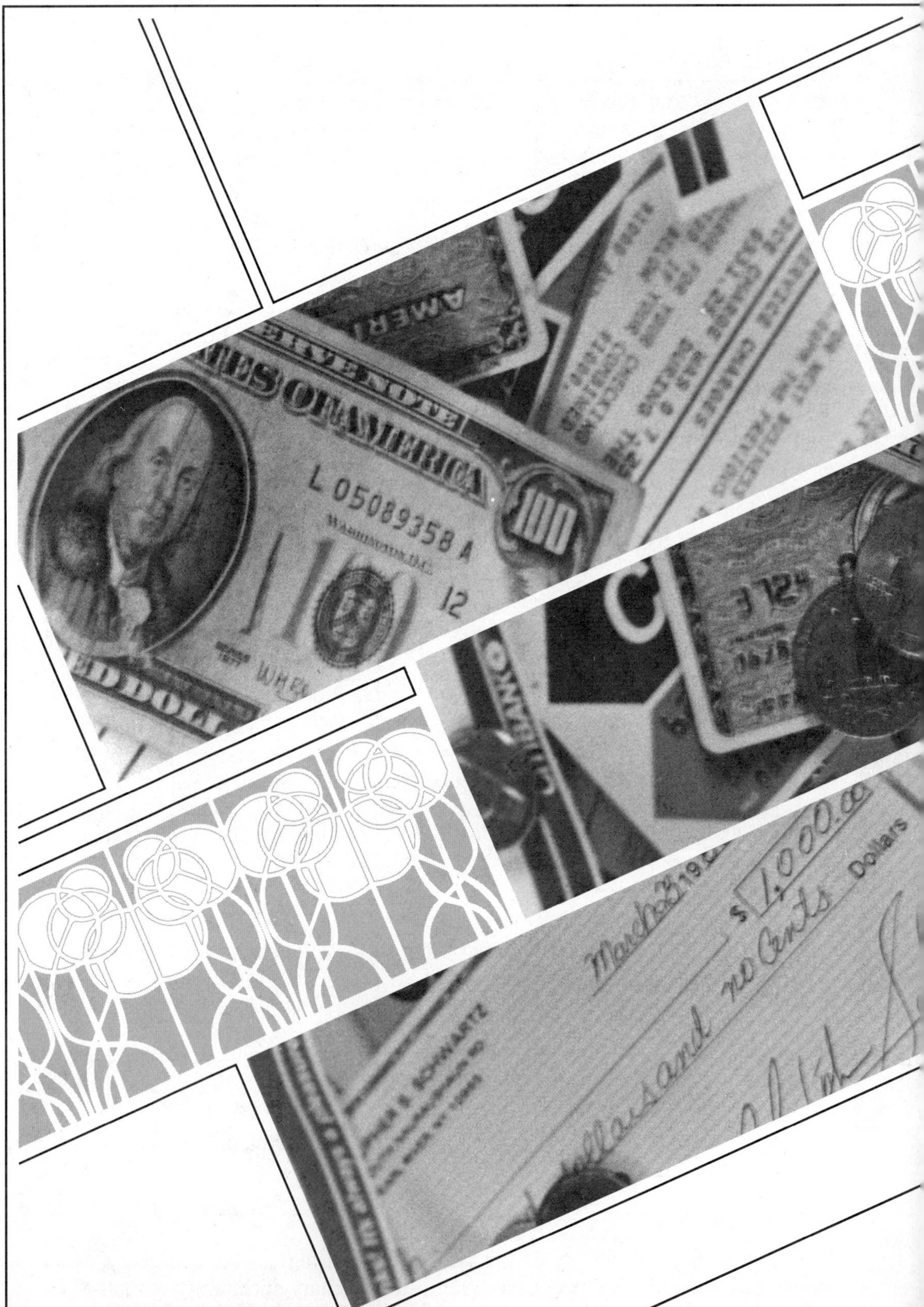

CHAPTER TWO

MONEY

MONEY   25

PRE-READING EXERCISE

Before reading this chapter, answer and discuss the following questions with your classmates and teacher. Compare your answers to those of your classmates.

This chapter is about money, banks, and paying university bills.

1. What are the hours of operation for banks in your country?

2. How common are automatic teller machines (ATMs) in your country? If they are not common, how do people get cash when the banks are closed?

3. Look at the photograph on the opposite page. What do you see in it? Think about these different types of money when you are filling out this questionnaire.

    How do people in your country usually pay for the things in the following list? If there is someone from your country in your class, work with him/her. Then compare your answers with those of your classmates.

ITEM	CASH	CHECK	CREDIT CARD
books (college textbooks)			
books, magazines, newspapers			
food from a supermarket			
meals in a restaurant			
clothing			
electric bills			
telephone bills			
tuition at university			
cassettes/records			
a stereo system			
a video cassette recorder (vcr)			
furniture			
airplane tickets			
vacations			
a refrigerator/stove			

4. For which of the previous things might a person or a family borrow money from a bank, credit union, or another family member?

   _____
   _____
   _____

5. What types of accounts at a bank do most university students have?

   _____

6. What is the average cost of university for one year in your country (tuition only, not including room, board [food], or books)? If there is a range of prices, give the average minimum and average maximum.

   _____
   _____
   _____

7. How do students pay for a university education in your country? (More than one answer is possible.)

   ____ Government scholarships (not to be repaid)
   ____ Government loans (to be repaid in the future)
   ____ Bank loans (to be repaid)
   ____ Loans from a family member (to be repaid)
   ____ Financial aid from the university, including:

       ____ Full or partial scholarships (not to be repaid)
       ____ Loans (to be repaid)
       ____ Work-study assistance (part-time work for students)
       ____ Teaching or research assistantships (part-time teaching or research responsibilities for students in M.A. or Ph.D. programs; these include a small salary and payment of tuition)

   ____ Parents or other relatives pay for all costs, including tuition, room and board, books, and other expenses.
   ____ Student's pay part of the costs by working in the summer and/or part-time during the school year.
   ____ Other (specify) _____

8. The first reading in this chapter is called "At the Bank." Which of the following things might be talked about in the reading?

   ____ soccer   ____ checkbooks   ____ credit cards
   ____ courses   ____ traveler's checks   ____ savings accounts
   ____ dormitories

A. VOCABULARY IN CONTEXT

Before reading the story "At the Bank," read the following paragraphs. Try to guess the meaning of the underlined words. Use the meaning of all the words in the paragraph to help you decide. Write down the words from the context that helped you choose the meaning of the underlined words.

1. Eric is a <u>sophomore</u> from New Jersey, and Walter is from Iowa in the Midwest. Because this is Eric's second year here, he showed Walter around town the first week of school.

    A <u>sophomore</u> is

    a. a type of engineer.
    b. a second-year student.
    c. a roommate.
    d. from Sophocles, Greece.

    What other words helped you choose the correct answer?
    Line_____   _____

2. Martha's friend works at the 1st National Bank in Greenville. She is a <u>bank teller</u>. When people come in to do business in the bank, she gives them money from their savings and checking accounts. Sometimes they give money to her, too.

    What is a <u>bank teller</u>?

    a. The president of a bank.
    b. A person who cleans a bank.
    c. A person who gives out and takes in money at a bank.
    d. A secretary at a bank.

    What other words helped you choose the correct answer?
    Line_____   _____

3. People <u>check</u> the following things. They <u>check</u>

    . . . to see if the baby is sleeping.

    . . . to see if the dinner is ready to eat.

    . . . to see if there is enough gas in the car.

    . . . to see when a dentist's appointment is scheduled.

    . . . to see how a word is spelled in a dictionary.

    Can you think of other things that people <u>check</u>?

    _____

    _____

28   Chapter 2

4. Gordon went shopping. Altogether, everything that he needed cost $27.82. He only had $10.25 in cash—a ten-dollar bill and a quarter. Luckily, he had his checkbook with him.

"Is it all right if I pay by check?" he asked the salesclerk.
"Yes, if your checking account is at a bank in Greenville," he replied.
"I have my account at 1st National," Gordon said as he wrote the check for $27.82.

Draw a line from each word at the left to the correct definition at the right.

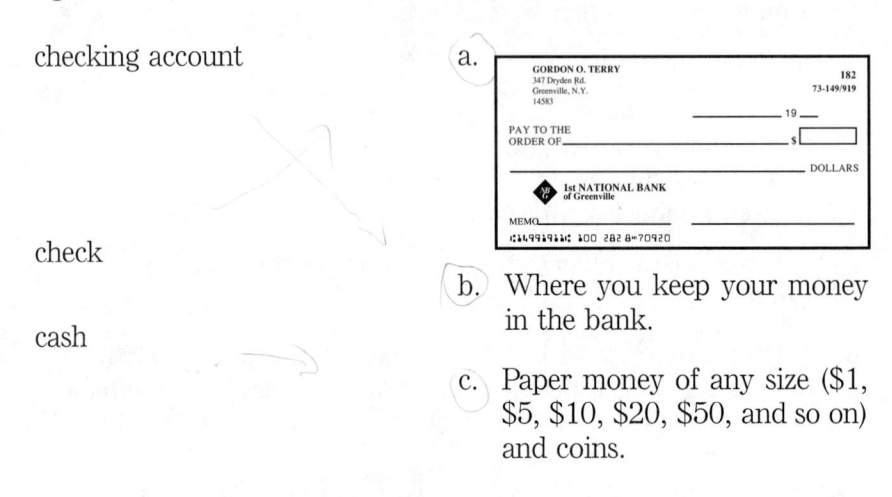

checking account   a. [check image: GORDON O. TERRY, 347 Dryden Rd., Greenville, N.Y. 14583, 182, 73-149/919, PAY TO THE ORDER OF, DOLLARS, 1st NATIONAL BANK of Greenville, MEMO]

check

b. Where you keep your money in the bank.

cash

c. Paper money of any size ($1, $5, $10, $20, $50, and so on) and coins.

5. Before Luis came to Furnell University, he worked for the state government. The government sent him to Furnell to get a master's degree. When he paid his tuition he got a receipt. He sent the receipt to the office where he worked. His office will give him the money back.

What does receipt mean?

a. Instructions for cooking something.
b. A piece of paper that says you have already paid some money for something.
c. A piece of paper for sending money by mail.
d. A traveler's check.

What other words helped you choose the correct answer?
Line _____ _____

When do you get a receipt?

a. When you pay money.
b. When you receive money.
c. When you earn money.
d. When you save money.

B. LONG READING

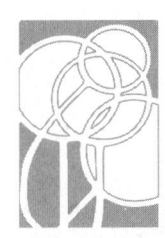

AT THE BANK

Walter and Eric are roommates in a dormitory at Furnell University. Eric is a sophomore from New Jersey, and Walter is from Iowa in the Midwest. Because this is Eric's second year here, he showed Walter around town the first week of school. Last Tuesday, they both went to the 1st National Bank near campus.

Eric had a check for $350 from his parents and $75 in cash. When they entered the bank, he filled out a **deposit slip** (1) for his savings account. The bank teller checked Eric's addition and made sure that the check was **endorsed** (2).

"There will be a three- or four-day delay before you can use the amount of this check, sir," she told him. "You cannot use it now. We have to collect it from your parents' bank in New Jersey first."

"That's no problem. This is spending money for the whole semester, so I don't need it immediately," Eric replied.

The bank teller went to the computer and added the $425 deposit to his account. She told him that the new balance was $473.82 and gave him a receipt.

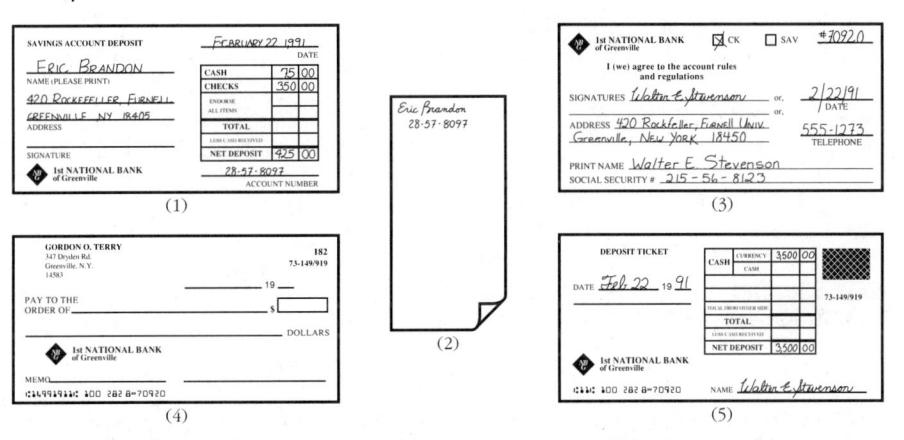

Meanwhile Walter went to the service desk. He had traveler's checks. He told the clerk there that he wanted to open a checking account. The clerk asked him to fill out a **signature card** (3) for the bank's records. Then he handed Walter a New Account Kit, which included the following items:

Instructions on how to (a) deposit and withdraw money, and (b) write a check.

An *order form* for 200 **personalized checks** (4) that he would receive in two weeks.

An *identification card* with the checking account number.

Ten checks (not personalized) to use while he waited for his personalized check order to arrive.

After the clerk had shown Walter the contents of the kit, he took out a **deposit slip** (5) and helped him fill it out.

"I don't have to wait before I can use this money, do I?" Walter asked the clerk.

"No, you don't," he replied. "Traveler's checks are just like cash. You can use them immediately. A check from this bank is okay, too. For a check from any New York State bank, there is only a few days' delay."

"That's good," Walter laughed, "because I have to use almost all of this money tomorrow to pay tuition at Furnell."

C. COMPREHENSION QUESTIONS

Choose the best answers to the following questions. Then write the paragraph and line where the correct answer is in the text, as you did in Chapter 1. You may look at the reading to help you find the correct answers.

1. Why couldn't Eric take money out of his savings account?

    a. Because it was cash.
    b. Because the bank needed to wait for the money to arrive from the bank in New Jersey.
    c. Because there is a thirty-four–day delay on all checks from New Jersey.

    Paragraph _____ Line _____

2. Eric deposited cash in his savings account. How much cash?

    a. $75.00
    b. $350.00
    c. $425.00
    d. $473.82

    Paragraph _____ Line _____

3. Why didn't Eric need the money he deposited immediately?

    a. He already had $75 in cash.
    b. He had already spent enough money.
    c. The money was for the entire semester.

    Paragraph _____ Line _____

4. How many checks were in Walter's New Account Kit?

    a. 200
    b. 10
    c. 3500

    Paragraph _____ Line _____

5. Why did Walter need to write a check the next day?

    a. To pay his Furnell University tuition.
    b. To return to Iowa.
    c. To give Eric $75 in cash.

    Paragraph _____ Line _____

6. Eric couldn't use his money immediately, but Walter could. In fact, Walter was going to write a check the next day. Why was this possible?

    a. Walter's check is from a New York state bank.
    b. Walter deposited $3500 in cash.
    c. There is no waiting period for traveler's checks.

    Paragraph _____ Line _____

MONEY 31

D. FILL-IN EXERCISE

Fill in the blanks with the correct words from the following list. Use the information in the sentences before and after the blank to help you decide which answer is correct. Each word must be used. No word can be used twice.

delay	endorse	deposited
balance	collect	deposit slip
kit	withdraw	tuition
	semester	

For example: The plane will be two hours late. We are sorry for the ___delay___. You can wait in the lounge.

1. I'm paying $1780 for my courses this semester at the Intensive English Program. How much is the _____ at your school?

2. After I deposited my paycheck, the _____ in my account was $743.89.

3. I need to _____ $5470 from my savings account. I'm buying a car this afternoon.

4. Charlie made sure his shaving _____ was complete. He put in his razor, some shaving cream, razor blades, and a bottle of after-shave lotion.

5. Harry forgot to sign the back of his paycheck. "Excuse me, sir," said the teller. "You'll have to _____ this check before I can deposit it."

6. A bank teller always uses an electronic calculator to check the arithmetic on a _____ .

7. I don't have enough money to pay my tuition. Maybe Furnell University will wait for a few months before they _____ the money from me.

8. "Did you put some money in the bank yesterday?" Jennifer asked her husband. "Yes, dear," he replied. "I _____ my paycheck—$345.00."

9. The fall _____ starts in September and ends in December.

E. WORD FORM CHART

Vocabulary Word	Adjective	Noun	Verb	Adverb
1. three- or four-day <u>delay</u>	delayed	delay	delay	
2. how to deposit and <u>withdraw</u> money	withdrawal*	withdrawal	withdraw	
3. 200 <u>personalized</u> checks	personalized personal	person personality	personalize	personally
4. a <u>deposit</u> slip	deposit*	deposit depositor	deposit	
5. how to <u>collect</u> it		collector collection	collect	
6. a <u>signature</u> card	signature*	signature	sign	
7. <u>instructions</u> on	instructive	instruction(s) instructor	instruct	
8. an <u>order</u> form	order*	order	order	
9. an <u>identification</u> card	identification*	identification	identify	
10. in <u>cash</u>		cash	cash	

*A noun used as an adjective in a compound noun.

Suffixes: The way a word ends often tells you what part of speech it is. If a word ends in "-tion" it is usually a noun. The "-tion" ending, called a suffix, may also be "-ation" or "-ition." It is usually added to a verb: *inform*, a verb, changes to *information*, a noun.

At the top of the next page are the suffixes used in the word form chart. Fill in the blanks with the correct parts of speech.

MONEY 33

-ize	changes an adjective to a verb
-ly	changes a(n) _____ to an adverb
-or/-er	changes a(n) _____ to a(n) _____
-al (has 2 uses)	changes a noun to a(n) _____
	changes a verb to a(n) _____
-ive	changes a(n) _____ to an adjective
-tion	changes a verb to a(n) _____
-ity	changes a(n) _____ to a noun
-ify	changes a noun to a(n) _____

G. WORD FORM EXERCISE

Choose the correct word form and fill in the blank. Number (1) is done for you. Look at (1) on the Word Form Chart to choose the correct answer for question (1) in this exercise, and so forth. Name the part of speech in the blanks at the right margin.

1. Look at that snow! I hope it doesn't __delay__ my airplane flight this afternoon.
   Part of speech __verb__

2. How much did you __withdraw__ last week? I need to subtract it.
   Part of speech __✓__

3. Every __person__ in the class said something. They all took part in the discussion.
   Part of speech __N__

4. I need a __deposit__ slip. Where can I find one?
   Part of speech __✓__

5. Gordon has stamps from all over the world. He is a stamp __collect__.
   Part of speech __✓__

6. He forgot to put his __signature__ on the check. The bank refused to accept it.
   Part of speech __✓__

7. I really like that __instructor__. She's very organized and clear in her classes.
   Part of speech __N__

8. When did you __order__ that car? You've been waiting for it for six months!
   Part of speech __✓__

9. What kind of insect is this? Maybe the biology department can __identify__ it.
   Part of speech __✓__

10. I don't have enough spending money at home, so I'm going to the bank to __cash__ a check.
    Part of speech __✓__

Chapter 2

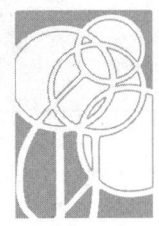

H. VOCABULARY REVIEW READING

CASHING A CHECK

Lee went to the teller at the Midland Bank. She wanted to cash a check to get some spending money for the weekend.

"Hi. I'd like to cash a check," she said to the teller.

"Do you have an account with us?" the teller asked.

"Yes, I do. I'm going to make the check out to 'cash,' okay?"

"That's fine, but in general I suggest that you make checks out to yourself. Then nobody can cash them except you. It's safer."

Lee made the check out to herself. When she finished writing and endorsing it, she handed it to the teller. Then the teller asked Lee for some identification. Lee took out her driver's license and showed it to her.

"How would you like the money?" the teller asked.

"Please give me one twenty, two tens, and ten ones," answered Lee.

She put the cash in her purse and opened her checkbook again. She subtracted the fifty-dollar withdrawal from her account. Her new balance was only seventy-five dollars. She decided to spend her money very carefully.

I. COMPREHENSION QUESTIONS

Answer the following questions. You may look at the reading, if necessary, to help you find the correct answers.

1. To whom did Lee make out the check?

   a. Herself, Lee Smith.
   b. Her mother.
   c. Cash.

   Paragraph _____ Line _____

2. How much did Lee have in her account before she cashed her check?

   _____

   Paragraph _____ Line _____

3. What kind of identification did Lee show the teller?

   a. A student ID.
   b. An I-20 form.
   c. A driver's license.

   Paragraph _____ Line _____

4. What did Lee do after she received her cash from the teller?

   a. Showed her identification.
   b. Subtracted her withdrawal.
   c. Endorsed the check.

   Paragraph _____ Line _____

J. SHORT READING

WORKING

Sarah Anne is a good student, but her parents have very little money. She does not have to pay tuition because she has a scholarship. But she needs money for necessities such as rent, food, and books, as well as for spending money. She is going to work as a work-study student in the chemistry laboratory to earn money.

During the first week of classes Sarah Anne went to the chemistry laboratory for her first afternoon of work.

The laboratory technician met her. "Hi," she said. "I'm Martha."

"I'm Sarah Anne." Then she added, "I'm very glad to be working in a laboratory this year, because I want to study medicine. Can I start work immediately?"

"Yes," said Martha, "but first you'll have to fill out these forms. We need to know your name, address, and identification number before we can start to pay you."

36 Chapter 2

K. COMPREHENSION QUESTIONS

Choose the best way to complete the following sentences. You may look at the reading, if necessary, to help you find the correct answers.

1. Sarah Anne is going to work because

    a. she has to pay tuition tomorrow.
    b. she needs money.
    c. she needs an address.
    d. she wants to meet Martha.

    Paragraph _____ Line _____

2. Sarah Anne wanted to start work

    a. today.
    b. tomorrow.
    c. next week.
    d. on Monday.

    Paragraph _____ Line _____

3. Before starting work Sarah Anne had to

    a. study medicine.
    b. be a good student.
    c. pay tuition.
    d. fill out some forms.

    Paragraph _____ Line _____

L. FILL-IN EXERCISE

Review the following vocabulary words by using them to fill in the blanks in the following sentences.

filled out	**withdrawing**	**spending money**
tuition	**deposited**	
endorse	**collects**	

In September, Lee put $3183 in her savings account. She _____ _____ all the money she had saved from her summer job. Her money included both checks and cash. She _____ the deposit slip. Part of the $3183 was $140 in cash. Another part of her money was the last check from her summer job, for $236.71. The bank teller noticed that Lee's signature was not on the back of it.

"I'm sorry, Miss. You forgot to _____ this check," she said.

MONEY   37

The last part of the $3183 was $2806.29 from her mother's checking account in California. The teller told her not to use the money from the two checks until the bank received it from the California banks.

"Does this mean that I can't pay Furnell until the 1st National Bank of Greenville _____ the money from my mother's bank in California?" Lee asked.

The bank teller told her she was right. She also said that the university would wait five or six days for her _____ and her housing payment.

"Many students pay their bills one or two weeks late," the teller said.

Lee's new balance was $3793.59. She was very pleased to have so much money in her account. She would be rich for a week, but she knew that she would then have to take out over $3000 to pay the university. It made her unhappy to think about _____ that much money from her account. She wouldn't have very much left for _____ after that.

STRATEGIES

USING CREDIT CARDS

PRE-READING EXERCISE

The next reading is about the use of credit cards. Please answer the following questions to help everyone in your class (including yourself) understand how often people in your country use credit cards instead of cash or checks. This will also show how they feel about credit.

Note: The words "most people" in the questions mean the people in your country whom you know about.

1. How many credit cards do most people have? _____

2. Do most people save extra money until they have enough to buy something expensive, or do they borrow money? _____

3. What do most people do when they want to borrow money to buy something expensive?

   They ask for a loan from _____ parents.
   _____ friends.
   _____ a bank.

   or

   They use credit cards from _____ a bank.
   _____ a large department store.

VOCABULARY WORDS

You are going to read and discuss some information about credit cards that was shortened from a university economics textbook called *Personal Finance**. In textbooks, you will often find definitions of technical vocabulary words. *Here are some words from the reading and their definitions. Read them now, and come back to them while you are reading if you need to.*

1. **Advantage** (noun): a benefit or good point (**dis**advantage is the opposite, meaning a bad or negative aspect of something).

2. To **avoid** (verb): to stop or prevent something from happening.

3. **Bill** (noun): a detailed account statement of things sold or work done for which a person must pay.

4. To **borrow** (verb): to use someone else's money with the plan to return it in the future, perhaps with some interest as payment.

*From *Personal Finance: An Integrated Planning Approach,* 2d Ed., by Winger and Frasca. Copyright 1989, Merrill Publishing Company. Reprinted by permission of the publisher.

5. **Consumer** (noun): someone who buys something.
6. **Convenience** (noun): something that makes life easier.
7. **Department store** (noun): a large store with many sections or departments that sells many different things such as clothing, furniture, appliances, etc.
8. **Loan** (noun): money that is borrowed from another person or a bank.
9. To **owe** (verb): to be under the obligation to return money to someone.
10. To **save** (verb): to keep and accumulate instead of spending or using.

READING THE TABLE OF CONTENTS IN A UNIVERSITY TEXTBOOK

If you were taking an economics course in personal finance, you would learn about credit cards during your course. But if you were not a finance student, and you wanted to find out as much as you could about credit cards, you might look in a consumer economics textbook such as *Personal Finance*, as well as talk to friends who already have credit cards and several banks that offer credit cards.

How could you find out exactly where to look in a large textbook? The first place is the **Table of Contents**. In *Personal Finance*, the table of contents gives a short title for each of the five parts in the book.

```
                TABLE OF CONTENTS

        Part One: The Basic Framework
        Part Two: Spending, Borrowing, and Saving
        Part Three: Protecting against Losses
        Part Four: Investing for the Future
        Part Five: Long-term Planning
```

QUESTIONS

1. Which part do you think will explain <u>credit cards</u>? Why?

2. Can you think of other information that might be in this textbook? In which part would it be?

40   Chapter 2

Now look at the **chapter titles** in Part Two:

> **PART TWO: SPENDING, BORROWING, AND SAVING**
>
> Chapter 6: Cash Management: Funds for Immediate Needs
> Chapter 7: Consumer Credit: Buying Now
> Chapter 8: Consumer Durables: Satisfying Your Continuing Needs
> Chapter 9: Housing: The Cost of Shelter

QUESTIONS

1. In which chapter do you think credit cards will be found? Why?

2. Can you think of different topics that might be in the other chapters?

You have found the chapter that deals with credit cards. *Now read the following section in Chapter Six that gives advantages and disadvantages of using credit cards. Look back at the vocabulary list if you have questions while you are reading.*

Ch. 6   Personal Finance

ADVANTAGES AND DISADVANTAGES OF CREDIT CARDS

ADVANTAGES

1. **Used for emergencies**, when something expensive breaks and needs to be fixed or replaced immediately. Many people think that this is the most important reason for having credit cards.
2. **Used to avoid inflation**, when you want to buy now to get cheaper prices instead of waiting until later, when the price will go up.
3. **Used as a shopping convenience**, when you do not want to carry cash or checks, and you want to have a record of what you have spent every month. Credit cards also make it easier to shop by telephone or mail.
4. **Used as a loan**, when you want to spend more money than you now have, and you know you will have more money in the future to pay the money back.

DISADVANTAGES

1. **Possibility of spending too much**: Because you are using plastic cards instead of cash or checks, it is easy to forget how much you have spent. Keeping a written record each time you use the credit card can help you avoid this problem.
2. **High cost of credit**: The interest rate for credit cards is the highest of all types of loans. If you use credit cards as a way to borrow money, it is important to find the card with the lowest interest rate. You can also find out about consumer loans from banks that probably have a lower interest rate.
3. **High credit payments in the future**: The more you use credit cards now, the more money you will need to pay to the bank each month. That means less money will be available to spend on other things you want.

VOCABULARY IN CONTEXT EXERCISE

1. Look at the first advantage, "Used for emergencies." What are some examples of emergencies for which you might use a credit card?

   _____

   _____

2. What are some examples of "medical emergencies"? _____

   _____

3. Look at the second advantage, "Used to avoid inflation." Which of the following is an example of "inflation"?

   Price of a 13 inch color television:
   a. 1989 = $275 1990 = $315
   b. 1989 = $275 1990 = $275
   c. 1989 = $305 1990 = $275

COMPREHENSION QUESTIONS

Answer the following questions. Look back at the reading to find the answers.

1. Thinking about the spending habits of people in your country (as you discussed in the beginning of this chapter), which <u>advantage</u> do you think is the most important to your compatriots? Why?

   _____

2. Which <u>advantage</u> is the most important to you, now, as a student in the United States? Why?

   _____

3. Which <u>disadvantage</u> is the most important to you?

   _____

4. Look at the following list of sections from Chapter Six of *Personal Finance*. If you do not have a credit card and you want to get one, which section of this chapter will give you information about getting one? (You have already read one section.)

   Chapter Six: Consumer Credit: Buying Now and Paying Later

   _____Credit Cards

   _____Advantages and Disadvantages of Credit Cards

   _____Protection against Credit Card Fraud

   _____Obtaining Credit

   _____Resolving Credit Problems

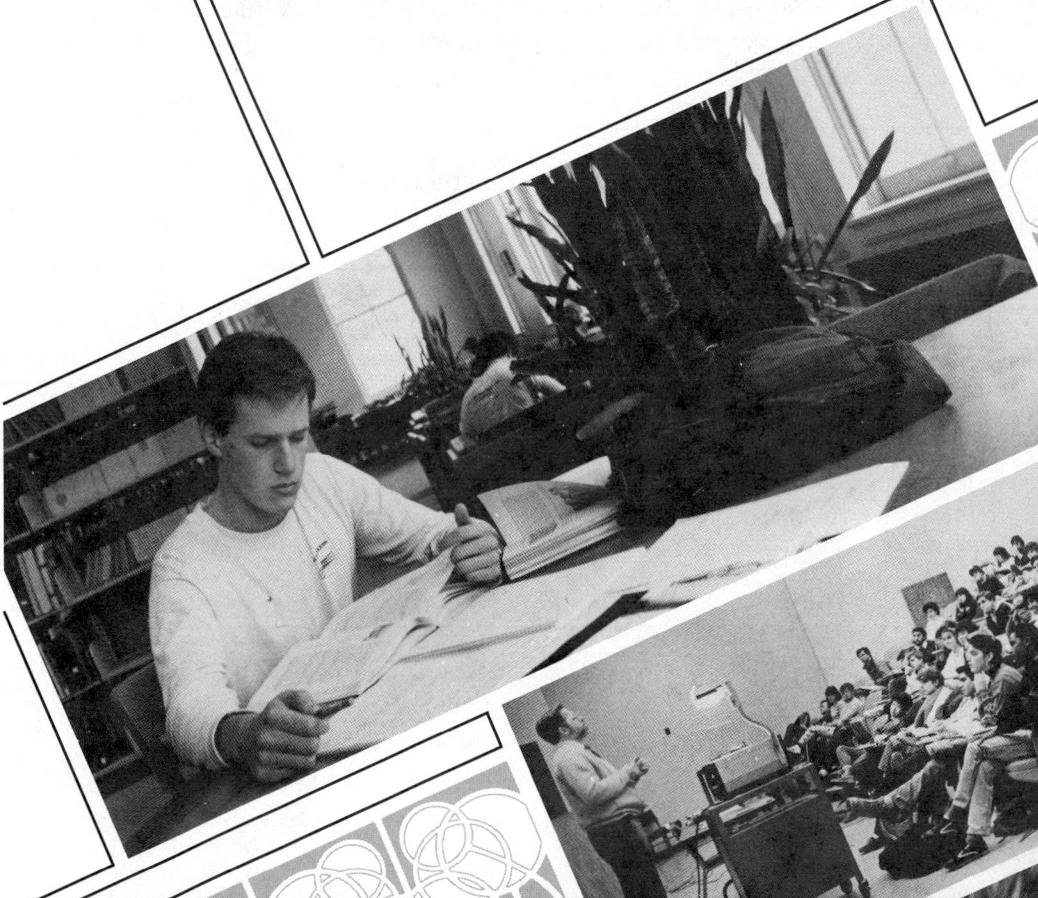
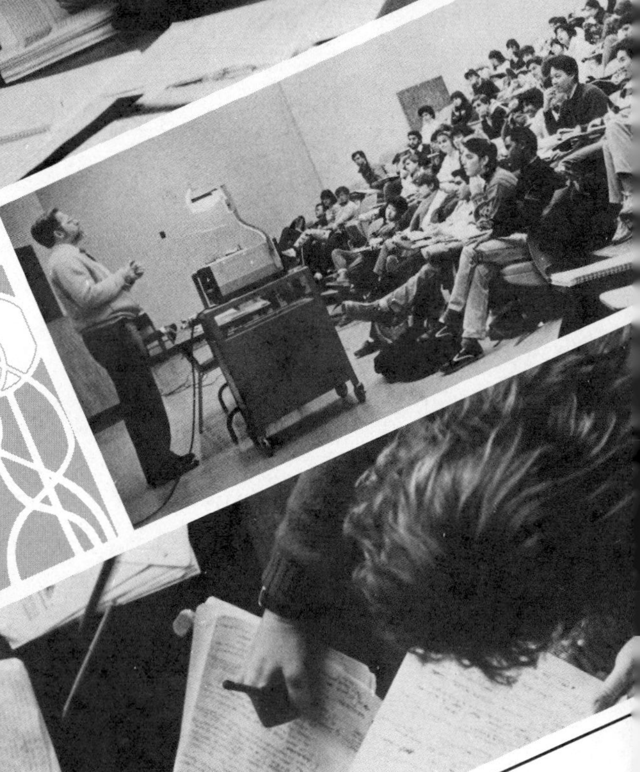

CHAPTER THREE

STUDYING

STUDYING   45

PRE-READING QUESTIONS

This chapter is about *studying* in an American university. Before starting the chapter, read the following outline. It describes how a university in the United States is organized.

THE UNIVERSITY IN THE UNITED STATES

There are universities of many different sizes in the United States, but all of them have the same basic organization.
Each university includes:

A. A COLLEGE OF LIBERAL ARTS (also called ARTS AND SCIENCES) with individual departments in

1. *the humanities*: literature, languages, arts, philosophy, etc.
2. *the sciences*: mathematics, physics, biology, chemistry, etc.
3. *the social sciences*: political science, economics, sociology, anthropology, and history.

B. OTHER COLLEGES OR SCHOOLS such as colleges of

1. engineering
2. architecture
3. education
4. business administration

C. A GRADUATE SCHOOL offering degrees at the master's and doctoral level.

D. One or more PROFESSIONAL SCHOOLS (after 2–4 years of undergraduate studies) such as

1. a law school
2. a medical school
3. a school of dentistry

There are over 3000 postsecondary schools in the United States. Over fifty percent of these are **four-year colleges**. They are organized as in letter A of the outline above, **College of Liberal Arts**. These colleges do not usually offer graduate degrees, except perhaps in education or business administration.

The type of education that students receive in a four-year college is called a **liberal arts education**. This means that the students are required to do very general studies in the first two years of school, taking courses from all three main areas: the **humanities**, the **sciences**, and the **social sciences** (see A.1, 2, and 3 above). In the third and fourth year, students concentrate on their **major**, taking most courses in only one area.

1. Use the information from the outline and paragraphs above to fill in the following chart.

```
                    Liberal Arts College
         _____|_____
        |                    |                  |
   [          ]         [          ]       [          ]
   _____           _____         _____
   _____           _____         _____
   _____           _____         _____
   _____           _____         _____
```

2. Make a simple chart or outline that describes either:

   a. how the university system in your country is organized,

   or

   b. how your specific college or university is organized.

3. What are the major differences in organization between colleges and universities in your country and in the United States?

   _____
   _____
   _____
   _____
   _____

4. What does the word "college" refer to in your country? In the United States, most people use it to mean the same as "university." This may be because over half of all postsecondary schools are four-year colleges, not large universities.

   _____
   _____

5. The title of the first long reading in this chapter is "Advice to Freshmen." "Advice" means suggestions or recommendations to help someone to do something well. Where do you think this long reading might be from? (See checklist at the top of the next page.)

Check one or more answer.

_____ a letter from a student's father

_____ a wall of a hall in a dormitory

_____ the student newspaper

_____ a textbook in a political science course

_____ a city newspaper

_____ a book of American short stories

6. What kind of advice would you give to first-year university students in your country? Compare your answers with your classmates' answers. After you have read the long reading, come back to this list to see how your list compares to the reading.

A. VOCABULARY IN CONTEXT

Before reading the article "Advice to Freshmen," read the following sentences. Try to guess the meaning of the underlined words from the context. Choose the correct meaning of the word. Write the words that helped you choose it.

1. Sometimes it's sunny and beautiful in Greenville. In that case I walk to school. But often it's rainy and cold. In that case I take the bus.

   In that case means

   a. in that box.
   b. maybe.
   c. in that building.
   d. if that is true.

2. How important is going to class? To some extent the answer depends on the professor. Some instructors announce that they require attendance. In that case you really should go to class.

   An instructor is

   a. a radio announcer.
   b. a paper telling how to do something.
   c. a person who teaches.
   d. a detective.

   What other words helped you choose the correct answer?
   Line _____ _____

48   Chapter 3

To require attendance means to

a. praise students who come to class.
b. make students come to every class.
c. write a list of students in each class.
d. make students listen.

What other words helped you choose the correct answer?
Line _____   _____

3. Once in a while it is better to stay in bed and sleep than to get so tired you cannot think. However, it is not a good idea to skip class more than a few times.

To skip class is

a. not to go to class.
b. to attend class.
c. to sleep in class.
d. to argue with the teacher.

What other words helped you to choose the correct answer?
Line _____   _____

At a university skipping class once in a while means

a. only once a year.
b. two to three times a semester.
c. once a week for some students.
d. never.

What other words helped you choose the correct answer?
Line _____   _____

*While you are reading the following two paragraphs, try to understand the difference between the word **class** and the word **course** in English. Then, answer the following questions.*

4. After the first week of classes, Martha asked Luis, "What's your favorite course this semester?"
   He answered, "My favorite course is rural sociology. I have three classes a week on Monday, Wednesday, and Friday at 9:15. There are about fifteen students in the class. Everyone says this course is very difficult, but I think it's going to be interesting."
   Gordon complained to Lee about his advanced organic chemistry course. "The professor isn't very interesting and the students don't seem to care about the course. In fact, the whole class seems bored. I saw one student asleep in class today. It's too bad I have to take this course, but it's required."

A class refers to (more than one is possible)

a. the time.
b. the place.
c. the subject you are studying.
d. the students.

A course refers to (more than one is possible)

a. the time.
b. the place.
c. the subject you are studying.
d. the students.

5. I want to talk to Professor Smith. He has office hours on Thursday afternoons. I have a lab at that time, so I will have to make an appointment to see him at a different time.

Office hours are

a. 9 to 5.
b. the time when a professor is free to see students.
c. a church service.
d. the time when a professor does research.

An appointment is

a. a memo.
b. a telephone call.
c. an agreement to meet someone at a certain time.
d. a little book for notes.

6. Don was sick. He felt so bad that he went to bed in the afternoon. He fell asleep and missed the party that evening.

He missed the party. He

a. was late to it.
b. did not go to it.
c. attended it.
d. disliked it.

B. LONG READING

The following article appeared in the Furnell University student newspaper, *The Furnell Daily Star*. It appeared after the first two weeks of classes. The student who wrote it gives somes suggestions about attending classes and doing well in school. *Read the article and do the comprehension exercise.*

THE FURNELL DAILY STAR

25¢

Warmer, see p. 2   Monday, January 15, 1990

Advice to Freshman

You have been at Furnell University for two weeks now. As usual, you need enough time to sleep and eat. You also want to spend time with your new friends and get some exercise. But, after the first two weeks of classes, you have probably concluded that there isn't enough time to do all these things, because you also have to attend classes, go to labs, do assignments and write papers.

Soon you will be in a situation like this one: You are going to have a quiz in your ten o'clock class. You studied for it until 3 a.m. You also have an eight o'clock. Should you sleep late and skip the eight o'clock class?

To some extent the answer depends on the professor of the course. Some instructors announce that they require attendance. In that case you really should go to class. Some don't say anything. In that case *you* have to decide. Once in a while it is better to stay in bed and sleep than to get so tired you cannot think. However, it is not a good idea to skip class more than a few times.

If you have to skip a class, ask another student for the class notes, announcements and the assignment. Also, come to the next class prepared. If you miss class because you are sick, tell the instructor afterward. He or she may let you make up the work. If you have an important appointment, tell the instructor about it before you miss the class.

Here is another common problem. You took the quiz. Even after studying very hard, you could not answer all the questions. In high school you always got every answer right. What went wrong? Nothing. High school work is easy, so a good student is supposed to get a perfect score. In college the teacher wants to challenge even the best students. Therefore, almost nobody answers every question correctly.

But maybe there were some very basic ideas in that course you did not understand. Go see the teacher during his or her office hours. Most teachers will gladly explain things again. Of course, they will not be pleased to repeat what they said in class to someone who skipped class.

Maybe you really should get up for that eight o'clock class!

STUDYING 51

C. COMPREHENSION EXERCISE

Complete each sentence in the way that best agrees with "Advice to Freshmen." Write the column, paragraph, and line that helped you decide.

1. According to the article, a good student in college must
   a. go to every class, no matter how he/she feels.
   b. go to class unless there is a good reason not to.
   c. stay in the dormitory and study.
   d. make excuses to the teacher.

   Column _____ Paragraph _____ Line _____

2. According to the article, a good student in college must also
   a. know the answer to every quiz question.
   b. answer only interesting questions.
   c. know the answer to every question the teacher asks.
   d. know the answers to a lot of quiz questions but maybe not the hardest ones.

   Column _____ Paragraph _____ Line _____

3. If you cannot go to class one day,
   a. do not bother the teacher with excuses.
   b. tell the teacher the reason for your absence.
   c. tell another student the reason for your absence.
   d. you are not a good student.

   Column _____ Paragraph _____ Line _____

4. Daily attendance is required
   a. at all American universities.
   b. only in elementary and high schools in America.
   c. for bad students only.
   d. by some college professors.

   Column _____ Paragraph _____ Line _____

5. Furnell students usually have
   a. announcements to make in class.
   b. a lot of free time.
   c. a lot of work and not much time.
   d. perfect quiz scores.

   Column _____ Paragraph _____ Line _____

6. If a student doesn't understand an important part of the lesson, he or she
   a. will never be a good student.
   b. should ask another student for class notes.
   c. should get a perfect score.
   d. should ask the instructor to explain it.

   Column _____ Paragraph _____ Line _____

D. FILL-IN EXERCISE

Fill in the blanks in the following passage. Use each word in the list once and only once. Do not change the form of the word.

advice	professor	easy	correctly
depends	freshman	decided	
high	studied	high school	

Last year I was a (1) __freshman__, a new student in college. I wanted to take a Spanish course, but I did not know whether to take Beginning Spanish or Intermediate Spanish. Then a (2) __professor__ gave me some good (3) __advice__. "You (4) __studied__ Spanish for two years when you were in (5) __high school__," she said. "The course you take here in college (6) __depends__ on your placement examination score. Your score is very (7) __high__, so you probably will not have any problems in Intermediate Spanish. It will be fairly (8) __easy__ for you.

I (9) __decided__ to take the intermediate course, and I am glad I did. I enjoyed the course a lot. When I went to Mexico this summer, I understood Spanish well. Also, the Mexicans often told me that I pronounced Spanish (10) __correctly__.

E. FILL-IN EXERCISE

Fill in the blanks with the correct words from the following list. Each word must be used once. No word can be used twice. Do not change the word in any way.

announcement	concluded	situation
assignment	impossible	are supposed to
basic	lab	right
challenge	repeat	

1. Joanne wasn't in any of her morning classes. She usually goes to class every day. I __concluded__ that she was sick.

2. There is no way to go back. Going back is __impossible__.

STUDYING   53

3. Tell me about the political ___situation___ in your country. Do people like the president?

4. The ___assignment___ for tomorrow is to read pages 7 to 15.

5. A place where students do work with equipment is called a(an) ___lab___.

6. The teacher made a(an) ___assignment___ today. He said, "The next quiz will be on Tuesday."

7. The teaching assistant said, "Everybody please do problem 17; it's important." So we ___supposed to___ do it.

8. The course is difficult, but it is very interesting. It's a(an) _____.

9. When you say something again, you ___repeat___ it.

10. The most important, fundamental parts of something are its ___situation___ parts.

11. The laboratory assistant in Chemistry Lab will show you the _____ procedure to follow in the experiment.

F. WORD ASSOCIATION

Fill in the blanks with either "teachers," "students," or both words.

_S_	attend class	_S_	take notes in class
_S_	do homework	_T_	prepare for class
_S_	assign papers	_S_	do assignments
_S_	go to labs	_T+S_	hand in papers
_T_	make announcements	_T+S_	hand out papers
_S_	take quizzes	_T_	give classes
_S_	take attendance	_S+T_	go to classes
_S_	attend labs	_T_	give quizzes
_T_	give assignments	_S_	pass exams
_ST_	write term papers		

54 Chapter 3

G. WORD FORM CHART

Vocabulary Word	Adjective	Noun	Verb	Adverb
1. <u>Daily</u> Star	daily	day		daily
2. it will be <u>impossible</u>	impossible possible	impossibility possibility		possibly
3. do your <u>assignments</u>		assignment	assign	
4. you cannot <u>think</u>	thoughtful	thought	think	thoughtfully
5. come to the next class <u>prepared</u>	prepared	preparation	prepare	
6. an <u>important</u> appointment	important	importance		
7. a <u>prefect</u> score	perfect	perfection	perfect	perfectly
8. answer every question <u>correctly</u>	correct	correction	correct	correctly
9. please to <u>repeat</u>	repetitive	repetition	repeat	repeatedly
10. ask... for the class <u>notes</u>		note(s)	note	

Prefixes and Suffixes: In addition to *suffixes*, which are added to the end of words and usually change the part of speech, there are *prefixes*, which change the meaning of words. "Pre-," for example, means before. In the case of prefixes, below, fill in the blank with the meaning that the prefix adds to the word. For suffixes, fill in the blanks with the correct part of speech.

Prefixes: im-_____* means   _____
            re-_____ means   _____

Suffixes: _____-ance   changes a verb to a(n) _____
            _____-ful   changes a(n) _____ to an adjective
            _____-ible/able   changes a verb to a(n) _____
            _____-ment   changes a(n) _____ to a noun

*as used in "impossible," not "important"

STUDYING 55

I. WORD FORM EXERCISE

Choose the correct word form from the preceding Word Form Chart and fill in the blanks. Look at number (1) on the Word Form Chart to choose the correct answer for question (1) in this exercise, and so forth. Name the part of speech in the blanks at the right margin.

1. How much work can you do in a ___day___?

    Part of speech _____

2. We cannot go by car, plane, or train, so only one ___possible___ is left. We have to take the bus.

    tay trái

    Part of speech _____

3. How much homework does Professor Smith ___assignments___? (He usually tells us to read an article each week.)

    Part of speech _____

4. ___Think___ carefully before you decide.

    Part of speech _____

5. He was not _____ for class and made many mistakes.

    Part of speech _____

6. Let us think about the ___importance___ of grades. Do we really have to worry about them so much?

    Part of speech __N__

7. He did the quiz ___correctly___. There were no mistakes.

    Part of speech _____

8. The teaching assistant ___prepared___ all the exams and gave them to the professor.

    Part of speech _____

9. She got a bad grade because she skipped class ___prefect___.

    Part of speech _____

10. It's very important to take good ___notes___ in your university courses so that you can study them later.

    Part of speech _____

J. VOCABULARY IN CONTEXT

Before reading "Problems with Chemistry," read the following paragraph. Try to guess the meaning of the underlined word. Use the meanings of all the words in the paragraph to help you decide.

Sarah Anne took Spanish 101 last semester. She became sick during the semester and missed more than two weeks of classes. Therefore, she didn't take all of the weekly quizzes. She passed all the quizzes she took, however, so she passed the course.

To pass a quiz is

a. to take it.
b. to answer all the questions on it.
c. to complete it successfully.
d. to do badly on it.

K. SHORT READING

PROBLEMS WITH CHEMISTRY

Ellen sat down in the library next to her friend Don, threw down her chemistry textbook, and began to cry. Don asked her what was wrong. Ellen explained that she had studied all night for her chemistry quiz. When she took the quiz she had been very tired. Even after studying all night, there were a lot of questions she hadn't been able to answer.

"I don't think I passed the quiz, Don," she said. "The teaching assistant is going to think I didn't study at all when he sees how badly I did on it."

"Maybe you were too tired to think well. Nobody can think without sleep. Take my advice. Before the next quiz, decide to study chemistry for no more than two hours. After that do your assignments for your other classes. Then go to bed," Don told her. Ellen seemed to feel better after listening to his suggestions.

She asked him, "Don, how long did it take you to decide what to major in? I was thinking about majoring in chemistry, but after this, I am really not sure."

"It took me a couple of semesters, I guess. I was always interested in plants and flowers, so horticulture seemed to be a natural choice for me. But I still have problems with some of my courses, you know," he told her, adding some more advice. "After the next quiz, if you still don't understand something, ask Gordon about it. He's the teaching assistant. Part of his job is to help serious students like you who really want to learn."

STUDYING 57

L. COMPREHENSION EXERCISE

Complete the following statements. You may look at the reading if necessary.

1. According to this story, it is important when studying for quizzes or exams to (more than one is possible)

    a. go to a movie the night before.
    b. get enough sleep.
    c. get help from the teaching assistant, if necessary.
    d. study all night the night before.

2. Ellen was crying because

    a. she spilled acid in chemistry lab.
    b. she had not studied for the chemistry quiz.
    c. she thought she hadn't passed the quiz.
    d. Gordon had refused to help her.

3. Don probably thinks that

    a. chemistry is easy.
    b. Daphne is childish.
    c. studying is the most important thing.
    d. studying is important, but sleep is important, too.

4. Part of a teaching assistant's job is

    a. to pass chemistry.
    b. to help students understand.
    c. to study all night.
    d. to do the assignments for his students.

M. VOCABULARY REVIEW READING

Read the following story quickly. Then answer the questions that follow.

TAKE MY ADVICE

Before Walter finished high school, he was accepted by Furnell University as a freshman for the next academic year. He wasn't sure what to major in, but he knew he didn't need to decide until his sophomore year. When he arrived in Greenville in September, he decided to take several very different courses—chemistry, literature, and economics.

Walter had been a good high school student but not an excellent one. He got almost all B's and a few C's. He had done his homework most of the time and once in a while he had skipped class. When he got to Furnell, he didn't change his study habits. As a result he got a bad grade on the first test in chemistry—65 percent, or D. When the teaching assistant gave back his quiz, he also have him some advice.

"Look, Walter, I know you're having problems with this course," Gordon told Walter. "Remember that the instructor requires attendance. In other courses it might be okay to skip class once in a while, but not in this one. A good grade in chemistry depends on attendance, good homework, and going to lab every week. If you continue to do poorly on the quizzes, you're going to have problems."

Walter thought about his advice a lot over the weekend. "The teaching assistant was serious. I'm doing poorly, and I might fail chemistry. In that case I would have to leave Furnell. I don't want to go home and find a job!" That weekend he started studying very hard. In addition, he started to do all his assignments and go to lab every week. After a month, he was able to answer almost all the quiz questions correctly.

"I'm happy to see that you're doing better in this course," the teaching assistant said to Walter.

"Yeah. Me too. It's a challenge to study every afternoon when I feel like playing football or video games. But now I know that Chemistry 102 is not an impossible course."

N. COMPREHENSION QUESTIONS

Answer the following questions. You may look at the reading to help you answer the questions.

1. In this reading, what was a challenge for Walter?

    a. To skip class once in a while.
    b. To change his study habits and do well in chemistry.
    c. To find a job at home.
    d. To major in chemistry.

2. If Walter failed chemistry at the end of the semester, what would he need to do?

    a. Study hard for his other courses.
    b. Play video games every afternoon.
    c. Look for work in his hometown.
    d. Go to lab every week.

3. What advice did the teaching assistant give Walter? (Circle all the correct answers.)

    a. Play video games every afternoon.
    b. Skip class.
    c. Start studying a lot.
    d. Do his homework.
    e. Take a literature course.
    f. Play football.
    g. Find a job.
    h. Go to class every day.

STRATEGIES

DOING LIBRARY RESEARCH FOR THE TERM PAPER

PRE-READING EXERCISE

Research means a careful study of a subject area. People often do research to find out what other people have written on the topic. A *research paper* or *term paper* organizes this information and presents any original ideas the student may have. High-level research may include some original ideas and experiments to support them.

In a university, library reference librarians or their aides can help you in your research. It is their job to show you where to look for information when you need help.

Here are some examples of reference materials that librarians can show you how to use. Discuss them with your class.

1. The card catalog, by subject, for books
2. Encyclopedias
3. *The Reader's Guide to Periodical Literature*, for magazines and journals
4. *The New York Times Index*, for the newspaper

List other reference books that you know of. Discuss them with your class.

_____

_____

Have you written any term papers? What were the topics?

_____

_____

Do you have to write any research papers for other courses you are taking? Which ones?

_____

_____

STARTING YOUR RESEARCH IN THE LIBRARY

A university library has many different information sheets to show people how to use the library. The following is a list of eight different information sheets available at the reference desk at Olin Library on the Furnell campus. Look at the photograph at the beginning of this *Strategies* section to see where these sheets are.

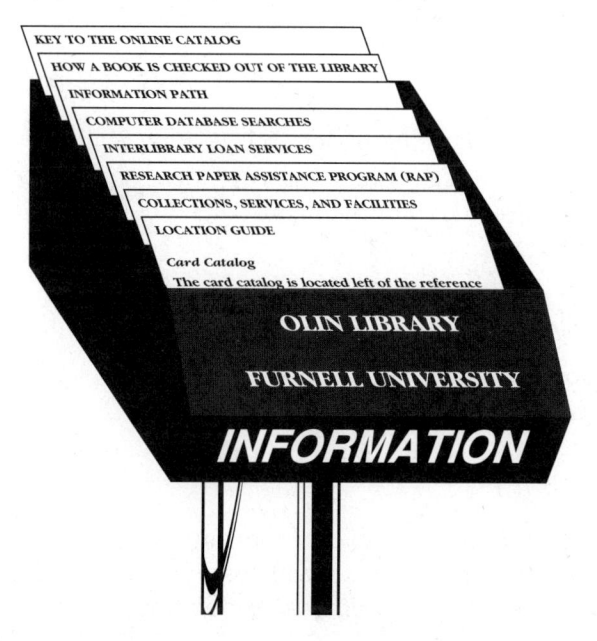

- KEY TO THE ONLINE CATALOG
- HOW A BOOK IS CHECKED OUT OF THE LIBRARY
- INFORMATION PATH
- COMPUTER DATABASE SEARCHES
- INTERLIBRARY LOAN SERVICES
- RESEARCH PAPER ASSISTANCE PROGRAM (RAP)
- COLLECTIONS, SERVICES, AND FACILITIES
- LOCATION GUIDE

Card Catalog
The card catalog is located left of the reference

OLIN LIBRARY

FURNELL UNIVERSITY

INFORMATION

Assume you are a student in Dr. Klammer's American history course. You are ready to start doing research for your term paper. Read the above titles of information sheets to see which ones can help you.

1. Which sheet will help you if you do not know where to find the magazines and academic journals? _____

2. Which sheets might help you if you want to know more about using the computer to do your research? _____

3. Which sheet will tell you what to do if the library does not own one of the books you need for your research? _____

4. Which sheet will be the most helpful to you in starting your research? Why? _____

You have chosen the correct information sheet to get help in researching your term paper. Now read it to find out what you need to do next.

RESEARCH PAPER ASSISTANCE PROGRAM (RAP)

What It is

It is your chance to get professional help with your research paper. You sign up for an appointment with a reference librarian. The librarian will spend time with you talking about your term paper topic and the best way to start your research.

What It isn't

It is *NOT* help in writing the paper. The Writing Skills Center can give you help in such things as organizing your ideas. At the library we offer assistance in finding the information you need before you can organize it into a term paper.

How Much Time It Takes

We spend about half an hour with you. We will be happy to spend more time if you need it.

How I Can Sign Up

Fill out the *RAP form* (available at the Information Desk) and give it to a reference librarian. In it you will state your term paper topic. The librarian will schedule your personal appointment.

What Is the Difference Between This and the Assistance Given at the Information Desk?

RAP gives you a private appointment with a reference librarian, someone who specializes in helping people find information. Before your appointment he/she has looked at your topic and has chosen some reference books that might contain information related to your research paper.

If you do not have time to make an appointment, but just go to the information desk, you will still speak to a reference librarian. However, you might not get the two advantages listed above: careful preparation and uninterrupted time. First, the librarian will not have had time beforehand to research your topic. Second, you may be interrupted by other people needing help.

In either case, the reference librarians are here to help you get started on your research paper. They can make your work a lot easier!

OLIN LIBRARY—FURNELL UNIVERSITY

COMPREHENSION QUESTIONS

1. Who helps the students in the Research Paper Assistance Program?

2. Who helps students organize their ideas for their term papers?

3. Why do you need to make an appointment?

4. Where can you go for help if you cannot make an appointment?

5. Who do you think can help students choose the topic for their papers?

6. Does your college library have a program like RAP? If not, whom should you see for this type of help?

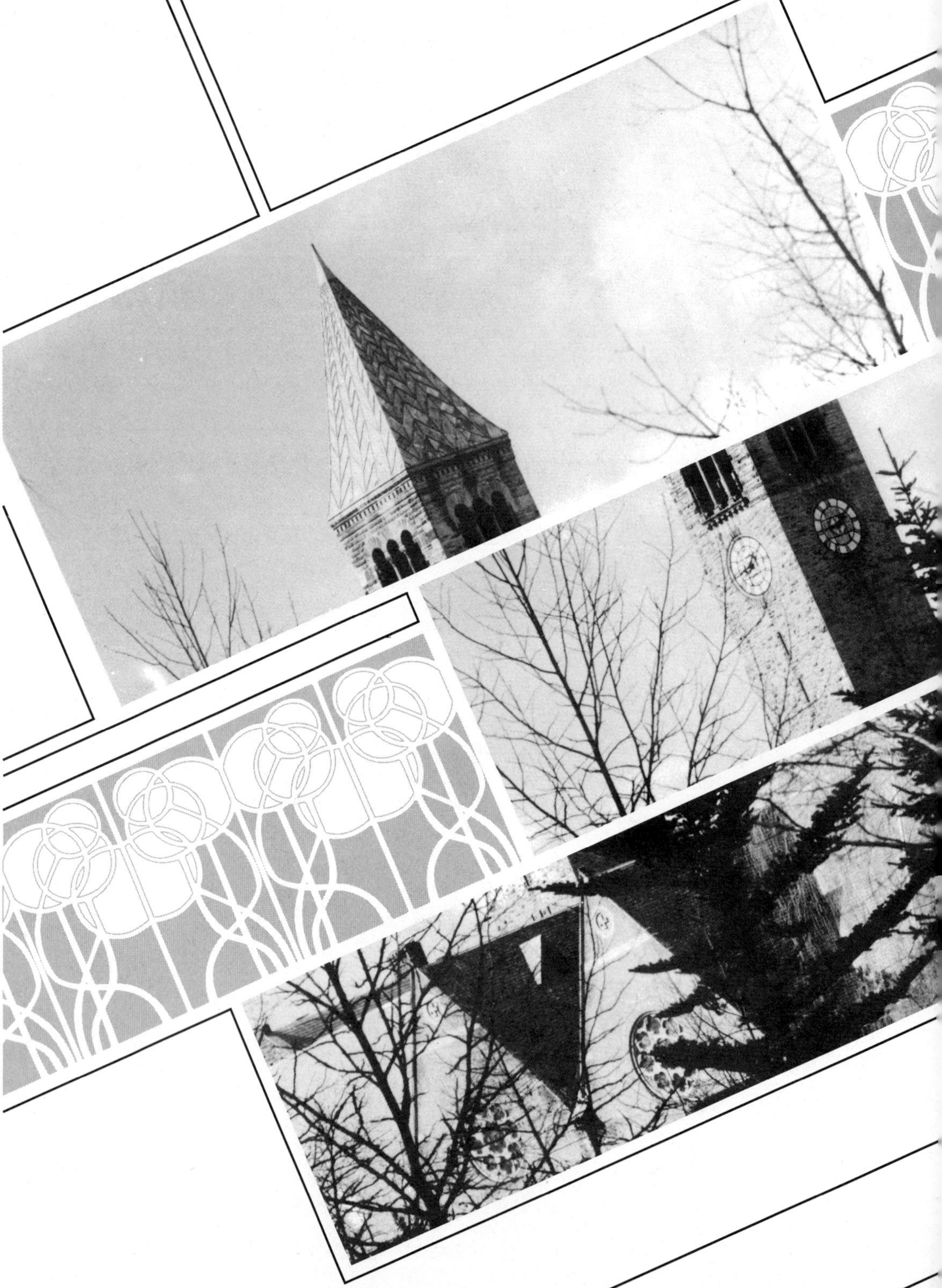

CHAPTER FOUR

TIME

TIME 67

PRE-READING QUESTIONS

*Before reading this chapter, discuss the following questions with your classmates and teacher. Compare your ideas about **time** with those of people from other countries.*

1. What are your first impressions of the American attitude toward time?

   _____

2. Have you had any humorous or embarrassing experiences related to time in the United States?

   _____

3. The first reading in this chapter describes a dinner party. The guests have different ideas about what it means to be **on time** to the party.

   Interview a classmate and write down the following information about his or her country. Then share what you have learned with the class.

   In _____ if you are invited at   it's okay to arrive at

   (dinner parties)   _____   _____
   (cocktail parties)   _____   _____
   (evening parties)   _____   _____
   (outdoor picnics)   _____   _____
   (group study sessions)   _____   _____

4. Fill in the time of the day when people **in your country** usually do the following things and compare them with your classmates'.

   wake up   _____
   eat breakfast   _____
   go to class or work   _____
   take a morning tea or coffee break   _____
   eat lunch
       (or midday dinner)   _____
       (for how long?)   _____
   go back to work or school   _____
   take an afternoon tea or coffee break _____
   leave school or work   _____
   eat dinner   _____
   watch the evening news on TV   _____
   go to sleep   _____

68 Chapter 4

5. When does the academic year begin and end?
   _____

6. When are the important exams? _____
   _____
   _____

7. Name each school holiday and give the approximate dates.
   _____
   _____
   _____
   _____
   _____

A. VOCABULARY IN CONTEXT

Before reading the story "Time for Dinner," read the following paragraphs. Try to guess the meaning of the underlined words. Use the meanings of all the words in the paragraph to help you decide.

1. There was a small <u>potluck dinner</u> at Luis and Martha's apartment last weekend. Martha invited four students from the Chemistry 102 course: Daphne, Don, Ellen, and Walter, as well as Gordon, the teaching assistant, and a friend of Martha's, Sarah Anne. Each brought a dish to share—meat and rice, vegetables, salad, bread, and dessert. Martha and Luis supplied the drinks.

   What is a <u>potluck dinner</u>?

   a. A dinner party where the hosts (Luis and Martha) cook all the food.
   b. A dinner party where the women bring the food.
   c. A dinner party where the cafeteria supplies the food.
   d. A dinner party where each person brings one part of the meal.

2. Martha was expecting her guests to bring meat and rice, a vegetable dish, a salad, dessert, and bread. Gordon arrived first. He brought a

beef casserole that smelled delicious. He gave it to Martha, who heated it before serving it.

What does beef casserole mean?

a. Soup with meat and vegetables.
b. Meat with rice or noodles.
c. Hamburgers.
d. Steak.

3. They ate and complimented each other on the food. Luis asked Daphne, "Where did you learn to make this delicious dessert?"

What does compliment mean?

a. Complicate things.
b. Tell people that you like their food or clothing.
c. Help each other serve the food.
d. Put salt and pepper on the food.

4. Lee would like to live abroad. Daphne, who has already lived in foreign countries, says it is very interesting.

To go abroad means to

a. go to a university.
b. go home.
c. go on a trip by boat.
d. go to foreign countries.

B. LONG READING

TIME FOR DINNER

Martha, the laboratory assistant, gave a small potluck dinner in her apartment. She invited four students from the Chemistry 102 course: Daphne, Don, Ellen, and Walter, as well as Gordon, the teaching assistant. She also invited her friend Sarah Anne. Each brought a dish to share—meat and rice, vegetables, salad, bread, and dessert. Martha and her husband, Luis, supplied the drinks.

It was 7:25. Martha had told everybody to come at 7:30. Unfortunately, it had taken her and Luis longer to clean their apartment than they had planned. Luis was going into the bathroom with a towel and clean clothes when Gordon arrived. Everybody knew that

Gordon always started his early-morning chemistry class at 8 sharp, so Martha wasn't surprised to see him arrive five minutes early.

"Hi Gordon! I'm sorry, but we're not ready yet. I'd forgotten that some people come on time," Martha laughed. "Oh, your beef and rice casserole smells delicious! Make yourself at home. Have something to drink while I finish getting ready."

"Thanks, Martha," Gordon answered. "Take your time. I'll entertain anyone who comes before you're finished."

A few minutes after 7:30 Walter arrived with a salad. At the same time Luis returned from the bathroom. Martha joined them soon afterwards for a drink. Then Sarah Anne arrived with three loaves of French bread.

Don and Ellen arrived together at five to eight. Don was a little angry at Ellen. He had waited about twenty minutes for her when he picked her up at her sorority house. Don was like Gordon—always on time or even early.

"When we first started dating you used to wait for me even longer. Now, I'm getting better, aren't I?" asked Ellen.

"I guess so," Don admitted reluctantly. "It looks like we're not even the last to arrive tonight. It's almost 8:15 and Daphne still isn't here. I sure am starving! And my vegetable dish is probably getting cold, too. My parents would be really angry at anyone who came for dinner even ten minutes late."

Gordon nodded in agreement. "Let's eat."

Just as they were starting to eat, Daphne came in the door, carrying a beautiful chocolate cake.

"Hi, guys!" she said cheerfully. "Hope I'm not too late. I'm never on time for dinner parties, but I usually arrive just in time to eat!"

As they ate, they complimented one another on the food that each had brought.

"Where did you learn to make this delicious dessert?" asked Luis.

"When I lived in South America I had a friend who was an excellent cook. She taught me to make this cake," Daphne said. Then she added, "I also learned a different meaning of 'on time' while I was there. Half an hour late is almost early there. Most people arrive an hour after the party starts, so 'on time' means one hour late."

Don was amazed. "It's a good thing I don't live there. I'd go crazy."

Gordon agreed wholeheartedly.

TIME   71

C. COMPREHENSION QUESTIONS

Choose the best answers to the following questions.

1. What is an important idea in this story?

    a. None of the guests was on time to the potluck dinner.
    b. Gordon arrived early, but Daphne came forty-five minutes late.
    c. People have different ideas about what "on time" means.
    d. People who have lived abroad are always an hour early for parties.

2. Who arrived at the party at 7:30 sharp?

    a. Gordon.
    b. Walter.
    c. Don and Ellen.
    d. Nobody.

D. IMPLICATIONS

*The answers to the following questions are not stated directly. They are **implied** or **suggested**. Let's look at an example.*

Daphne went to the chemistry department to ask about her grade on the chemistry exam. When she returned to the dormitory she was smiling.

It is implied but not stated that

a. Daphne got a good grade on the exam.
b. Daphne got a bad grade on her exam.

Daphne is probably smiling because she is happy about her grade. Therefore, (a) is the correct answer.

Now answer the following implication questions about the story "Time for Dinner."

1. Luis was carrying his towel and clean clothes when Gordon arrived. Where was Luis going?

    a. To get some soda from the Pepsi machine.
    b. To the laundromat to wash his clothes.
    c. To the bathroom to take a shower.
    d. To the beach.

2. In the story, Daphne said, "Half an hour late is almost early there. Most people arrive an hour after the party starts, so 'on time' means one hour late."

   Don was amazed, "It's a good thing I don't live there. I'd go crazy."

   Why would Don not like living there?

   a. Because they eat chocolate cake all the time.
   b. Because they never go to parties.
   c. Because "on time" means one hour early.
   d. Because they have different ideas about being early and late.

E. FILL-IN EXERCISE

Review the following vocabulary words by using them to fill in the blanks in the following sentences.

provides	intended	going out with
extremely hungry	confessed	
and also	prepared	

1. The person who invites people to his/her house for a potluck supper usually ____provides____ the plates, silverware, glasses, and napkins.

2. Ellen and Don ____prepared____ to go to a late movie after the potluck supper.

3. How long has Ellen been ____going out with____ Don?

4. Don was ____extreme hungry____ when Daphne finally arrived at the potluck dinner.

5. Daphne ____confessed____ that she was always late to parties.

6. Unlike the other students at the party, Don lives with his parents, his brother and sister, ____and also____ his cat.

7. At the party Gordon asked Ellen whether she was ____intended____ for her next chemistry quiz. Ellen replied, "Well, not quite. There are a couple of things I really don't understand. Could I come to your office on Monday to get some help?"

TIME 73

F. WORD ASSOCIATION EXERCISE

*Read the following paragraph and try to understand the terms **on time**, **late**, and **in time**. Then do the following exercise.*

The class was supposed to start at 8:00. Gordon and Don arrived early, at 7:55. Walter and Daphne were on time. They hurried in at 8:00 sharp. Ellen was late. She came at 8:05. Fortunately, the quiz began at 8:10, so she was in time to take the quiz.

Fill in the blanks with one of the following:

on time   in time   late

1. The appointment with the dentist was for 3:30. Jane got there at 3:40. She arrived _____ for the appointment.

2. Ellen's ride to Washington, D.C., was supposed to leave at 10:15. She got to the student center at 10:29, one minute before the driver was ready to drive away. She arrived _____ to catch her ride.

3. Gordon's interview was at 4:15. He got there at 4:15 sharp. He arrived _____ .

4. The pregnant woman and her husband got to the hospital only twenty minutes before the baby was born. They got there _____ for the doctor to help deliver the baby.

5. My little brother Tommy loves cartoons. He always arrives at the exact minute when they begin at the movie theater. He always gets there _____ .

6. Walter overslept and was twenty-five minutes late for his exam. Fortunately, he finished it before the end of the class period. He arrived _____ to finish the exam.

7. The train arrived at exactly 6:25 and left at 6:35, on schedule. It came into the train station and left _____ .

8. Walter and his date got to the dance at 8:30, when it was supposed to start. Everybody else arrived at about 9:30, at the same time that the dancing started. Walter and his friend got there _____ . Everybody else arrived _____ to dance.

9. My appointment with the doctor was for 11:15. I ran and arrived at the office at 11:25, tired and out of breath. The doctor didn't call me until 11:45. Even though I arrived ten minutes *late* for my appointment, I was *in time* to see the doctor. The doctor was _____ , too.

G. WORD FORM CHART

Vocabulary Word	Adjective	Noun	Verb	Adverb
1. <u>Unfortunately</u>, it had taken ... longer.	unfortunate fortunate	fortune misfortune		unfortunately fortunately
2. "Hi, guys," she said <u>cheerfully</u>.	cheerful	cheer	cheer (up)	cheerfully
3. "I guess so," Don <u>admitted</u> reluctantly.	admitted	admittance	admit	admittedly
4. Don admitted <u>reluctantly</u>.	reluctant	reluctance		reluctantly
5. Gordon agreed <u>wholeheartedly</u>.	wholehearted halfhearted			wholeheartedly halfheartedly
6. Martha wasn't <u>surprised</u> to see him ... early.	surprised surprising	surprise	surprise	
7. Don was <u>amazed</u>.	amazed amazing	amazement	amaze	amazingly
8. I sure am <u>starving</u>.	starving	starvation	starve	
9. Gordon <u>agreed</u>.		agreement	agree	

Prefixes:
un- means _____

TIME 75

H. WORD FORM EXERCISE

Choose the correct word form and fill in the blank. Look at number (1) on the Word Form Chart to choose the correct answer for question (1) in this exercise, and so forth. Name the part of speech.

1. The boy was __fortunate__ to have an aunt and uncle who took care of him when his parents died.

    Part of speech __Adj__

2. Your sister is sad. Whey don't you __cheer up__ your sister with some of your jokes?

    Part of speech __V__

3. The __admitted__ criminal was in prison for five years.

    Part of speech __Adj__

4. The soldier left his wife and children with great __reluctance__ to go abroad to fight. (chiến đấu)

    Part of speech __N__

5. Luis and Martha wrote a letter to the newspaper about equality. Sarah Anne agreed with it __wholeheartedly__. She thought it was completely correct.

    Part of speech __A__

6. "Wasn't that news __surprised__?" she exclaimed. "I never thought that old car could win a race."

    Part of speech __A__

7. To my __amazement__, I won the first prize in the cooking contest.

    Part of speech __N__

8. How many children __starve__ in the world while we waste so much food every day?

    Part of speech __V__

9. After a long talk, Don and Ellen came to an __agreement__. He promised to dress better. She promised to be on time.

    Part of speech __N__

76   Chapter 4

I. SCANNING

What is scanning?   *Scanning* means reading to find specific information to answer a question. When you scan, you do not read every word on the page. That would take too long. Instead, your job is to find the location of the answer in the text as quickly as possible.

Key words help you scan.   When you scan, your eyes look over the reading quickly for important words (key words) that may be close to the information you want to find. You choose these key words from the important ideas in your question. When you find one of your key words in the text, you stop scanning and read more carefully to find your answer. Let's try an example of finding key words in questions and scanning for answers. Look back at the reading on page 50, from the *Furnell Daily Star*. Your question is "What score should a good high school student get?" You know the whole article is about advice for college students. The important idea in your question is *high school* and *score*. Look quickly for these words in the reading without rereading every word. Can you answer the question?

Question words also help you scan.   Many English questions begin with *question words* such as *where*, *when*, *who*, or *what*. Question words tell you what kind of answer to expect. For example, here are some possible answers to a *where* question. All of them are *places*:

On Buffalo Street.

In the dormitory.

Abroad.

In Greenville.

The answer to a **where** question will be a place, usually in the form of a prepositional phrase.

*Look at the following **where** question from the reading (Section B) in this chapter. Scan the reading for a place, then find the answer.*

1. Where was the potluck dinner? ___Martha's appartment___
   Paragraph __1__ Line __2__

The following is a **when** question. Here are some possible answers to **when** questions. They are all times or dates.

At 1:45 PM.

On Sunday.

In the summer.

On August 28, 1967.

TIME 77

You will find that with a little practice your eyes can find numbers on a page very quickly.

Now scan the reading in Section B to answer the following question. Let the key words (underlined words in the question) and question words help you scan.

2. **When** did <u>Don</u> and <u>Ellen</u> arrive at the party?
   At five to eight

   Paragraph _5_ Line _12_

Possible answers to **who** questions are names of people:

Dr. Coleman.
Mrs. Herman.
The professor.
The Jones family.

Usually, the capital letters of people's names are easy to find, so names can usually be found quickly.

3. **Who** brought the <u>vegetable dish</u> to the dinner?
   Don isty brought the vegetable dish to the

   Paragraph _6_ Line _8_

Possible answers to **what** questions are things:

A beef casserole.
A lot of books.
A withdrawal slip.
An old pickup truck.

4. **What** did <u>Daphne</u> bring to the party?
   cake

   Paragraph _____ Line _____

Now try to find the answers to some more questions. First underline the key words in the questions. Then decide whether the answer will be a place, a time, a person, or a thing. Finally, find the answer by scanning the reading until you find your key word(s), then reading carefully for the answer.

5. **How many** people were at the potluck dinner? _____

   Paragraph _____ Line _____

78 Chapter 4

6. **Which** course were most of these people taking at Furnell? _____
   Paragraph _____ Line _____

7. How long did Don wait for Ellen at her sorority house? _____
   Paragraph _____ Line _____

8. Now fill in the following table by scanning the reading: Discuss how to find the answers.

GUEST	TIME OF ARRIVAL	FOOD BROUGHT TO POTLUCK
Daphne	_____	_____
Don	_____	_____
Gordon	_____	_____
Sarah Anne	_____	_____
Ellen	_____	_____
Walter	_____	_____

J. SCANNING EXERCISE

Find the answers to the following questions. Look in the list on the next page for the name of the city in the left column (by alphabetical order). Then find the time in the column on the right. Do this as quickly as possible.

When it is 12 noon* in New York City, what time is it in _____?

Paris, France	_____
Juneau, Alaska	_____
Freetown, Sierra Leone	_____
Rio de Janeiro, Brazil	_____
Mexico City, Mexico	_____
Cairo, Egypt	_____
Honolulu, Hawaii	_____
Denver, Colorado	_____

*Eastern standard time (not daylight savings).

Beijing, China	1:00 A.M.†
Bombay, India	10:30 P.M.
Cairo, Egypt	7:00 P.M.
Caracas, Venezuela	1:00 P.M.
Denver, Colorado	10:00 A.M.
Freetown, Sierra Leone	4:00 P.M.
Honolulu, Hawaii	7:00 A.M.
Juneau, Alaska	9:00 A.M.
Lima, Peru	12:00 noon
London, England	5:00 P.M.
Manila, Philippines	1:00 A.M.†
Mexico City, Mexico	11:00 A.M.
New York, New York	12:00 noon
Paris, France	6:00 P.M.
Rio de Janeiro, Brazil	2:00 P.M.
Riyadh, Saudi Arabia	8:30 P.M.
Singapore	12:30 A.M.†
Sydney, Australia	3:00 A.M.†
Teheran, Iran	8:30 P.M.
Tokyo, Japan	2:00 A.M.†
Wellington, New Zealand	5:00 A.M.†

†The morning of the next day.

K. VOCABULARY IN CONTEXT

Before reading the story "It's Earlier Than You Think," read the following sentences. Try to guess the meaning of the underlined words from the context.

1. Mr. Hanover, a lawyer, said hello to the man who was walking into his office. "Good morning, Mr. Walsh. How are you today?"

   "Just fine," he replied, "but I'm not Mr. Walsh. My name is Alex Brown."

   "Oh, my goodness, Mr. Brown," said the lawyer as his face turned red. "I'm so embarrassed. How could I have made a mistake like that?"

   "Perhaps Mr. Walsh looks like me," Mr. Brown answered.

   People say, "oh my goodness" when

   a. they are sad.
   b. they work in an office.
   c. they are surprised.
   d. they have a professional job.

   Mr. Hanover said, "I'm so embarrassed!" What words in the same paragraph tell you what embarrassed means?

   _____ Mistake _____

   _____

2. Daphne showed Walter a picture of a very unusual new building in Paris. "Boy, is it strange!" said Walter.

By saying boy, Walter said that the building was

a. not strange.
b. a little strange.
c. for men only.
d. very strange.

L. SHORT READING

Read the following short reading and answer the comprehension questions that follow.

IT'S EARLIER THAN YOU THINK!

The kitchen clock said 7:50 A.M. Sarah Anne's roommate, Joanne, was eating breakfast in the kitchen of their apartment when she heard Sarah Anne pick up the phone. "Who are you calling this early in the morning?"

"A friend in California. It's a lot cheaper if I call before 8 A.M. Oh, wait. Someone's answering." Joanne heard Sarah Anne say hello and ask, "Is Nancy there?" A few seconds later she said, "Oh my goodness! I forgot. Don't wake her up; I'll call back later. I'm really sorry."

Joanne was very curious. "What happened?" she asked as Sarah Anne hung up the phone.

"Well," Sarah Anne answered. "I guess I was really excited about calling Nancy for so little money. I completely forgot that California is in a different time zone. It's three hours earlier there than it is here. Boy, am I embarrassed!"

M. COMPREHENSION QUESTIONS

Choose the best answer to the following questions. Do not look back at the reading.

1. What is an important idea in this short reading?

a. Sarah Anne talked to her friend in Los Angeles at 7:50 A.M.
b. Telephone rates are cheaper before 8 A.M.
c. You should never call anyone before 8 A.M.
d. There are different time zones in the United States.

2. It is implied that Nancy's roommate in California was

a. showering.
b. sleeping.
c. eating.
d. reading.

N. SCANNING

Before you scan this reading for specific facts, get an idea of its structure by reading the first paragraph and the first phrase in each of the other paragraphs. This should give you a good idea about where to look for information in the paragraph. Now scan to find answers to the following questions:

1. Are American lunch breaks long?
2. Do people come to evening parties exactly on time?
3. What do many Americans do while they get dressed in the morning?

How did you know in which paragraph to find each answer?

O. VOCABULARY REVIEW READING

CLOCKS AND WATCHES

For most Americans, clocks and watches are very important. They are always aware of them.

In the morning some people have to get up when it is still dark. Others sleep through several hours of sunlight. But both groups wake up when they hear their alarm clock ring. While they get dressed and eat breakfast, they listen to the radio, and the radio tells them again and again exactly what time it is.

On the way to work or school, people look at their watches. If they think they are going to be late, they hurry.

At work, Americans think it is important to arrive at meetings on time. Their lunch breaks are short, lasting only a half an hour or an hour. Late in the afternoon, they check their watches often to see how soon they can go home.

In the evening, however, Americans are more relaxed. They try to arrive on time, but they don't worry if they are a few minutes late to meet friends in a restaurant. Also, people who arrive a few minutes late to a movie are usually in time to see the main feature film. If a party at a friend's house starts at 8:00, some people come an hour later, and nobody minds.

Americans are used to living by clocks and watches. It is hard for them to understand that people in many parts of the world don't think that being on time is so important.

P. COMPREHENSION QUESTIONS

Answer the following questions about the short reading. Do not look at the reading to help you answer the questions.

1. What is an important idea in the reading?

   a. Americans hurry too much and should follow the example of more relaxed cultures.
   b. It is impolite to arrive more than an hour late to a party in the United States.
   c. Time plays a very important role in American culture.
   d. Americans hurry more at night than in the daytime.

2. Americans are used to

   a. being late to meetings and movies.
   b. waking up without an alarm clock.
   c. not worrying about time.
   d. checking the time often.

3. According to the reading, when people are a little late to a movie

   a. they have to wait for the next show.
   b. they usually arrive at the beginning of the feature film.
   c. they check their watches to see when they can go home.
   d. they go to a party instead.

   Is this answer stated directly or implied? _____implied_____

STRATEGIES

FINDING INFORMATION FROM A WEEKLY CLASS SCHEDULE

Walter's weekly schedule is at the top of the next page. The schedule includes the meeting times for all of the following: classes, laboratories (Spanish and chemistry), and study groups. Walter also wrote on the schedule the times when he eats his lunch and dinner and when he goes to the library to study. *Answer the following questions to understand Walter's schedule during the week.*

	Monday	Tuesday	Wednesday	Thursday	Friday
8:00	Chem 102 Lecture	Review Session TA	Chem 102 Lecture		Chem 102 Lecture
9:05					
10:10	History 101	English 105	History 101	English 105	History 101
11:15	Lunch	Freshman Comp	Lunch	Freshman Comp	Lunch
12:20	Economics 101	Lunch	Economics 101	Lunch	Economics 101
1:25	S	P	A	N	I	S	H	103
2:30	Language Laboratory			Chem 102 LAB	
3:35	Tennis Class		Tennis Class		
4:40					
	D	I	N	N	E	R
6:00	LIBRARY		LIBRARY		
7:00					
8:00	Chem Study Group	VOLLEYBALL	Chem Study Group	VOLLEYBALL	No STUDYING!
9:00					
10:00		LIBRARY		LIBRARY	
11:00					
12:00					

1. What courses is Walter taking? _____

2. Do any of his classes meet five days a week? If so, which one(s)? _____

3. Which days are easier for Walter: Monday, Wednesday, Friday (MWF) or Tuesday, Thursday (TTh)? Make a list below of his courses to find out. Decide with your classmates which days are easier.

      MWF   T Th

84   Chapter 4

4. Which of the activities on Walter's schedule are flexible, that is, can be changed according to his needs?

_____

_____

_____

5. Can you guess what a Chem(istry) Study Group is? Where do you think it might meet?

_____

_____

FINDING INFORMATION FROM AN ACADEMIC CALENDAR

PRE-READING EXERCISE

*Look at the following list of important dates. Put a check by the dates you think will be printed on an **official academic** calendar. Discuss your choices with your classmates.*

1. National holidays such as George Washington's and Martin Luther King's birthdays
2. The first day of spring
3. The first day of classes
4. Graduation ceremonies, when seniors graduate from Furnell
5. Father's day
6. The date that students can move into their dormitories
7. Thanksgiving vacation
8. Christmas day
9. Easter day
10. Channukah
11. Spring break
12. Exam dates
13. Dates for registration for the next semester
14. Birthstone and flower for each month
15. Your birthday

STRATEGIES   85

1. Can you think of any other dates that would be on an academic calendar?

　_____

　_____

2. How would a calendar for the people who work all year long at the university (such as administrators, secretaries, cafeteria workers, etc.) be different from an academic one that is only for students and faculty?

　_____

　_____

　_____

Now look at the Furnell 1986–87 calendar. Does it have the information that you and your classmates thought it would? What is *not* included that you think *should be* included?

FURNELL UNIVERSITY
CALENDAR FOR 1986–1987

New students report to campus	TUES SEPT 2
Returning students report to campus	SAT SEPT 6
First day of class	MON SEPT 8
Midterm exams	FRI OCT 10
Registration for spring term	MON OCT 27
	through FRI OCT 31
Thanksgiving vacation	THURS NOV 27
	through SUN NOV 30
Last day of fall term classes	FRI DEC 5
Reading days for exams	SAT DEC 6
	through SUN DEC 7
Fall term final exams	MON DEC 8
	through FRI DEC 12
Spring term begins	MON JAN 19
Midterm exams	TUES MAR 10
Spring break	SAT MAR 14
	through SUN MAR 22
Registration for fall term 1987	MON APR 6
	through FRI APR 10
Last day of spring term classes	FRI MAY 15
Reading days for exams	SAT MAY 16
	through SUN MAY 17
Spring term final exams	MON MAY 18
	through FRI MAY 22
Graduation	5:00 PM SUN MAY 24

COMPREHENSION QUESTIONS

1. Why do you think new students need to come to campus early?

2. When do students need to decide which courses to take in the spring? In the fall? _____

3. How long is Thanksgiving break? _____

4. How many reading (study) days are scheduled in each semester?

5. How long is spring break? _____

6. Approximately how many weeks are there between the midterm and final exams in both fall and spring semesters?
   Fall: _____
   Spring: _____

READING A COURSE OUTLINE

PRE-READING QUESTIONS

1. What kinds of work do students have to do for a university course in your country? Discuss this with your class. _____

2. Which of the following things does the teacher use to give a grade for each student? What percentage (%) is each worth?
   _____ short papers/projects (including class presentations)
   _____ midterm exam
   _____ final exam
   _____ research (term) paper
   _____ class participation (discussing the homework assignments, including readings from the textbook and any outside readings)
   Others: _____

3. How is a science course different from a humanities or social sciences course?

4. How is an upper-level course (third or fourth year) different from an introductory level course?

5. How is a graduate-level course different from an undergraduate-level course?

STRATEGIES 87

SCANNING FOR ANSWERS TO VERY SPECIFIC QUESTIONS

Look at the course outline to find the answers to the following questions. Do this as quickly as you can. Then read it carefully and answer the questions on the next page.

1. **When** does History 101 meet? _____
2. **How much** of the grade depends on the final exam? _40%_
3. **What** is Prof. Klammer's office room number? _305 Marshall hall_
4. **When** is the term paper due? _December 15_
5. **What** is the name of the textbook? _the book with many ..._

COURSE OUTLINE FOR HISTORY 101, DR. JANE KLAMMER

COURSE: History 101
"Introduction to American History"

CLASS: 363 Marshall Hall
    10:10–11:00
    M W F

INSTRUCTOR: Dr. Jane Klammer
OFFICE: 305 Marshall Hall
OFFICE HOURS:
    11:15–12:30 M W F
    3:35– 5:00 T Th
Other times by appointment

TELEPHONE: 255-4475

TEXTBOOK: Green, Robert P., Jr., et al., *The American Tradition: A History of the United States,* Charles E. Merrill Publishing Co,, Columbus, Ohio: 1984. (Available at the College Bookstore)

COURSE REQUIREMENTS:
mid-term exam: October 10   20% of the final grade
final exam: December 10   40% of the final grade
term paper due: December 15   40% of the final grade

    Attendance is not required, but you are responsible for *all* the information given in the class lectures. In the lectures I will talk about the chapters in the textbook and other material that I choose to supplement the course. The exams will cover all this information. Therefore, I advise you to come to class as much as possible. If you have to miss a class, be sure to get the class notes from another student.
    Your **homework assignments** are listed on the next page. You are supposed to read the chapter about which I will be lecturing *before* you come to class. This is to make sure that you understand as much as possible while taking notes in my lectures. Be prepared when you come to class. If there are any changes in the assigned homework readings, I will announce them in class.
    The **term paper** is 40 percent of your final grade. It should not exceed fifteen pages. (Anyone thinking of majoring in history may write twenty-five pages.) Before the midterm exam you will choose the topic for your paper.
    Have a good semester!

88   Chapter 4

Now read the course outline carefully and answer the following comprehension questions.

1. When should a student read chapter 2?

   a. Before Prof. Klammer talks about it in class.
   b. After Prof. Klammer talks about it in class.
   c. Before the midterm exam.
   d. Before the final exam only.

2. How does a student know what the homework assignments are?

   a. Prof. Klammer announces them in class.
   b. The student reads the list on the next page.
   c. Prof. Klammer gives a list every week in class.
   d. The student goes to the professor's office and asks.

3. If a freshman thinks that (s)he might major in history, what is the maximum length her/his paper can be?

   a. fifteen pages
   b. twenty-five pages
   c. ten pages
   d. no maximum

4. If a student cannot see Prof. Klammer during her office hours, what should (s)he do?

   a. See her after class.
   b. Call her at home.
   c. Ask another student.
   d. Make an appointment with her.

5. How are the percentages for final grade determination in Dr. Klammer's course different from what they might be in a history course in your country?

   _____
   _____
   _____

6. What other characteristics of this course are different from those in a similar university course in your country?

   _____
   _____

IF THIS IS YOUR FIRST VISIT
PLEASE FILL OUT THIS FORM
THANK YOU

CHAPTER FIVE

HEALTH

PRE-READING QUESTIONS

Before reading this chapter, answer the following questions with a partner from a different country. Compare your two systems, and then discuss the answers with your classmates.

1. Check the phrases which best describe the medical care that you receive in your country.

    Doctor:
    _____ A private doctor
    _____ A clinic, with many doctors
    _____ A family doctor, a general practitioner
    _____ A specialist (e.g., heart, ear, bone, etc.)

    Payment:
    _____ State-subsidized insurance (socialized medicine) pays 100 percent of medical bills.
    _____ State-subsidized insurance pays a large percentage of medical bills.
    _____ Private insurance pays 100 percent of the medical bills.
    _____ Private insurance pays a large percentage of the medical bills.
    _____ No insurance; each person is totally responsible for his/her own medical bills.

2. What type of health workers do you think are in a university health center? Look at the photographs for ideas.
   _____
   _____

3. What is the average cost per visit to the doctor?
    _____ family doctor, general practitioner
    _____ specialist (e.g., heart, ear, bone, etc.)

4. What is the average waiting time for making appointments?
    _____ a few days
    _____ a few weeks
    _____ a month or two

    In the doctor's office (before you see him/her after your scheduled time has past)? _____

5. What is the average amount of time that the doctor spends with you during your appointment? _____

94   Chapter 5

6. How does health care for university students differ from the situation you have discussed above?

   _____
   _____
   _____

7. Are there any medical problems that students suffer from more than other members of the population (people of different ages or occupations)?

   _____
   _____
   _____

8. Many Americans have become aware of the health consequences of the food they eat and the amount of exercise they get. Have you seen examples of this awareness at your university in the United States? How does this compare to the food and exercise habits of students and other people in your country? Discuss this with your partner and classmates.

9. The first reading in this chapter is titled "At the Clinic." What do you think it will be about?

   _____
   _____
   _____

A. VOCABULARY IN CONTEXT

Before reading the story "At the Clinic," read the following paragraph. Try to guess the meaning of the underlined words from the context.

Luis went to the Furnell University Health <u>Clinic</u>. He described his <u>symptoms</u> to the health associate. He said that he had a headache, a sore throat, and a bad cough. After the health associate had examined him, she told him that his throat was very red and his temperature was 102 degrees. She felt his neck and said that his neck glands were quite <u>swollen</u>. "I'm going to <u>prescribe</u> an antibiotic for you. Take one <u>capsule</u> every four hours."

HEALTH 95

1. A <u>symptom</u> is

   a. a medical complaint, for example, a headache.
   b. a medical history or former illnesses.
   c. a financial problem or a debt.

2. <u>Swollen</u> means

   a. painful.
   b. enlarged.
   c. dangerous.

3. When a doctor <u>prescribes</u> some medicine, he or she

   a. orders a medicine.
   b. gives some advice.
   c. gives a medical warning.

4. A <u>capsule</u> is

   a. something to drink.
   b. a pill.
   c. a short nap.

5. A <u>clinic</u> is

   a. the Chemistry Department building.
   b. where sick people go to get help.
   c. apartments for married students.

B. LONG READING

AT THE CLINIC

Luis had a headache, a sore throat, a bad cough, and a temperature. He had been sick for five days. Finally, his wife, Martha, convinced him to go to the Furnell University Health Clinic. He didn't have an appointment, so he knew he would have to wait.

As he entered the clinic, the receptionist asked him to fill out a sign-in slip. He wrote down his name, address, phone number, and I.D. number. Then he checked the reason for his visit to the clinic. He checked "cold, sore throat."

Luis waited in the waiting room on the second floor for about twenty minutes. Then, a nurse called his name and Luis followed her into an examination room. She took his temperature and told him the health associate would be in to see him soon. Luis asked the nurse if a health associate was a doctor.

Furnell University Health Services
VISIT RECORD

Please Print:
Name _Luis Rodriguez_
I.D. no. _513-27-8234_ Phone no. _277-2802_
Address (local) _28-B Habrouck Apts_

Do you have an appointment?

If not, nature of visit:
- ☐ Injury
- ☐ Dental
- ☐ Allergy shot
- ☐ Travel shots
- ☑ Cold, sore throat
- ☐ Dermatology clinic
- ☐ Eye clinic
- ☐ Gynecology clinic

PLEASE GIVE COMPLETED SLIP TO RECEPTIONIST

She explained that a health associate is not a doctor but has several years of medical education and training. When necessary, health associates consult with the clinic doctors.

After fifteen minutes the health associate came in. Luis described his symptoms to her. After she had examined him, she told him that his throat was very red, his neck glands were quite swollen, and his temperature was 102 degrees. "You've got a bad infection, Luis. I'm going to ask the doctor to prescribe an antibiotic for you. Take one capsule three times a day for ten days. You should also stay in bed for two days until your fever comes down. Drink a lot of liquid and rest as much as possible. If your infection doesn't clear up after five days, come back to the clinic or call me."

"Thanks a lot," said Luis, taking the prescription. He was glad that he had listened to his wife's advice. On his way home, he stopped at the drugstore and had his prescription filled.

When he got home, he took his medicine and went right to bed. Two days later his temperature was back to normal. By the time he had taken all the pills, he felt like himself again.

HEALTH   97

C. COMPREHENSION QUESTIONS

Choose the best answer to the following questions or the best way to complete the sentences. You may look back at the reading to help you find the correct answers.

1. Health associates
   a. are better trained than doctors.
   b. are not as intelligent as doctors.
   c. prefer working with students at a university.
   d. work closely with doctors at the clinic.

2. What does a receptionist do?
   a. Prescribes medicine.
   b. Takes people's temperatures.
   c. Cleans offices.
   d. Talks to people as they enter.

3. Which of the following were *not* symptoms of Luis' infection?
   a. A headache.
   b. A sore throat.
   c. A fever.
   d. A stomachache.

4. What did the health associate tell him to do?
   a. Drink a lot of liquid.
   b. Go back to class immediately.
   c. Take two capsules every four hours.
   d. Eat a lowfat diet.

5. Which of the following statements is true?
   a. Luis didn't have to wait for medical attention.
   b. The clinic gave Luis the necessary medicine.
   c. Luis' fever did not come down after he took the pills.
   d. His fever came down in two days.

6. It is implied that
   a. using a clinic is expensive.
   b. Luis' wife was also very sick.
   c. Luis hadn't wanted to go to the clinic for a long time.
   d. Luis did not eat or sleep well before he got sick.

7. A receptionist usually works at a reception desk. The suffix *-ist* is
   a. a noun suffix that means a *thing*.
   b. a verb suffix.
   c. a noun suffix that means a *person*.
   d. an adjective suffix.

D. FILL-IN EXERCISE

Fill in the blanks with the correct words from the following list. Each word must be used. No word can be used twice.

advice	fever	cold, sore throat
capsule	normal	checked
come down		

1. To indicate the reason for his visit, Luis checked the box labeled "___sore throat___."

2. When the nurse noticed his high temperature, she said, "You have a ___fever___."

3. Handing the patient a prescription, the health associate said, "Take one ___capsule___ every four hours."

4. Luis' wife noticed that he seemed to feel like himself again. "I'm so glad you're back to ___normal___," she said.

5. His temperature dropped quickly. He remembered that the health associate had said it would start to ___come down___ in two days.

6. The student filled out the sign-in slip. Because she had a deep cut that probably needed stitches, she ___checked___ the box that said "injury."

7. His wife convinced him to visit the clinic. Later he appreciated her ___advice___.

E. HOMONYMS

Homonyms are words spelled and/or pronounced alike but different in meaning. Sometimes one word can have several different meanings. You have probably noticed this when looking up a word in the dictionary. You often have to choose which definition is correct. To decide which one is best, you must think about the context.

The word *check* has several meanings, two of which were used in the story "At the Bank" in Chapter 2. Remember that Walter opened an account and immediately received ten *checks*. In this case, the word *check* is a noun. A check looks like this:

HEALTH   99

```
GORDON O. TERRY                                        182
347 Dryden Rd.                                    73-149/919
Greenville, N.Y.
14583
                                    _____ 19 ___
PAY TO THE
ORDER OF _____ $ _____
_____ DOLLARS
        1st NATIONAL BANK
        of Greenville
MEMO _____    _____
```

When Eric made his deposit, the bank teller *checked* to see if he had endorsed his check. Here, the word *checked* is a verb and means to look to see about something.

In this chapter, Luis *checked* the box labeled "cold, sore throat." In this context, *checked* is also a verb but means to make a mark like ✔. This is a third definition.

In Chapter 11 Don and Ellen will go to a restaurant. There, the word *check* will have a fourth meaning. "Ellen picked up the *check* that the waiter put on the table." *Check* is a noun in this case. It means a bill in a restaurant.

F. HOMONYM EXERCISE

*In this exercise, there are four sentences at the left, each using the word **check** with a different meaning. Match each sentence with the sentence or illustration on the right that means the same thing. Use the context to tell you which sentences match. You have to look at the context every time you see the word **check** or any other homonym in your reading.*

_b_ 1. My checks from 1st National Bank are each numbered at the top right.

a. After dinner I called the waiter over and asked for the bill.

_d_ 2. I checked to see if there was enough oil in my truck.

b. [check illustration]

_a_ 3. When we had finished our dinner, I asked for our check.

c. As I filled out the form for my passport, I put a ✔ in the box marked "renewal."

_c_ 4. While I was filling out my passport application, I checked "renewal," not "first application."

d. I thought there might not be enough oil in my truck. I looked to see how much there was.

G. WORD FORM CHART

Vocabulary Word	Adjective	Noun	Verb	Adverb
1. Luis had a sore throat.	sore	sore		
2. He checked the reason for his visit.		check	check	
3. Luis described his symptoms.	symptomatic	symptom		
4. His neck glands were quite swollen.	swollen	swelling	swell	
5. His prescription was filled.	prescribed prescription*	prescription	prescribe	
6. His temperature was back to normal.	normal abnormal	normality abnormality		normally
7. If your infection doesn't start to clear up...	clear		clear up	clearly
8. He took his medicine.	medical	medicine	medicate	

Suffixes: ▬▬-atic changes a noun to a (n) _____ .

*A noun used as an adjective in a compound noun.

HEALTH   101

H. WORD FORM EXERCISE

Choose the correct word form and fill in the blank. Look at number (1) on the Word Form Chart to choose the correct answer for question (1) in this exercise, and so forth. Name the part of speech in the blank at the right.

1. After falling off her bicycle, Daphne had a _____ on her leg for several days. It felt especially _____ when she sat down.

   Part of speech _____
   Part of speech _____

2. When you fill out an application, you are often asked to _____ your sex and ethnic background.

   Part of speech _____

3. A fever is _____ of a virus. But there are many other _____, too.

   Part of speech _____
   Part of speech _____

4. Soon after the bee stung Eric's arm, it began to _____ and get red. The _____ arm became painful, and he went to the clinic to have the _____ examined.

   Part of speech _____
   Part of speech _____
   Part of speech _____

5. She took the _____ capsules according to the doctor's directions, but the infection did not clear up. Finally the doctor gave her another _____.

   Part of speech _____
   Part of speech _____

6. It _____ takes only two or three days to see results from antibiotics. It is _____ to see symptoms continue longer than that.

   Part of speech _____
   Part of speech _____

7. This is not a common cold. It is a severe infection. However, this medicine should help _____ the infection quickly.

   Part of speech _____

8. Sarah Anne wants to be a doctor. She is going to apply to _____ school next year.

   Part of speech _____

I. VOCABULARY IN CONTEXT

Before reading the "Ronex" label, read the following paragraphs. Try to guess the meaning of the underlined words from the context.

1. Luis told the doctor his symptoms. "I have a bad cough and nasal congestion." The doctor said, "I'll give you some medicine for the cough and something else for your stuffed-up nose. Here are your prescriptions."

    Nasal means

    a. an illness.
    b. related to the nose.
    c. cough medicine.
    d. a congested chest.

2. Rats were eating the chicken feed on Don's family's farm. Don's father put rat poison near the chicken house to kill the rats. After the rats ate the poison, he found twelve dead rats and saw several more sick ones.

    Poison is

    a. a fence to keep animals away from a chicken house.
    b. a dead animal.
    c. something that causes death or sickness when eaten.
    d. food for farm animals.

3. Professor Brown announced, "Your papers may be from ten to twenty-five pages long. I will not take any papers exceeding twenty-five pages in length."

    A paper exceeding twenty-five pages is

    a. more than twenty-five pages long.
    b. less than twenty-five pages long.
    c. less than ten pages long.
    d. more than ten pages long.

J. SHORT READING

Answer question (1) by looking quickly at the following label of an over-the-counter drug. Then answer the other questions after you have read the label thoroughly.

RONEX

A SAFE, EFFECTIVE DECONGESTANT/ANALGESIC
FOR TEMPORARY RELIEF OF NASAL CONGESTION,
HEADACHE, PAIN, ACHES, AND FEVER
DUE TO COLDS, SINUSITIS, AND FLU

WARNING: Do not give to children under six or use for more than 10 days unless directed by physician. Individuals with high blood pressure, heart disease, diabetes or thyroid disease should use only as directed by a physician. In case of accidental overdose, call a physician or poison control center immediately.

DOSAGE: Adults — TWO CAPSULES every four hours not exceeding eight capsules in 24 hours. Children 6-12 should take only ONE CAPSULE every four hours not exceeding four capsules in 24 hours.

FORMULA: Each capsule contains 17 mg phenylpropanolamine POL, 380 mg acetaminophen.

STORE AT ROOM TEMPERATURE

1. Match the following:
   a. Dosage   _c_ Ingredients
   b. Warning   _d_ Doctor
   c. Formula   _a_ How much and how often
   d. Physician   _b_ Things to be careful of

2. Which symptoms will Ronex not relieve?
   a. A headache.
   b. A stomachache.
   c. A stuffy nose.

3. A thirteen-year-old can
   a. not take this medicine.
   b. take two capsules every eight hours.
   c. take one capsule every four hours.
   d. take the adult dosage.

4. Temporary relief means
   a. complete and permanent disappearance of symptoms.
   b. relief of one but not all symptoms.
   c. symptoms may return when medicine is stopped.

5. Who thinks Ronex is safe and effective?
   a. The poison control center.
   b. Most physicians.
   c. The manufacturer of Ronex.

6. An over-the-counter drug
   a. must be prescribed by a doctor.
   b. can be bought without a prescription.
   c. is safe and inexpensive.

7. Which of the following is implied about dosages?
   a. A child could take two capsules and then wait eight hours before taking more.
   b. Nervous adults should not take Ronex.
   c. An overdose may be extremely dangerous.
   d. Ronex should be kept in the refrigerator.

K. PREFIXES

Look at the Word Form Chart (Section G). What noun suffixes are there that you have seen before? What adverb suffix is there? What prefix is there? Here are some prefixes that will be used in the following Short Readings:

Prefix	Meaning	Example
im-/in-	not	impolite, impossible, inappropriate
pre-	before	prejudge, preview
over-	too much	overdo, overcook
under-	too little, less than	undervalued, underrepresented, underestimate
un-	not	undo, untie, unwrap
dis-	not	disagree, disapprove
re-	back, again	redo, reproduce, review

These Short Readings are not hard. You know most of the words in them already. Some of the new words are made up of words and prefixes you also already know.

L. SHORT READING

A SEMINAR REPORT

Sarah Anne is a sophomore. She is a pre-med student. This means that after college she wants to attend medical school, if possible, and become a doctor. She is taking courses that will prepare her to study medicine, such as biology, second-year chemistry, and statistics. She is also taking courses that are unrelated to her major: Spanish and a seminar in sociology.

In a seminar, the professor does not lecture. Instead, the students give reports and discuss them. Sarah Anne chose to talk about "The High Cost of Health Care in the United States." She noticed that unprepared students often gave bad reports. Therefore, she went to the library and read several articles. She made notes of all her thoughts. Then she wrote a summary of her report.

HEALTH   105

M. COMPREHENSION QUESTIONS

Choose the best way to complete the following sentences. You may look back at the reading to help you find the correct answers.

1. It is implied that Sarah Anne's major is
   a. biology.
   b. Spanish.
   c. sophomore year.
   d. sociology.

2. It is implied that when Sarah Anne gives her report, she will be
   a. noticed.
   b. chosen.
   c. unprepared.
   d. prepared.

3. A student can be a pre-med student
   a. after he or she becomes a doctor.
   b. after going to medical school.
   c. only during sophomore year.
   d. before going to medical school.

4. Sarah Anne wrote
   a. several articles.
   b. her whole report.
   c. a summary of her report.
   d. a bad report.

N. MAIN IDEA INTRODUCTION

People read in different ways for different purposes. In some reading situations you want to understand and remember all the details you are reading. For example, when you read a detective story, you need to remember all the details for the story to make sense and be exciting. When you read a textbook, you need to analyze and understand all the details for a later quiz or lecture.

In some other reading situations, however, you do not need to learn all the details. You only want to learn the *topic* of the reading, the *main idea*, or the *organization* of the reading. For example, you may want to know the topic of a reading to decide whether to read it carefully. You may want to understand the main idea of a reading to know the opinion of an author. You may want to understand the organization of a reading to be able to find where answers to questions are located, so you can answer certain questions quickly. It is important to reach your general understanding goal quickly, without reading everything. This is called skimming.

*First skim this reading to find the main idea, then read it carefully. Read **only** the first and last paragraphs and the first sentence of the second paragraph. After skimming this reading, answer the following questions about the main idea.*

O. SHORT READING

THE HIGH COST OF HEALTH CARE IN THE UNITED STATES

The cost of health care in the United States is very high. The time and money that doctors spend on their medical education is probably one reason for this problem.

A visit to a doctor's office costs from fifteen to fifty dollars. It is almost impossible for people to pay for the medical care they need. Many people in the United States think that doctors are overpaid. Most doctors, however, disagree. They say that they were required to study medicine for a very long time, first as undergraduates, then as graduate students. Tuition for many years of medical education costs a lot of money. Doctors argue that it is necessary for most medical students to borrow money from a bank to pay their tuition. Because this money must be repaid to the bank, young doctors need to receive a lot of money for their work. So, they charge people high prices for medical care.

Therefore, it is possible that the high cost of medical care in America is unnecessary. Because high tuition is one cause of high costs, one way to lower costs would be to have medical schools that are free or have low tuition.

P. MAIN IDEA EXERCISE

1. What is the *main idea* of this article?

    a. A visit to your doctor's office can cost as much as $50.
    b. American students often borrow money from banks to pay tuition.
    c. Medical care in the United States costs a lot of money because doctors like to be rich.
    d. The high cost of tuition in medical school is one reason for the high costs of American health care.

2. Now look at each of the following explanations and discuss why it is or is not the best answer to the question.

    a. This is a detail, an example of how high medical costs are. It is not the main idea.

b. This is an idea related to the main idea. Some students must borrow money to pay the high tuition in medical school.
c. This is an opinion of many people in the United States. But it is not related to Sarah Anne's main idea.
d. This is the main idea. All the sentences in the middle paragraph support this main idea.

Q. COMPREHENSION QUESTIONS

Answer the following questions. Look back at the prefix chart on p. 104 if necessary.

1. It is impossible for some people to pay for their medical care. These people
    a. do not want to pay for medical care.
    b. want to pay for medical care.
    c. cannot pay for medical care.
    d. can pay for medical care soon.

2. Many people say that doctors are overpaid. They say that doctors
    a. are paid too much.
    b. are paid too little.
    c. are paid too early.
    d. are paid too late.

3. When people say that doctors are overpaid, most doctors disagree. The doctors
    a. say the same thing.
    b. return the money.
    c. do not agree.
    d. go to medical school.

4. Medical students often borrow money from a bank. Later, when they are doctors, it must be repaid. They must
    a. charge people lower prices.
    b. go to the bank more often.
    c. pay by check or credit card.
    d. give the money back to the bank.

5. Maybe the high cost of medical care is unnecessary. Maybe it is
    a. very necessary.
    b. not needed.
    c. very important.
    d. the price you have to pay.

R. VOCABULARY IN CONTEXT

Before reading the following article about tamper-resistant packaging, read the following paragraphs. Try to guess the meaning of the underlined words. Use the meanings of all the words in the paragraph to help you decide.

1. The packages the products come in are very different each from another. Detergent comes in bright boxes of two, five, ten, and twenty pounds. Perfume is sold in very small, beautiful bottles, containing as little as one ounce. Food comes in cans with colorful labels, boxes covered with paper, glass jars with pictures on them, or—in the case of fresh fruit and vegetables—without much packaging at all.

   A package is
   a. the fruit you buy at a supermarket.
   b. the covering that protects a product and attracts people to buy the product.
   c. the different weights of a product that you can buy, from one ounce to twenty pounds.
   d. the items that you can buy at a department store.

2. On the side of Gordon's house, there is an electric meter that measures how much electricity Gordon and his housemates use. Above the meter is a sign that says:

   > **No Tampering
   > under Penalty of Law
   > Property, Greenville Electric Co.**

   If someone opens the meter to change the numbers on it, the electric company can call the police.

   When you tamper with something, you
   a. turn it on.
   b. destroy it.
   c. open it and change it.
   d. read the numbers on it.

3. Examples:
   a. We lick the glue on an envelope to seal a letter.
   b. A pack of cigarettes is sealed with clear cellophane and paper.
   c. Good wine is sealed with a cork.
   d. People in Greenville try to seal or insulate their houses well in the winter to keep the heat in and the cold out.

Put a check to the left of things that are sealed.

- ___ 1. A dinner plate.
- _e_ 2. A bottle of beer.
- _d_ 3. A coffee cup.
- _k_ 4. A cigarette.
- ___ 5. A loaf of bread.
- ___ 6. A can of coffee.
- _a_ 7. A TOEFL test booklet.

S. SHORT READING

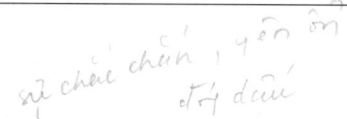

SAFETY-SEALED PACKAGING

Some people died in Chicago in 1982 after taking a pain reliever called Tylenol Extra Strength Capsules. Police found cyanide, a deadly poison, inside some of the remaining capsules in one of the bottles of pills. Someone had opened the capsules and filled some with cyanide. The killer took them to a drugstore and put several poisoned capsules in some bottles on the shelves.

The killer was able to tamper with the Tylenol capsules because the capsules and bottles were not safely sealed. They could be opened and closed easily, without the buyer discovering that someone had put poisoned capsules inside. Unfortunately, a few other poisonings occurred in other cities after this.

Neither the drug companies nor the U.S. government want this to happen again. The U.S. government has passed laws concerning safety-sealed packaging, which cannot be opened before the user buys the drug. The illustration shows the following five types of tamper-resistant packaging.

- a. Inner seal bottles, such as you find on instant coffee.
- b. Plastic shrink bands that go over the top of bottles to seal them, such as you find on wine bottles.
- c. Dose packaging, where each pill or capsule is sealed separately.
- d. Metal bands, such as you find on soft drinks.
- e. Capsules that lock, so they cannot be pulled apart.

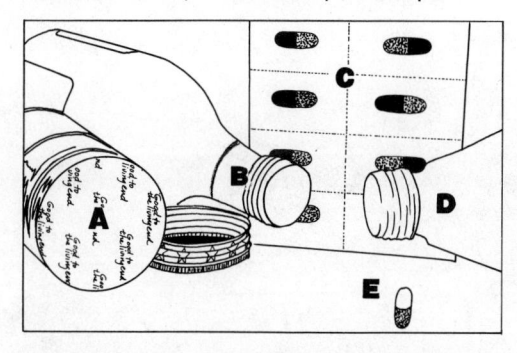

The customer should always check the bottle or container before buying it to make sure that no one has already opened it. With this new packaging, it is possible to see if anyone has tampered with the drug that you are going to buy.

110   Chapter 5

T. COMPREHENSION QUESTIONS

Choose the best answer to the following questions. You may look back at the article to help you find the answer.

1. The main idea of this article is that
    a. it is terrible that someone poisoned a bottle of pills in Chicago.
    b. because of recent poisonings, the U.S. government has passed laws to ensure tamper-resistant packaging of drugs.
    c. there are five types of tamper-resistant packaging.
    d. the drug companies disagree with the government regulations about packaging.

2. What is the purpose of safety-sealed packaging?
    a. To keep children from opening the container.
    b. To stop the air from entering the bottle.
    c. To stop someone from tampering with the drug.
    d. To make people want to buy the drug.

3. Which of the following should you do before you buy a drug? (More than one is possible.)
    a. Tamper with the container.
    b. Check the seal on the container.
    c. Make sure no one has opened it.
    d. Take two capsules every four hours.

STRATEGIES

READING A TEXTBOOK CHAPTER OUTLINE

PRE-READING EXERCISE

Read the following two situations. Make sure you understand the vocabulary. Then discuss the possible answers with your partner or group. Write down other reactions that you can think of.

1. You are lost in the woods far from anyone. You see a dangerous animal. You think that it is ready to attack you. Which of the following will probably happen to you?

   __ I will be very scared.
   __ My heart rate will increase.
   __ I will perspire.
   __ I will feel weak and dizzy.
   __ My stomach will be upset.
   __ My legs and hands will shake.
   __ Other: _____

2. You need to take an oral exam in your major field of study. If you do not pass the exam, you will not be allowed to continue your studies at your university. A group of four professors will ask you questions about the courses you have completed so far. Which of the following will probably happen to you just *before* and *during* this oral exam?

   __ I will have bad dreams about the exam.
   __ I will have a stomachache.
   __ My hands will feel cold.
   __ My heart rate will increase.
   __ My eyes will twitch uncontrollably.
   __ I will breathe quickly and not very deeply.
   __ My mind will jump around, making me unable to concentrate.
   __ Other: _____

The situations above are very different, but they have something in common. Both are very *stressful situations* that cause certain physical and

112   Chapter 5

emotional *reactions*. Can you think of other stressful situations that people experience? *(List them below, with any other reactions that you did not discuss in (1) and (2).)*

Stressful Situations	Reactions
_____	_____
_____	_____
_____	_____
_____	_____

Many of these stressful situations are very common. What can we do to minimize the harm these reactions to stress cause our bodies and minds?

Ways to behave to avoid harmful reactions to stress:

_____

_____

One place to find information about stress is a psychology textbook. In a textbook called Introduction to Psychology, *there is a chapter about stress. Read the* **title** *of this chapter and the* **introductory paragraph** *and do the exercise that follows.*

Emotional Stress: Its Causes, Effects, and Resulting Behavior

Introduction

Stress makes people afraid or worried. It is caused by difficulties in our lives, such as uncertainty about the future. Many people have physical reactions to emotional stress, ranging from minor problems, such as headaches, to serious conditions, such as ulcers or even cancer. There are ways to *cope with*, or take action about stress, so that it does not make us "worried sick."

STRATEGIES 113

Exercise: *Do this exercise with two or three of your classmates and then discuss your answers with the rest of your class.*

1. What does the above expression *cope with* mean?
   _____

2. There are three major parts to this chapter. What do you think they are? Look at the title of the chapter and the introduction above to help you. List them below.

   Outline:
   I. _____

   II. _____

   III. _____

3. Look at your notes from the pre-reading exercise. Write them into the outline under I, II, or III.

   Now look at the chapter outline from the college textbook on page 114, Introduction to Psychology. While you are reading the outline, think about the ideas that you wrote down.

COMPREHENSION QUESTIONS

Answer these questions with your partner or group.

1. Look back at the ideas that your group wrote down in each of the three major sections before you read this outline. Are there any ideas that are not included in this outline? Are they too *specific* or too *general* for an outline?

2. In which section of the outline might these topics be found?

   ___ using alcohol and drugs to forget stressful situations
   ___ spouse and child abuse as a result of stress
   ___ regular exercise as "medicine" for a stressful lifestyle
   ___ cancer seen as a result of stress

3. What do you think is the difference between the two types of coping, III. A., Defensive, and III. B., Active?
   _____
   _____

Emotional Stress: Its Causes, Effects, and Resulting Behavior

Chapter Outline

I. Causes of Stress

    A. What Is Stress?
    B. Daily Problems
    C. Cyclical Deadlines
    D. Holiday Pressures
    E. Financial Worries
    F. Life Changes

II. Effects of Stress

    A. Anxiety
    B. Frustration
    C. Chronic Illnesses
    D. Serious Medical Problems

III. Resulting Behavior

    A. Defensive Coping (Fight or Flight?)

        1. Aggression
        2. Avoidance

    B. Active Coping

        1. Controlling Irrational Thoughts
        2. Learning to Express Feelings
        3. Lifestyle Changes

            a. Nutrition
            b. Meditation and Other Relaxation Methods
            c. Exercise to Reduce the by-products of Stress

IV. Summary

STRATEGIES 115

4. Which parts of the chapter deal with the kinds of stress that international university students experience?

_____
_____

5. In your opinion, what are the ways that most university students deal with the stress found in university life? Which ways are harmful or destructive, and which are helpful or constructive?

Destructive Behavior	Constructive Behavior
_____	_____
_____	_____
_____	_____
_____	_____

READING A CHART

PRE-READING EXERCISE

In the outline of the chapter called *Emotional Stress*, the heading "*serious medical problems*" is listed as a major sub-topic in the section about the *effects of stress*. Below is a chart called The Century's Top Five.

LOOKING BACK

THE CENTURY'S TOP FIVE

As Americans took up smoking and changed their diets, heart disease, cancer and other 20th-century ills surpassed infectious diseases. Below are annual U.S. deaths.

1986
1. Heart disease — 763,380
2. Cancer — 465,440
3. Stroke — 147,390
4. Accidents — 93,990
5. Chronic lung disease — 75,220

1970
1. Heart disease — 735,542
2. Cancer — 330,730
3. Stroke — 207,166
4. Accidents — 114,638
5. Pneumonia and influenza — 62,739

1950
1. Heart disease — 535,705
2. Cancer — 210,733
3. Stroke — 156,751
4. Accidents — 91,249
5. Diseases of early infancy — 60,989

1930
1. Heart disease — 251,153
2. Pneumonia and influenza — 120,171
3. Cancer — 114,186
4. Kidney disease — 106,679
5. Stroke — 104,345

1910
1. Heart disease — 75,429
2. Pneumonia and influenza — 73,983
3. Tuberculosis — 73,028
4. Acute intestinal infections — 54,795
5. Stroke — 45,461

1900
1. Pneumonia and influenza — 40,362
2. Tuberculosis — 38,820
3. Acute intestinal infections — 28,491
4. Heart disease — 27,427
5. Stroke — 21,353

USN&WR—Basic data: U.S. Dept. of Health and Human Services

116   Chapter 5

1. Look at the chart quickly. What do you think the chart gives information about? Complete the title with another word. You need to find a word that is more general than all the examples that you see in the chart.

   The Century's Top Five _____

2. Look quickly at the names of the illnesses listed. If there are some names that you do not know, find out what they mean from someone in your class.

3. Now look at the way the chart is organized. There are six years represented. Which six years are they? How are they organized in the chart? Write the six years from the chart.

   _____   _____   _____

   _____   _____   _____

4. How many medical problems are listed for each year? _____

5. Which number from 1–5 is the *highest* cause of death? _____
   The *lowest* cause of death? _____

Directions: You are now ready to find very specific facts in this chart. Do Part One by yourself. Then compare your answer with a partner. Answer the questions in Part Two together.

PART ONE

1. What was the third cause of death in 1970? _____

2. When did heart disease become the leading cause of death in the United States? _____

3. How many Americans died of pneumonia and influenza in 1900? ____

4. True or False? The fifth cause of death in 1986 killed more or less the same number of people as the first cause of death in 1910.

5. True or False? Heart disease killed more than twice as many Americans as cancer in the following four years:
   _____ 1930 _____ 1950 _____ 1970 _____ 1986

6. What are the top three causes of death for the same years listed in (5)? They are each listed below, next to the different types of lines that are used in line graphs.

Heart disease	× × × × × × × × × × × × × × × × × × × ×
Cancer	+ + + + + + + + + + + + + + + + + + + +
Stroke	....

   Look at the statistics from the preceding chart for heart disease, cancer, and stroke in the years shown on the following line chart. Plot the points and connect them with the type of line shown above.

Quantity
(in thousands)

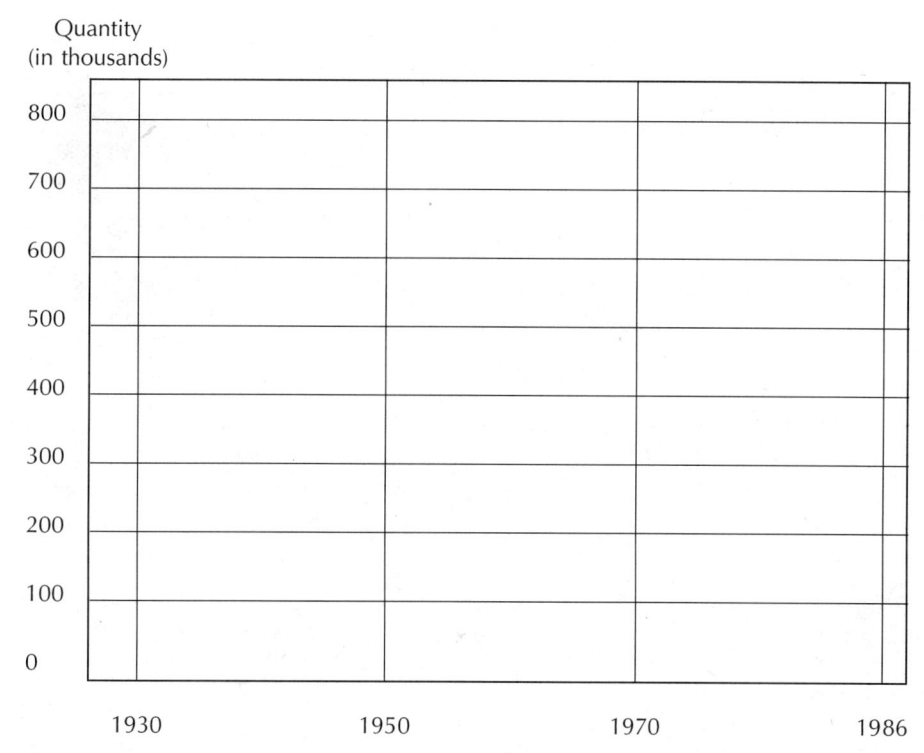

	1930	1950	1970	1986
800				
700				
600				
500				
400				
300				
200				
100				
0				

7. How is this graph helpful to you in understanding the statistics in The Century's Top Five?

PART TWO: DISCUSSION QUESTIONS

1. Why do you think that diseases of early infancy are no longer leading causes of death in the United States?

2. What types of cancer do you think are related to changes in lifestyle in the 20th century?

3. Which causes of death in 1986 do you think are related to the stressful nature of American life? Why?

4. Which "killers" do you think are related to environmental pollution? Which types of pollution are most harmful?

5. What do you think the top five causes of death in *your* country are today?

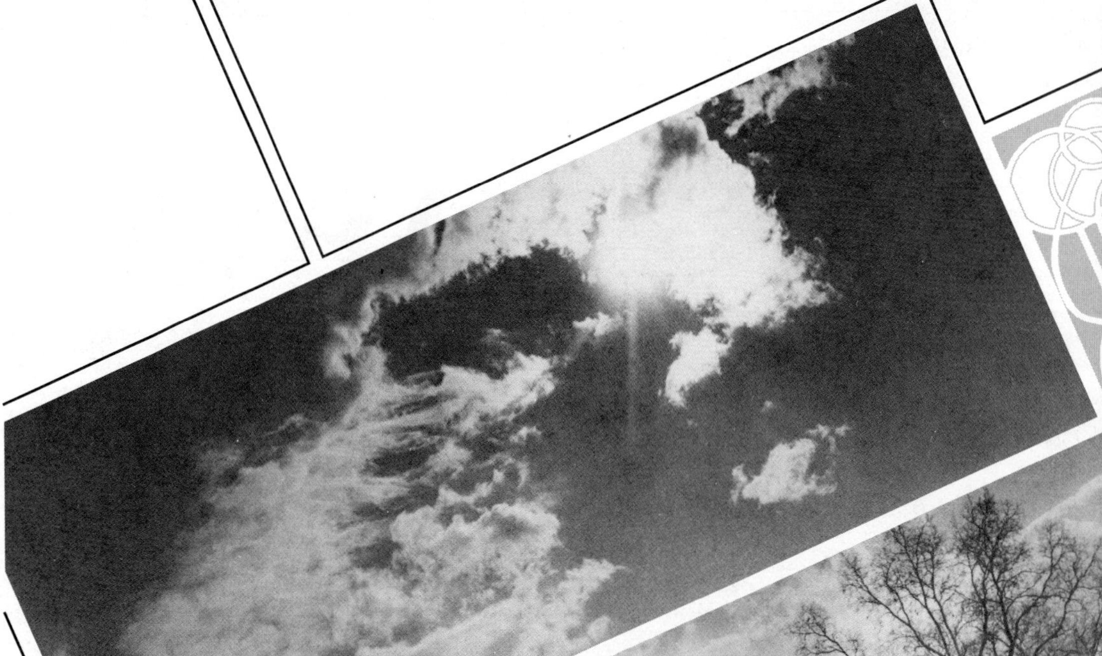

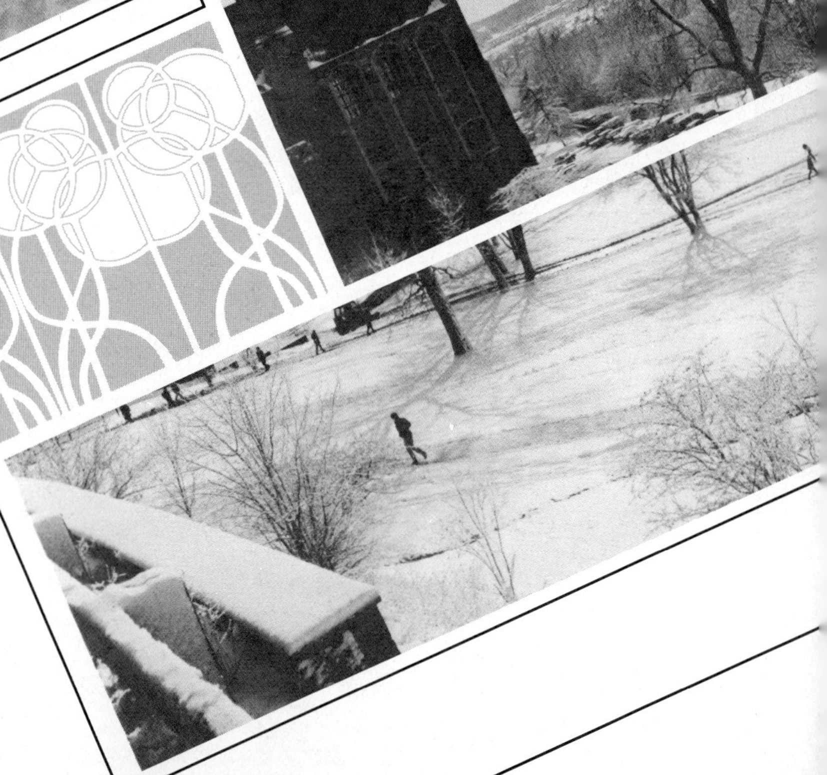

CHAPTER SIX

WEATHER

WEATHER   121

PRE-READING QUESTIONS

This chapter is about weather. The weather in your country is probably different from the weather in your town or city in the United States. *Answer the following questions about the climate in your country and how it differs from the weather in the United States. Discuss these answers with your classmates.*

Just as there are different climates in the United States, the weather in one part of your country may be different from that in another part. When answering questions about your country, talk about the region you are from.

1. How does the weather in your country differ from the weather in this photograph of winter in Greenville?

   _____

   _____

2. How many different seasons are there?   1   2   3   4

3. Which group of words would best describe your climate?

   _____ dry and hot   _____ dry and cold
   _____ humid and hot   _____ humid and cold

4. On a scale of four, rate the weather in your country:

   very predictable   1 2 3 4   unpredictable

   usually sunny   1 2 3 4   usually overcast, grey

   green vegetation   1 2 3 4   brown vegetation

5. Are heating or air conditioning costs a large expense in your country? Which? How much per year?

   _____

   _____

6. What do people use to heat/cool their homes?

   _____

   _____

7. How do they make their homes more energy efficient (so that they use less fuel to heat/cool them)?

   _____

   _____

122   Chapter 6

8. How is your climate different from the one in which you are living now? Use some of the characteristics from the preceding questions when making the comparison.

9. What do you miss the most about the weather in your country?

10. Do people in your country trust the weather forecasts on television or in the newspapers?

A. VOCABULARY IN CONTEXT

Before reading the story "The Thunderstorm," read the following paragraphs. Try to guess the meaning of the underlined words from the context.

1. It began to rain hard. The thunder was very loud and they saw lightning in the sky. Their clothes were damp and they felt chilly. They put on their extra sweaters.

   Thunder is *sấm*

   a. a bad rainstorm.
   b. the sound of birds.
   c. the loud sound of electrical storms.
   d. a flash of light in the sky during a storm.

   Damp means *ẩm ướt*

   a. quite cold.
   b. a little wet. *mát*
   c. slightly torn.
   d. very dirty.

   Chilly means *lạnh buốt*

   a. very tired.
   b. a little cold.
   c. quite frightened. *làm cho sợ hãi*
   d. somewhat nervous.

WEATHER 123

2. "Look," said Lee, reaching for her camera, which was under her seat. "There's a flock of geese flying overhead." After she got the camera out of her pack, she took a photograph of the V-shaped flock.

To reach for something means

   a. to drop something in the water.
   b. to put out your hand to get something.
   c. to put something away.
   d. to take a photograph.

3. Lee and Daphne were in the dormitory getting ready for a canoe trip on the lake. They were putting a picnic lunch, extra sweaters, water to drink, and a camera into their packs. It was a beautiful day.

To get ready for a quiz the next day you

   a. wash the dishes.
   b. ask about your grade.
   c. study your notes and the text.
   d. take a long trip.

A pack is

   a. something you use to cook food.
   b. the ball in a hockey match.
   c. something you use to carry things on your back.
   d. a defensive soccer player.

B. LONG READING

THE THUNDERSTORM

It was a Saturday morning. Lee and Daphne were in the dormitory getting ready for a canoe trip on the lake. They were putting a picnic lunch, extra sweaters, water to drink, and a camera into their packs. It was a beautiful day—not too hot, not too cold, not too windy. It was a perfect day for a canoe trip.

Lee and Daphne rented a canoe at Seneca State Park and started up the lake. They planned to go three or four miles to a little island close to the shore. They wanted to have a picnic there and return about four o'clock. The sun was shining and the lake was calm.

"Look," said Lee, reaching for her camera, which was under her seat. "There's a flock of geese flying overhead." When she got the camera out of her pack, she took a photograph of the V-shaped flock.

They canoed for thirty minutes, enjoying the pleasant weather. Suddenly, Daphne noticed some black clouds in the sky ahead. She felt a cool wind on her face, and she started getting a little worried. The sky began to get cloudy, and she felt a sudden chill.

"Lee, do you feel raindrops?" she asked. "It looks like there's going to be a thunderstorm."

They decided to go to the shore. The lake was quickly getting rougher as the storm approached. As they pulled the canoe out of the water, they heard thunder. It began to rain hard. Together, they turned the canoe over on the ground and ran under a large rock to wait for the end of the storm. The thunder was very loud, and they saw lightning over the lake.

"Just in time!" said Lee. "We can't go anywhere now, so let's have our picnic."

Their clothes were damp, and they felt chilly. They put on their extra sweaters and tried to enjoy the picnic lunch they had brought.

The storm had begun very quickly. It ended quickly too. The sun came out again, and the wind stopped blowing. Lee and Daphne put the canoe back in the water. They went several miles up the lake before returning to the state park. It had been an almost perfect day for a canoe trip.

C. COMPREHENSION QUESTIONS

Choose the best answer to the following questions or the best way to complete the sentences.

1. Why did Lee and Daphne expect a perfect day for a canoe trip?
   a. It was early spring.
   b. It was Saturday.
   c. It was raining in the morning.
   d. The weather was beautiful.

WEATHER   125

2. Which of the following things in nature did Lee and Daphne not want to see?
   a. Flocks of geese.
   b. The sunshine.
   c. The black clouds.
   d. The calm lake.

3. Daphne and Lee
   a. felt that their trip was ruined by the weather when they returned home.
   b. thought quickly to keep themselves and the canoe dry.
   c. returned home early because of the storm.
   d. had a picnic on an island close to the shore three or four miles up the lake.

4. It is implied but not directly stated that Daphne and Lee
   a. hoped to see some beautiful natural things.
   b. were 100 percent certain that it was not going to rain or get cold on the canoe trip.
   c. drank the lake water.
   d. had never canoed before.

5. When Daphne said "Just in time," she was thinking that
   a. they had a lot of time for lunch.
   b. they almost got wet.
   c. they were late for the storm.
   d. it was a beautiful day.

D. FILL-IN EXERCISE

Fill in the blanks with the correct words from the following list. Each word must be used. No word can be used twice.

approached	shore	ground
raindrops	lightning	turned over
rent	flock	island

1. Don first knew it was raining when he saw ____raindrops____ on the windows of his pickup truck.

2. Some children were playing on the beach along the ____shore____ of the lake.

3. During the thunderstorm they saw ____lightning____ flash brightly in the sky.

4. A ____flock____ of Canada geese flew over the house this morning. I had never seen such a large group of birds before.

5. Would you like to ____rent____ a canoe and go around the lake this afternoon?
6. They lived in a small house on an ____island____ in the middle of the lake.
7. The pilot said, "Please fasten your seat belts," as the plane ____approached____ the airport.
8. At a picnic, people usually sit at a picnic table or on the ____ground____.
9. Eric ____turned over____ his check so that he could endorse it.

E. WORD FORM CHART

Vocabulary Word	Adjective	Noun	Verb	Adverb
1. A <u>canoe</u> trip	canoe*	canoe / canoeing	canoe	
2. A <u>picnic</u> lunch	picnic*	picnic		
3. The sun was <u>shining</u>.	shiny	sunshine	shine	
4. Some black <u>clouds</u>	cloudy	cloud		
5. She felt a sudden <u>chill</u>.	chilly	chill	chill	
6. They heard <u>thunder</u>.	thunder*	thunder	thunder	
7. Their clothes were <u>damp</u>.	damp	dampness	dampen	
8. <u>Suddenly</u> Daphne noticed some . . . clouds.	sudden	suddenness		suddenly

Suffixes:

▪-y changes a noun to a _____.

▪-ness changes an adjective to a _____.

▪-en changes an adjective to a _____.

*A noun used as an adjective in a compound noun.

WEATHER 127

F. WORD FORM EXERCISE

Choose the correct word form and fill in the blank. Look at number (1) on the Word Form Chart to choose the correct answer for question (1) in this exercise, and so forth. Name the part of speech in the blank at the right.

1. _____canoe_____ is my favorite sport. I'm glad there's a lake nearby.

   Part of speech __N__

2. Tom: "What do you want to do next Saturday?"
   Helen: "I'd like to go on a _____pinic_____. How about you?"

   Part of speech __N__

3. My new car is very _____shiny_____. After a Greenville winter, the paint will be dull, I'm sure.

   Part of speech __Aj__

4. I am unhappy that it is _____cloudy_____ today. I wanted to go for a walk in the woods, but I am afraid it will rain.

   Part of speech __Aj__

5. Do you think it is _____chill_____? I can close the window if you would like me to.

   Part of speech __N__

6. I heard _____thunder_____ in the middle of the night. I looked out the window and saw lightning in the sky.

   Part of speech __N__

7. I can't put anything in my basement because of the _____damp_____ there.

   Part of speech __Aj__

8. Her mother's _____suddenly_____ death was a shock to the whole family.

   Part of speech __Ad__

G. MORE THAN ONE WAY TO SAY IT

Read the following sentences. Try to understand the meaning of the underlined word from the context. Then find a word from the list that means the same thing and write it above its synonym.

sunny	upper	report	in the low 50s
cloudy	chance	precipitation	in the high 50s

1. In Greenville, the weather <u>forecast</u> can be found in the newspapers, on the radio, and on television. You can also call up a weather number on the telephone.

2. Greenville's weather is rarely <u>clear</u>; there always seem to be a few clouds in the sky.

3. Furnell students see a big difference between temperatures <u>of 51–53 degrees</u> and <u>57–59 degrees</u>. They would never go sun bathing in those lower temperatures, but if the sun is shining, you might find some of them out in their bathing suits on a day of 58 degrees.

4. It rarely gets into the <u>high</u> 90s in Greenville, except in the months of July and August.

5. Why is upstate New York so green and lush? Probably because of all the <u>rain</u> it gets.

6. There is almost always the <u>possibility</u> of rain in Greenville.

7. Furnell students from sunnier climates find the many <u>overcast</u> days to be very depressing.

H. SHORT READING

Read "A Weather Forecast." Then do the comprehension questions that follow.

A WEATHER FORECAST

Two weeks after the thunderstorm, Lee and Daphne planned a second canoe trip.

"I'm free Saturday and Sunday," Lee said.

"Me too. Either day would be fine for me," agreed Daphne. "But let's read the weather forecast very carefully this time before we decide when to go."

Weekend Weather Forecast for the Greenville Area

Cold Saturday, low temperatures in the upper 40s. High near 55 degrees. Overcast with possible clearing late in the day. Winds from the southeast to 15 miles per hour. Much warmer Sunday with highs near 70 degrees. Lows in the mid-50s. Mostly sunny with periods of cloudiness. Light winds from the south. Chance of precipitation 60 percent on Saturday, 10 percent Sunday.

WEATHER 129

I. COMPREHENSION QUESTIONS

Scan the weather forecast again to help you answer these questions. Choose the best way to complete the sentences.

1. According to the forecast, Saturday will be
   a. cold and mostly cloudy.
   b. cloudy and warm.
   c. rainy and warm.
   d. warm and mostly clear.

2. Sunday will probably be
   a. rainy and warm.
   b. cold and cloudy.
   c. cloudy and warm.
   d. warm and clear.

J. SCANNING EXERCISE

*This is a chart for converting degrees centigrade (°C) to degrees Fahrenheit (°F). Using the chart, **scan** to find the answers to the following questions.*

1. Which would be a more comfortable air temperature for swimming in a lake, 25 degrees F or 25 degrees C?

   _____

2. Where Lee lived, it was sometimes 5 degrees C on the coldest mornings of the year. How cold is that in degrees F?

   _____

3. It is usually 10 degrees F warmer at Gordon's house in town than at Don's farm on the hill. The average temperature at Gordon's house is 30 degrees F in the winter. What is the average temperature at Don's house in Centigrade?

   _____

4. If the temperature range in New York City is from 1 degree to 100 degrees F, what is the range in degrees C?

   _____

5. Which is colder, 1 degree C or 15 degrees F?

   _____

K. FILL-IN EXERCISE

Fill in the blanks with the correct words from the following list. These words have already been used in this chapter. Each word must be used once. No word can be used twice. Do not change the words in any way.

sunshine	cloudy	chilly
chill	forecaster	unfortunately
shore	snowstorm	

Luis and Martha went walking in Sapsucker Woods near the Furnell campus. It was a sunny but _____ day, late in October. Luis had brought a camera in hopes of taking some interesting pictures of the beautiful fall colors in the woods. Martha had a sore throat and a cough, but she decided to go because the weather was beautiful.

As the young couple walked through the woods, they came to the _____ of a small lake. They saw geese and ducks swimming in the water and flying overhead. The _____ on the water was very pretty. They were glad to be outside.

Suddenly Martha felt a _____ and noticed that it was getting colder. She put on her wool hat, and Luis put on the hood of his coat. They both put on their gloves and started to walk faster in order to stay warm.

In a few minutes, it started to snow. The sky was _____, and the wind was very cold on their faces. _____, Luis had forgotten to take pictures of the woods before it got cloudy.

Martha said to Luis, "We should probably go back now. It's getting really cold and hard to see in this _____." She did not want to get any sicker than she already was.

Luis agreed. "Do you know which way the car is?"

Neither Luis nor Martha knew which way to walk. It was impossible to see anything because of the heavy snow. At first, both Luis and Martha were worried, but then they saw their red car through the snow.

Luis and Martha got into the car. They drank the hot coffee that they had brought with them. Listening to the car radio, they heard the weather _____ talk about the first snowstorm of the year. They decided to listen to the weather report before they went on their next walk in the woods.

WEATHER 131

L. VOCABULARY REVIEW READING

Skim this reading to find the main idea. Remember, this means reading the first and last paragraphs, as well as the first sentences of the other paragraphs. Then answer the following question about the main idea.

1. What is the main idea of this reading?

   a. The temperature in Greenville falls below 0 degrees Fahrenheit in winter.
   b. Letter carriers must deliver mail in all different types of weather, which makes their job very difficult.
   c. Letter carriers have to find a place to stay dry during rain and snowstorms.
   d. Most people give their letter carriers cool drinks in the summer.

A HARD JOB

Have you ever thought about where letter carriers go in the middle of a rainstorm? While you are safe in your home, office, or car, watching the raindrops on the windows, letter carriers are trying to keep dry. Often they cannot, and they end their workday feeling damp and chilly. As we know, the weather forecast is sometimes wrong.

In July and August, when the weather gets hot, the mail still has to be delivered. While you sit in your cool house or air-conditioned office, letter carriers are walking their five miles a day in the worst heat of the year. As the sun shines hot on their faces, they probably wish one of those rainstorms would come and cool them off.

Fall and winter bring their own troubles, too. Unexpected chilly days in the fall can give letter carriers a bad cold. Then come the freezing temperatures of winter. How many sidewalks covered with snow and ice can they walk on without breaking their necks?

Letter carriers in Greenville not only have to carry heavy packs on their five-mile routes, but they often have to do it in terrible weather. Working in the high 90s in the summer to below 0 degrees Fahrenheit in winter, walking through rain and snowstorms, letter carriers deserve more respect than they usually receive.

On the next 98-degree summer day, why don't you offer your letter carrier a cold glass of lemonade and a cool spot to drink it in?

132   Chapter 6

M. COMPREHENSION QUESTIONS

Choose the best answer for the following questions.

1. It is implied that something can be done in winter to help letter carriers. What?

    a. Give them ice cream.
    b. Keep ice and snow off your sidewalk.
    c. Help them deliver the mail.
    d. Read the weather forecast to them.

2. How does the unpredictability of the weather affect mailmen?

   _____

   _____

N. SKIMMING AND SCANNING EXERCISE

First skim the short reading, "Temperate Climates," to understand its structure: its main topic and the locations of its subtopics. Work with a partner to find out which subtopics are in which paragraphs.

Main topic: _____

Subtopic paragraph 1 _____

Subtopic paragraph 2 _____

Subtopic paragraph 3 _____

Now scan the same short reading to find the answers to the following questions. Remember to carry out two important steps when you scan:

1. Look at the question word in each question to help you decide what sort of information the answer will be. A person or place will be capitalized. Numbers and times are easy to find.

2. Decide what the key words of the question are. Move your eyes quickly over the text looking for those words or their synonyms.

WEATHER 133

Scan to find the answers to these questions.

1. What are the two major zones of temperate climates?

2. How low does the average temperature go in a warm temperate climate in Fahrenheit degrees?

3. Where do we find the western or Mediterranean type of warm temperate climate?

4. How many months in each year can the average temperature drop below 6 degrees Centigrade in a cool temperate zone?

5. Which cool temperate zone has frequent changes in weather conditions?

O. SHORT READING

TEMPERATE CLIMATES

There are many different types of climates in the world. This article discusses the various types of temperate climates, that is, the climates that are free from very high and very low temperatures.

The world's temperate regions are divided into warm and cool zones. In the warm temperate zones, the average temperature does not drop below 43 degrees F or 6 degrees C in the coldest month of the year. This is the lowest possible temperature for growing plants all year round. There are two different kinds of warm temperate regions. One is the western or Mediterranean type (dry, hot summers and mild, wet winters) found on western coastal belts and across southern Europe. The other kind is called the eastern or China type. This kind of climate is influenced by trade winds and is wetter, with mild winters and hot, humid summers.

The cool temperate zones, on the other hand, have a cold season. There are as many as five months a year when the average temperature goes below 43 degrees F or 6 degrees C. There are two different kinds of cool temperate zones. One type is called a maritime zone, with frequent changes in weather conditions. The other is called a continental region, with warmer summers and cold winters.

P. VOCABULARY IN CONTEXT

Read the following short paragraphs. Try to guess the meaning of the underlined words from the context.

1. Gordon watched the Furnell hockey team practice before the game. "They're good. They'll win," he said. Gordon was right. Two hours later, they won the game, 5 to 3. Gordon had predicted their win.

   When you predict something, you tell about it
   a. after it happens.
   b. before it happens.
   c. incorrectly.
   d. reluctantly.

2. Greece was part of the Turkish Empire for almost four centuries, from 1455 to 1829.

   A century is
   a. a decade.
   b. a guard or soldier.
   c. a king or emperor.
   d. one hundred years.

3. Plants grow best under the right conditions. There must be good soil, enough sun, and enough water.

   Good conditions for studying are
   a. a quiet place with enough light.
   b. an assignment.
   c. undergraduates and graduate students.
   d. land, sun, and water.

4. Don's father made his plans for spring planting in advance. It was still winter when he decided exactly what to plant and where to plant it.

   Lee bought her plane ticket in advance. She bought it
   a. immediately before she got on the plane.
   b. sometime before the day that she left on her trip.
   c. while she was getting on the plane.
   d. after she was already on the plane.

5. We went to watch the baseball game, but just before starting time, it began to rain. They announced that the game was delayed, so we waited. A half an hour later, they announced that it was canceled, so we went home.

   When something is canceled,
   a. it is delayed.
   b. it will take place later.
   c. it will not take place.
   d. it will go very badly.

Q. SHORT READING

WEATHER FORECASTING

Many people listen to the weather forecast on the radio in the morning so that they will not overdress on warm days or underdress on cold days. Other people do not listen, because weather forecasts are very often incorrect. These people say that weather forecasters are unable even to predict when it will rain, so they probably do not know anything. This shows a misunderstanding of weather science.

Weather scientists, or meteorologists, have been studying the weather for more than a century. Although some things are still unexplained, they understand the causes of different types of weather. However, they cannot always predict what will actually happen. For instance, they may know that conditions are right for snow. However, if the temperature goes up a few degrees, or if the wind changes direction just a little, the conditions will not be right for snow anymore. Such small changes are still unpredictable.

Meteorologists are using computers to give more useful information in advance. For example, meteorologists hope that in the future people will not buy prepaid airline tickets and later find that their flight is delayed or canceled because of snow. Meteorologists know that their science is still imperfect, but they think it is perfectible.

R. COMPREHENSION QUESTIONS

Choose the best way to complete each sentence.

1. The main idea of "Weather Forecasting" is that weather scientists
    a. understand everything about the weather.
    b. understand very little about the weather.
    c. are not weather forecasters.
    d. are learning how to make better predictions.
2. If you underdress on a cold day, you will probably be
    a. cold.
    b. hot.
    c. well-dressed.
    d. dirty.
3. When weather forecasts are incorrect, they are
    a. quite right.
    b. early.
    c. not right.
    d. too long.

STRATEGIES

PRELIMINARY STEPS IN RESEARCHING A TOPIC

PRE-READING EXERCISE

What do you know about *acid rain?* Discuss this topic to see how much you and your classmates already know about the topic.

Read the following statements about acid rain. Which ones did you already talk about with your classmates?

*Decide if each one is a **cause** (C), **effect** (E) or possible **solution** (S) to the problem of acid rain.*

1. ____ Whenever fossil fuels, especially coal, are burned, sulfur dioxide and nitrogen oxides are released into the atmosphere.

2. ____ Acid rain may cause the soil to release metals, which may be toxic to fish, into lakes.

3. ____ New coal-fired power plants in the United States are required by law to remove up to 90 percent of the sulfur from their waste gases before they are released into the atmosphere.

4. ____ Winds carry pollution from coal-burning industries across political boundaries, until it falls to earth with rain or snow.

5. ____ Reduced and more efficient per-capita use of energy as a nation-wide policy would automatically decrease the production of pollutants responsible for acid rain.

For his course on "Soils and the Environment," Don had to do a research paper. He had heard about the problem of acid rain in the newspaper and in political discussions, but was not sure what it meant. He thought it sounded like an interesting problem, since it was very current and seemed controversial.

STRATEGIES 137

To get started on learning more about this topic so he could write about it, Don went to the library and asked a reference librarian. The librarian suggested looking in an encyclopedia and then trying *Editorial Research Reports,* which has articles about interesting current issues.

Don then looked in a general encyclopedia. He wanted to find a clear definition of acid rain and some current ideas about it. Especially, he wanted to find areas where there might be some disagreement about acid rain. If the experts disagree, then he could give his own opinion and support that opinion in his paper. He expected to find three possible areas of controversy: *the sources of acid rain, its distribution and effects,* and possible *solutions.*

Read the encyclopedia article on the next page. Match each of these three areas of controversy with the paragraph from the encyclopedia article that discusses it. Write some words or phrases that are examples or explanations of each aspect.

Sources	**Distribution and Effects**	**Solutions**
Paragraph 1	_____	_____
Examples	_____	_____
	_____	_____
	_____	_____
Paragraph 2	_____	_____
Examples	_____	_____
	_____	_____
	_____	_____
Paragraph 3	_____	_____
Examples	_____	_____
	_____	_____
	_____	_____

138   Chapter 6

> **ACID RAIN** is a term for rain, snow, or other precipitation that has been polluted by acids. The acids are produced when water vapor in the air reacts with chemical compounds given off by automobiles, by factories, and by power plants and other sources that burn coal or oil. These chemical compounds consist chiefly of sulfur dioxide and nitrogen oxides, which form sulfuric acid and nitric acid when they react with water vapor.
>
> Acid rain falls over large areas of eastern North America and northwestern and central Europe. It has polluted thousands of lakes, rivers, and streams, causing the death of fish and other aquatic life. Some scientists believe acid rain may also damage buildings, statues, crops, forests, and soil.
>
> Acid rain can be reduced by limiting the amount of sulfur and nitrogen compounds released into the air. For example, several types of devices have been developed to remove these compounds from substances that pass through industrial smokestacks. Scientists have also found ways of decreasing the effects of acid rain. For instance, lime can be added periodically to acidified lakes. The lime helps temporarily restore the lakes by neutralizing the acid. The lime temporarily restore the lakes by neutralizing the acid.

Since Don is studying horticulture, not chemistry, he is most interested in the effects of acid rain on plants. He wants to find some areas of disagreement. These are often indicated by words like "may," "possible," "believe," "uncertain," and "suggest." With these words in mind, what is the controversial issue in the paragraph about the distribution and effects of acid rain?

_____

_____

_____

What is one possible solution offered in the article?

_____

_____

Don began to think that the issue of the *effects of acid rain on plants* might be a general direction for his paper.

Next Don went to *Editorial Research Reports*. The librarian showed him that there was an index to the last ten years, not counting the most recent year. The librarian further explained that each year was divided into two volumes, since there were too many pages for each year to fit into one volume.

Find the two articles about acid rain in the index. Why did Don choose the second one?

EDITORIAL RESEARCH REPORTS
Subject-Title Index
To Reports
January 1977-December 1987

	Year	Vol.	Page
Abortion			
Abortion: Decade of Debate	1983	I	25
Abortion: Policy	1987	II	534
Acid rain			
Acid Rain	1980	I	445
Acid Rain: Canada's Push for U.S. Action	1986	I	165
Acquired immune deficiency syndrome. See AIDS			
Adolescents and youth. See also Colleges and universities; Education, Elementary			
AIDS Dilemmas	1987	II	578
Juvenile Justice	1979	II	541
Juvenile Justice	1986	II	873
Pressures on youth	1982	II	589
Teenage Drinking	1981	I	349
Teenage Pregnancy	1979	I	205
Troubled Teenagers	1987	II	346
Youth Suicide	1981	I	429
Youth Unemployment	1977	II	765
The Youth Unemployment Puzzle	1983	I	213
Adoption			
Independent Adoption	1987	II	646
Issues in Child Adoption	1984	II	857
Advertising			
Access to Legal Services	1977	II	557
Direct Marketing Boom	1984	II	877
Media Reformers	1977	II	973
Postal Service Changes	1987	II	518
Trends in Advertising	1981	II	653
Aeronautics. See Aviation; Space programs			
Affirmative action. See Discrimination in Employment			
Africa. See also Angola; Libya; Rhodesia; South Africa			
African Policy Reversal	1978	II	501
International Relief Agencies	1985	I	61
Strategies for Economic Turnabout	1986	II	813
Aged and aging. See Elderly			
Agent Orange			
Agent Orange: The Continuing Debate	1984	II	489
Agriculture. See also Food supply; Forests and forestry; Pesticides			
Access to Federal Lands	1981	II	693
Advances in Agricultural Research	1981	I	369
Agriculture: Key to Poland's Future	1981	II	837
Farm Finance	1986	I	265
Farm Policy's New Course	1983	I	233
Genetic Breakthroughs	1986	I	1
Migrants: Enduring Farm Problem	1983	I	413
Tobacco Under Siege	1984	II	737
AIDS (acquired immune deficiency syndrome)			
AIDS Dilemmas	1987	II	578
AIDS: Spreading Mystery Disease	1985	II	597
Air Force, U.S. See Armed forces			
Air Pollution. See also Acid rain			
Air Pollution Control: Progress and Prospects	1980	II	841

	Year	Vol.	Page
Air Pollution Countdown	1987	II	618
Environmental Conflicts in the 1980s	1985	I	121
Synthetic Fuels	1979	II	621
Toxic Substance Control	1978	II	741
Volcanoes	1983	II	781
Airlines. See Aviation			
Alaska.			
Alaska: 25 Years of Statehood	1983	II	921
Alcohol			
America's New Temperance Movement	1984	II	937
Teenage Drinking	1981	I	349
Troubled Teenagers	1987	II	346
Alzheimer's disease			
Mystery Disease of the Elderly	1983	II	841
American Indians. See Indians of North America			
American Telephone and Telegraph Co.			
Breaking Up AT&T	1983	II	941
Telecommunications in the 80s	1983	I	89
Andropov, Yuri V.			
Russia under Andropov	1983	I	1
Angola			
Angola and the Reagan Doctrine	1986	I	21
Animals. See also Wildlife			
Animal Rights	1980	II	561
Zoo Renaissance	1987	II	457
Anorexia			
Anorexia Nervosa and Other Eating Disorders	1985	II	657
Antarctic Regions			
Future of Antarctica	1982	I	469
Antitrust law			
Breaking Up AT&T	1983	II	941
Broadcasting Deregulation	1987	II	630
Business Mergers and Antitrust	1982	I	21
Corporate Takeovers	1987	I	77
Deregulating Electric Power	1987	II	602
Oil Antitrust Action	1978	I	101
Apartheid. See South Africa			
Apparel. See Clothing and dress			
Arab countries. See Middle East; names of specific countries			
Architecture. See also Housing			
Historic Preservation	1984	I	105
Trends in Architecture	1982	I	45
Argentina			
Democratic Revival in South America	1984	II	837
Armaments. See also Arms control; Chemical warfare; Firearms; Nuclear weapons; Space warfare			
America's Arms Sales	1979	I	325
Lasers' Promising Future	1983	I	373
Third World Arms Industries	1987	I	181
Armed Forces. See also Vietnam War			
American Involvement in Lebanon	1984	I	169
American Military Strength Abroad	1980	I	105
Draft Registration	1980	I	425
Military Pay and Benefits	1978	I	421
Women in the Military	1981	II	489

140 Chapter 6

```
Vol.  I                              Mar.  7
No.   9                              1 9 8 6

ACID RAIN:

Canada's Push
For U.S. Action
by
Roger Thompson

                                              page

INTERNATIONAL IRE                              167
    Canada's Complaints Get Summit Notice      167
    Reactions to Envoys' $5 Billion Proposal   168
    Scientific Consensus on Causes, Sources    171
    Uncertain Effects on Forests and Health    174

U.S. POLICY DILEMMA                            176
    Clean Air Act's Lack of Acid Rain Control  176
    Ten-Year Legal Battle over Tall Stacks     176
    New England vs. Midwest and Ohio Valley    177

CLEAN COAL TECHNOLOGY                          180
    Finding a Middle Ground for Advancement    180
    Promising Ways for Burning Coal Cleanly    181
    Economic Advantages of Innovative Designs  182
    Legal Incentive for Utilities Not to Change 183
```

This is the *title page* to the article in *Editorial Research Reports* about acid rain. The subtitle, "Canada's Push for U.S. Action" refers to the disagreement between Canada and the United States about solutions to the problem of acid rain. This problem is not the focus of Don's paper. Which section of the article might be about Don's interest?

He does not have time to read all seventeen pages of this article, especially since the part that interests him is only two pages, and he may not be interested in all of that.

There are six paragraphs in the section in which Don is interested. Skim the article on the next page. Here are the topics of the paragraphs. Number them according to their order in the article (1–6).

Uncertain Effects on Forests and Health

____building material damage

____cause of forest damage—acid rain? same with crops

____more on study of air danger

____effects on breathing air

____effects on human health—water, fish

____intro, data on decline of forest growth

Which paragraphs would be most helpful to Don? What do you think Don could do next to find information about his topic? (See the mini-unit at the end of this book for the continuation of Don's research into acid rain.)

Uncertain Effects on Forests and Health

Acid rain once was thought to be the prime cause of a decline in forest growth in the United States and Europe, but current research has not established a cause-and-effect relationship. Damage figures, however, continue to mount, according to the World Resources Institute study. It reported that the extent of damage to West German forests rose from 34 percent in 1983 to 55 percent last year, while 10 percent of the trees in southern Scandinavia and Czechoslovakia have been damaged. In the United States, stands of red spruce in high elevations in Vermont have declined by about half. Similar declines have been reported in the Adirondacks and the southern Appalachians.

Though the cause of this damage has not been clearly established, acid rain remains a prime suspect. It may harm trees by removing nutrients from the leaves or by altering the soils in which the trees grow. However, observed growth declines also may result from drought, temperature extremes, insects, heavy metals (such as aluminum), ozone, or other pollutants. Writing in *The Environmental Forum* magazine, two forest industry researchers summed up the current state of scientific knowledge: "[O]ver the past years, forest products industry scientists have studied all major forest locations having undiagnosed damage symptoms. Not only were we unable to conclude that this forest damage is definitely linked to acid rain, but industry scientists also could not positively conclude that other specific air pollutants—acting singly or together—were the culprit." Likewise, damage to crops from acid deposition under natural conditions has not been documented. Years of research in this area "suggest that acid deposition's impact on agriculture is not a cause for concern," said a 1984 General Accounting Office (GAO) report.

Acid deposition does have a well-recognized potential to damage building materials, such as stone, paint, steel, and zinc. Dry deposited SO_2 and sulfate, a secondary product of SO_2, combine on moist surfaces to form sulfuric acid, which is more corrosive than acid rain. It is difficult to determine, however, which portion of damage is done by pollutants swept in from long distances and which is done by those emitted locally. It is equally difficult to apportion damage between acid deposition and other factors, such as weathering. Nonetheless, a 1985 draft study by EPA, Brookhaven National Laboratory, and the Army Corps of Engineers set a preliminary midpoint estimate of $3.5 billion for annual building materials damage caused by acid deposition.

Direct effects of acid deposition on human health so far have not been proven. There is some fear of indirect effects, such as contamination of fish or drinking water supplies. It is thought that acidified water can contribute to elevated levels of dissolved mercury, which in turn can produce toxic concentrations of mercury in fish. However, no human health problems have been associated with mercury dissolved by acid rain.

Some researchers see a larger threat from breathing extremely small particles of sulfur dioxide. Sulfates contribute to poor visibility across much of the United States, including national parks in the West, where copper smelters are the primary source. Sulfates mixed with other particulates "could be responsible for about 50,000 premature deaths a year, particularly among people with preexisting respiratory or cardiac problems," concluded the Office of Technology Assessment (OTA). It is not known, however, whether harmful effects are caused by sulfates or other particulates with which they are associated.

While the OTA study is widely cited by environmental groups, William H. Megonnell, an environmental specialist at the Edison Electric Institute, an industry research and information organization, says it has no validity. "The study concluded that deaths attributable to sulfates ranged from 1 to 150,000, so they came up with 50,000 as a midpoint," he said. "It has absolutely no scientific credibility."

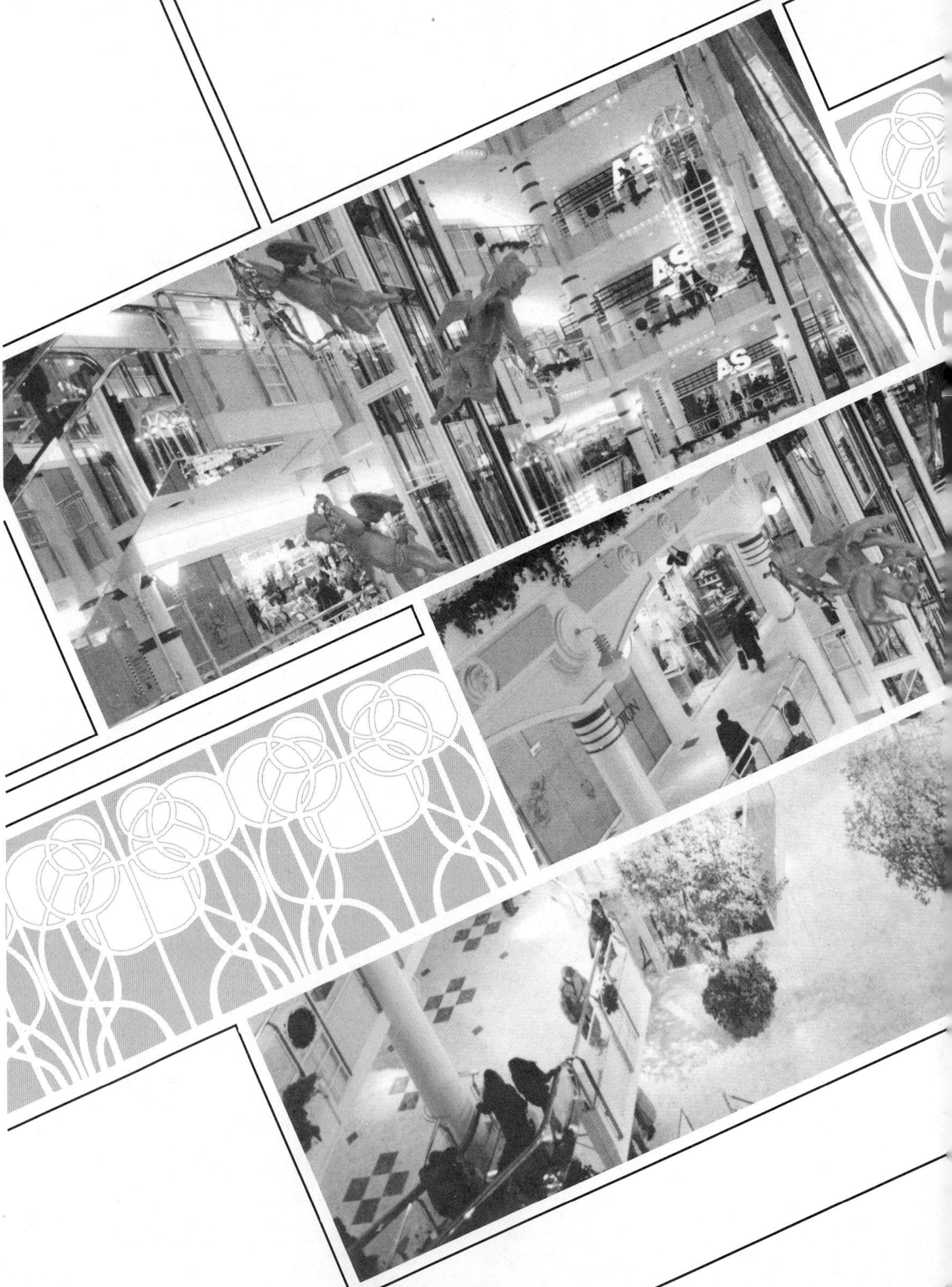
AS
AS
AS

CHAPTER SEVEN

SHOPPING

PRE-READING QUESTIONS

1. What you see in the drawing is a pedestrian mall in Greenville. It is located in the downtown area. The street that used to run down the middle is now only for pedestrians (people who walk), not cars. There are several small parks and a playground for children in the middle of the mall. Is there anything like this in your country? In your city in the United States?

Answer the following questions about your country. When you discuss these with your classmates, compare them with the situation in your town in the United States.

2. List the shops that are in your neighborhood, that is, within walking distance or a short car or bus ride. _____

3. How often do people who cook meals in your family (you, your spouse, your parents, etc.) go food shopping? _____

4. How often do you go shopping for other things besides food (books, clothing, presents for others, appliances, etc.) _____

5. List the things that you buy very frequently (more than two or three times a week). _____

6. List some things that you buy very infrequently (only three or four times a year). _____

7. When you want to go shopping for things other than food, where do you go? _____
   to a neighborhood shop ____
   to a shop downtown, in the town or city center ____
   to a shopping mall, a huge building with many stores under the same roof ____

8. What types of stores are there in shopping malls in your country? ____
   _____
   _____

9. What are the hours of operation of shops in your country? _____
   _____
   _____

10. Have you ever bought something over the phone or through the mail? What types of things can you buy in this way? _____
    _____
    _____

11. Can you think of other ways that shopping in the United States is very different from shopping in your country? List some things that you would like to discuss with your classmates that are not covered in the questions above. _____
    _____
    _____
    _____

12. In the long reading in this chapter, Lee and Daphne go to a shopping mall one Saturday morning. Why do you think they decide to go there instead of to the shopping area near Furnell University? _____
    _____
    _____

    Can you guess what things they might need to buy?

    ____ soft drinks   ____ Furnell shirts   ____ car parts
    ____ shoes   ____ textbooks   ____ a tape recorder
    ____ medicine   ____ a refrigerator   ____ greeting cards
    ____ clothing   ____ groceries   ____ candy bars

    After you read the long reading, come back to this question to see how many of your answers were correct.

SHOPPING 147

A. VOCABULARY IN CONTEXT

Before reading the story "At the Mall," read the following paragraphs. Try to guess the meaning of the underlined words from the context.

1. I spent all day at the mall. I had a lot of different things to do and buy, and I didn't want to waste time driving all over town. I went to a bookstore, a card shop, a bank, a furniture store, and a flower shop. Then I had lunch and finished up by going to a clothing store. I got all these errands done in a very short time.

   A mall is

   a. a large store with many departments.
   b. a large parking lot.
   c. a shopping center with many stores.
   d. a furniture store with a restaurant.

   Which of the following are errands? (eran) đi lang thang

   a. Buying stamps at the post office.
   b. Doing the grocery shopping.
   c. Going to the library to study.
   d. Brushing your teeth.
   e. Taking some clothes to the drycleaner.
   f. Cashing a check at the bank.
   g. Buying some shampoo and vitamins at the pharmacy.
   h. Returning some books to the library.
   i. Going swimming at the university pool.
   j. Having dinner at a restaurant.

2. Martha was browsing in a discount drugstore. She wasn't looking for anything special, and she had a few minutes before catching the bus. She was amazed at the prices. Everything was much less expensive than at the pharmacy near campus. She decided she would come back the next time she needed something from a drugstore.

   To browse is to (bruze) đọc lướt qua

   a. shop for medicine and cosmetics in a drugstore.
   b. have a snack while waiting for someone.
   c. wait a long time for a bus.
   d. look around a store without planning to buy anything.

   A discount store

   a. sells vitamins.
   b. has low prices.
   c. is for browsing.
   d. is a store on a college campus.

148   Chapter 7

3. Sarah Anne came home from the department store with ten pairs of stockings. Her roommate Joanne asked her why she had bought so many pairs of stockings.

"They were such a good <u>bargain</u>, I had to buy them," Sarah Anne told her. "They're usually $1.50 each pair, but today they were on sale for $.69. That's less than half price! I'm sure that I'll use them all this year at school."

What does a <u>bargain</u> mean?

a. Something that costs $.69.
b. Something that is much cheaper than usual.
c. Something that you buy ten of at one time.
d. Something that you buy at a department store.

B. SKIMMING AND SCANNING EXERCISE

First skim the following long reading called "At the Mall." What are the different kinds of stores that Sarah Anne and Lee went to on their shopping trip? You will find this information at the beginning of each paragraph, so it is not necessary to read the whole paragraph. Write the kinds of stores on the lines. Your teacher will tell you when to start and stop.

1. _____
2. _____
3. _____
4. _____
5. _____

Now scan the reading to find the specific information you need to answer the following questions. Write down the location of the answer in the text. Your teacher will tell you when to start and stop. The questions are arranged in the same order that the answers occur in the reading. For example:

How did Sarah Anne and Lee get to the mall? _____by bus_____

Paragraph __2__ Line __1__

1. What did Lee buy in the shoe store? _____
   Paragraph _____ Line _____

2. What did Sarah Anne want to buy in the card shop? _____
   Paragraph _____ Line _____

3. What was the price of the book Lee bought? _____
   Paragraph _____ Line _____

4. Name the three different ways that Sarah Anne and Lee paid for their purchases:
   1. _____ Paragraph _____ Line _____
   2. _____ Paragraph _____ Line _____
   3. _____ Paragraph _____ Line _____

C. LONG READING

AT THE MALL

One Saturday morning Lee complained to Sarah Anne, "I have so many things to do I'll never have time to study for our exam in statistics. I have to buy shoes and a birthday present and return a sweater . . . "

"Let's take a bus to the shopping mall," Sarah Anne suggested. "There are about thirty stores there. It will be full of shoppers, of course, because everyone shops on Saturday morning, but we'll be able to get our errands done quickly and still have time for lunch. Then you can go home and study all afternoon."

At the mall, their first stop was a shoe store. Lee looked for running shoes, while Sarah Anne browsed. A salesperson offered to help her, but Sarah Anne said, "I'm just looking, thank you." Lee was fortunate to find a pair of shoes on sale. The price was reduced from $35.95 to $28.95. "These shoes are marked down. I'll save seven dollars, and they fit me well," she said to Sarah Anne as she paid for them by credit card.

Next they made a quick stop at a small card shop so Sarah Anne could buy an anniversary card for her aunt and uncle in Alabama. There were lots of cards for sale, but she didn't like the selection.

Next to the card shop was a large bookstore where Lee looked for a birthday present for her sister in California. She skimmed a couple of books about canoeing. The price of the one she chose was $15.95. It cost more than she wanted to spend, but it was the perfect gift for her sister. Meanwhile, Sarah Anne bought a dictionary.

The next stop was a discount drugstore. Sarah Anne wanted to pick up some vitamin C tablets, because she had already had two colds that semester. Lee offered to hold her package while she read the labels and picked out some tablets. As Sarah Anne had expected, the vitamins were much cheaper than at the small pharmacy in town. She was glad she had compared prices before buying.

The last stop before lunch was a women's clothing store. Lee returned a very expensive green wool sweater she had bought there. She exchanged it for a blue one that cost less, so she received a small refund. At the same time, Sarah Anne decided to purchase a moderately priced cotton turtleneck. "This is a real bargain," she exclaimed. "It's not expensive, and it's excellent quality. It will last for years." Sarah Anne paid by personal check, because she had just enough cash left for lunch.

Sarah Anne and Lee were very tired from running around the crowded shopping center. But all their errands were done. They only had thirty minutes left before catching the bus to campus, so they stopped at a restaurant and hurriedly ate lunch.

D. COMPREHENSION EXERCISE

Choose the best answer to the following questions or the best way to complete the sentences. You may look at the reading to help you find the correct answers.

1. An important idea in this reading is that
   a. it is exhausting to shop at a mall, especially just before Christmas.
   b. you should always buy shoes on sale, if possible.
   c. Lee likes to do her shopping early in the day to avoid crowds.
   d. you can do a lot of different errands quickly at a shopping mall.

2. The book on canoeing was
   a. cheaper than Lee had expected.
   b. marked down in price.
   c. for sale in the card shop.
   d. exactly what Lee wanted to give her sister.

3. Lee wanted to do her errands quickly because
   a. she needed time to study for an exam.
   b. she wanted to save money.
   c. she had a lot of shopping to do.
   d. she wanted to be on time for the statistics exam.

4. Which of the following things are implied but not said directly in the reading? (Choose one or more.)
   a. Sarah Anne and Lee missed the bus to campus because they ate lunch.
   b. Vitamin C may prevent colds.
   c. Sarah Anne had already planned to buy a turtleneck before she went shopping.
   d. The same thing may have different prices in different stores.
   e. The shopping mall is only crowded at Christmas time.
   f. Sarah Anne did not buy any cards.

5. A *personal* check is a check
   a. from a company or store.
   b. from a bank.
   c. from the government or the United Nations.
   d. from a man or woman.

SHOPPING   151

E. FILL-IN EXERCISE

Read the following sentences. Try to understand the meaning of the underlined words from the context. Then find a word from the following list that is a synonym.

browsed	purchase	returned
price	marked down	shop
crowded	selection	shopping center
pharmacy	tablet	

1. I am going to the <u>mall</u>. There are several things I need to do at the _____.

2. The mall is very _____ around Christmas time. It's <u>full of people</u> doing last-minute Christmas shopping.

3. You <u>bought</u> a house for $105,000! Why did you _____ such an expensive one?

4. The jackets were <u>reduced</u> from $55 to $48. I wonder why they were _____ so much.

5. The <u>cost</u> of the book on canoeing is very high. I won't pay that _____.

6. Lee <u>took back</u> the sweater she bought last week. She _____ it because it was too small.

7. The <u>choice</u> of vegetables at the A & Z is terrible. I prefer the _____ at Leader Supermarket.

8. When I graduate from Furnell, I want to buy my own <u>store</u> and go into business for myself. I hope to get a flower _____.

9. Gordon <u>was looking around</u> the bookstore while he waited for Daphne to buy a textbook. He found an interesting book about the Canadian wilderness while he _____.

10. Luis had to go to a <u>drugstore</u> to get his prescription filled. He went to the Hillside _____.

11. Suddenly Luis remembered that he had forgotten to take his <u>pill</u>. He reached for the bottle and took out a _____.

F. WORD ASSOCIATION EXERCISE

Look at these sentences from "At the Mall."

There were lots of cards <u>for sale</u>.

This sentence tells us that it was <u>possible to buy</u> cards. They were available to buy.

She found a pair of shoes <u>on sale</u>.

This means that the shoes were marked down, or <u>the price was reduced</u>. *Now read the sentences that follow. Decide if* **on sale** *or* **for sale** *applies in each case.*

1. Gordon doesn't use his guitar any more. It is _____for sale_____.

2. The sign on that house says _____for sale_____. I guess the family that lives there is moving to another house.

3. I try very hard to save money. As a result, I usually buy things _____on sale_____.

4. After the ski season is over in March, skis, poles, and ski clothes are always _____on sale_____ in Greenville.

5. Luis bought a new bicycle, so his old bike is now _____for sale_____.

6. These gloves are much cheaper than before. They are _____on sale_____.

7. Washing machines are _____on sale_____ at the appliance store in the mall. They are marked down $50.

8. Washing machines are _____for sale_____ at the mall. No store sells them downtown.

9. Don't buy your TV now. Wait until TVs are _____on sale_____. Why spend extra money?

10. There are some beautiful paintings in the library at Furnell. I wonder if they are _____for sale_____ or if they belong to the university.

G. WORD FORM CHART

Vocabulary Word	Adjective	Noun	Verb	Adverb
1. to the <u>shopping</u> mall	shopping*	shopping shop shopper	shop	
2. the <u>crowded</u> shopping center	crowded	crowd	crowd	
3. She didn't like the <u>selection</u>.	selective	selection	select	selectively
4. a <u>moderately</u> priced cotton turtleneck	moderate	moderation	moderate	moderately
5. Sarah Anne decided to <u>purchase</u> a...	purchase*	purchase	purchase	
6. <u>reduced</u> from $35.95 to $28.95	reduced refund*	reduction	reduce	
7. She received a small <u>refund</u>.		refund	refund	
8. and <u>hurriedly</u> ate lunch.	hurried	hurry	hurry	hurriedly
9. the one she <u>chose</u>	chosen	choice	choose	

*A noun used as an adjective in a compound noun.

154   Chapter 7

H. WORD FORM EXERCISE

Choose the correct word form and fill in the blank. Look at number (1) on the Word Form Chart to choose the correct answer for question (1) in this exercise, and so forth. Name the part of speech in the blank at the right.

1. The store was full of ___shopping___. You could hardly move.

   Part of speech ___Adj___

2. The children ___crowded___ into the movie theater for last Saturday's afternoon film.

   Part of speech ___Adj___

3. Gordon used to ___select___ his courses carefully after finding out about the professors, textbooks, and teaching assistants.

   Part of speech ___V___

4. Martha receives a ___moderation___ salary for her job as a lab technician. She would like to earn more, of course, but she can survive.

   Part of speech ___N___

5. The ___purchase___ price includes both the radio and its batteries.

   Part of speech ___N___

6. After Christmas, there is always a ___reduce___ of prices on winter clothes. You can save a lot of money.

   Part of speech ___V___

7. Sarah Anne bought a calculator on sale, but it didn't work. The store ___refund___ her money.

   Part of speech ___V___

8. Daphne was in a ___hurry___. She knew she was already late for the potluck dinner.

   Part of speech ___N___

9. I didn't find the dictionary I wanted at the campus store. The ___choose___ of books there is not very big.

   Part of speech ___V___

SHOPPING 155

I. FACT AND OPINION

It is important to be able to recognize the difference between a fact and an opinion. A **fact** is something that can be *proved* or *disproved*. Often, a fact includes numbers. For example, the following sentences state facts:

1. Every year 43,500,000 passengers pass through O'Hare Airport in Chicago.
2. The bus fare in Greenville, New York, is thirty-five cents.
3. The Carters have ten children.

An **opinion**, on the other hand, *cannot* be proved or disproved. It is possible to agree or disagree with an opinion. Sometimes an opinion includes adverbs and adjectives. For example, the following sentences are opinions:

4. Traveling is <u>dangerous</u>.
5. The Greenville bus fare is <u>cheap</u>.
6. The Carters have <u>too many</u> children.

If you count the number of people who travel through Chicago, you will be able to prove or disprove sentence (1). Then no one will be able to disagree. But you may easily disagree with sentence (4). It is clearly an opinion.

Read the following statements. Decide if they are facts or opinions. Write F for fact or O for opinion to the left of each statement. Be prepared to explain why you chose *F* or *O* in each case.

1. __O__ It is better to shop at a mall than to go to several different stores downtown.
2. __F__ There are thirty stores at the Greenville Mall.
3. __O__ It is important to read quickly on the TOEFL exam.
4. __O__ Americans are always in a hurry.
5. __F__ Lee spent too much time at the Mall on Saturday.
6. __F__ The parka was marked down six dollars.
7. __F__ Gordon used to take guitar lessons two times a week.
8. __F__ There are twelve months in a year.
9. __O__ May is the nicest month in Greenville.
10. __F__ A book on canoeing for $15.95 is a real bargain.

156 Chapter 7

J. VOCABULARY IN CONTEXT

Before reading the article "Market Research," read the following paragraphs. Try to guess the meaning of the underlined words from the context.

1. Professor Silverman bought his house for $75,000. Two years later he sold it for $80,000. He made a small profit on his house.

   To make a profit is to

   a. sell something you own soon after you buy it.
   b. reduce the price of something.
   c. sell something at a discount.
   d. sell something for more money than you paid for it.

2. Martha works as a lab technician in the Chemistry Department at Furnell University. She has a yearly income of $17,000. Her husband Luis is a graduate student. He also has a part-time job and earns about $4000 a year. Together, Luis and Martha have an annual income of about $21,000.

   Income is

   a. a wife's salary.
   b. the money received.
   c. the entrance to a building.

3. Even though he lives in Greenville, Luis prefers living in a big city. He likes the excitement, the fast pace of life, the various kinds of people and restaurants, the theater, and museums. His preferences match Martha's. She likes city life too. She loves the theater, playing frisbee in the park, and window shopping downtown. She and Luis don't plan to stay in a small town like Greenville after he finishes his degree at Furnell.

   If things match they

   a. are the same or go together well.
   b. compete with each other in many ways.
   c. are very different and contrasting.

K. VOCABULARY CHECKLIST

Here are the words that you will need to know when you read the article "Market Research." Put each word in the correct blank. Use each word only once.

company	consumers	product
questionnaires	data	

1. A group of people who are organized to work together to make money is a ____company____ .
2. Factual information that is used for scientific or practical decision making is called ____data____ .
3. People who buy things and use services are called ____consumers____ .
4. ____Questionnaires____ are written forms containing questions to be answered.
5. Something that is produced, usually for the purpose of selling or trading, is a ____product____ .

L. SHORT READING

Read the following article to find out what market research is.

MARKET RESEARCH

In order to make a profit, a company must make a product or provide a service that people will buy. Companies, therefore, often hire market researchers who study consumers and the various things that influence their shopping decisions. Market researchers collect information about products and the people they expect to buy them by using the telephone, personal interviews, and questionnaires. Then they analyze the information they collect and present new ideas to the company.

For instance, a market researcher might have the job of finding out why a specific company's products are not popular in a certain city. He or she has to study all the ways the products are being presented to the consumers. Is the price too high for their incomes? Do the products match the wants and needs of consumers? Do the advertisements reach the people who will probably buy the products? Does the product have a package that appeals to shoppers? Finally, do the stores display the product well?

The company will use the data that has been collected and analyzed by the market researcher to increase the sales of its products.

M. COMPREHENSION EXERCISE

Choose the best way to complete the following exercises. Do not look back at the reading.

1. The main idea of this reading is that marketing researchers
   a. worry about helping consumers keep prices low.
   b. try to help companies please consumers and therefore make a profit.
   c. advertise products in certain cities where sales are not going well.
   d. collect data from companies and give it to the consumers.

2. It is implied that marketing researchers might ask certain questions when they analyze the sales situation of a specific product. Circle the ones you think they would ask.

   a. Is the packaging appealing?
   b. Is this product safe for children?
   c. Does the product cost too much?
   d. Are the advertisements seen by shoppers who might by the product?
   e. Is the product made of too many scarce natural resources?
   f. Is there a more efficient way to make the product?

3. Circle all the words that name a "person or thing that does something."
   a. Researcher.
   b. Information.
   c. Consumer.
   d. Personal.
   e. Shopper.
   f. Decision.

N. VOCABULARY IN CONTEXT

Before reading the story "Supermarket Special," read the following paragraphs. Try to guess the meaning of the underlined words from the context.

1. Lee's dentist told her that she should not drink <u>soft drinks</u> so often. He said that ginger ale, cola, root beer, and fruit sodas all contain a lot of sugar. They cause problems with your teeth.

   <u>Soft drinks</u> are
   a. drinks made from fresh fruit without sugar.
   b. sweet, flavored drinks made with soda water.
   c. alcoholic drinks.
   d. nutritious drinks.

SHOPPING 159

2. It was 10 A.M. and Walter and Daphne were going to their next class, which started at 10:15. "I didn't have a big breakfast this morning, so I really need a snack before statistics class," Walter told Daphne on his way to the vending machines. He bought a candy bar, and Daphne got some yogurt.

   A snack is *on lot da*

   a. a small amount of food eaten between meals.
   b. a sweet dessert.
   c. food eaten at a meal.
   d. food eaten at breakfast.

3. Sarah Anne hoped to buy a calculator to help her with her statistics course. She saw an ad for a one-week special on calculators at a local department store. A calculator, regularly priced at $32.50, was offered for only $28.99.

   A special is

   a. a sale price for a product for a limited time.
   b. an unusual calculator used by statisticians.
   c. a special department selling low-priced items.
   d. a high-priced calculator in excellent condition.

4. Professor Kramer invited all the students from his ancient history course to his house for tea at the end of the semester. He went to the German bakery in Greenville and bought assorted pastries to serve with tea. He bought several kinds of cookies, a few cupcakes, a small cake, and some fruit turnovers. He wanted to offer his students many different types of pastries.

   Assorted means *chia ra*

   a. delicious.
   b. different types.
   c. expensive.
   d. one kind.

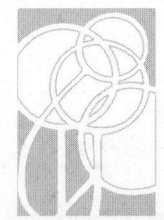

O. SHORT READING

Read the following and then do the Scanning Exercise.

A SUPERMARKET SPECIAL

   Walter and Eric decided to give a party in their dorm room. They planned to invite between ten and fifteen friends over on a Friday evening. Because they both had very little spending money left in their bank accounts, they wanted to be very careful to save money on beer, soft drinks, and snacks for the party.
   "Look, Walter," said Eric as he read the *Greenville Journal* on Wednesday afternoon. "The Supermart downtown is having a special on party food this week. Let's go down there right away. According to this ad, we should be able to save a lot of money."

160   Chapter 7

P. SCANNING EXERCISE

In the following illustration you will see the Supermart ad for a special on party drinks and snacks that Walter and Eric saw in the *Greenville Journal*. Scan the ad to find the answers to the following questions.

SUPERMART SPECIAL SUPERMART

SHOP NOW FOR YOUR PARTY NEEDS!

$1.89 / half gallon
JOHNSON'S
Famous home made flavor
Ice Cream
Johnson's VANILLA
Vanilla, chocolate, strawberry and assorted flavors

GREAT OFFER!!!!!
COLEMAN'S "PARTY PACKS"
3 SIX PACKS
of frosty ginger ale
$6.10

Fresh Salted **Peanuts**
12oz. jar
SALT MEISTER
$1.59
regularly $1.98

TRY THIS HEALTHY SNACK
Sesame Bran Crackers
delicious
nutritious
low in calories
Now through Saturday only
89¢/box

Riteway Diet Soda
2 calories per can
$2.10
per six-pack!

Qurly-Q PRETZELS Snappy Flavor
Low-calorie treat!!!!
2 BAGS now
$1.79

BYRNE'S CRISPY Potato Chips
12 oz. bag
ONLY **$.98**
reg. $1.29

1. How much will Eric and Walter save if they buy two jars of salted peanuts during the Supermart special?

    a. $1.59
    b. $.39
    c. $.78
    d. $.14

SHOPPING 161

2. How many different kinds of Johnson's ice cream are on special at Supermart this week?

   a. Three.
   b. Ten.
   c. Five.
   d. None.
   e. Many.

3. Gordon, Martha, and Sarah Anne are trying to lose weight. Walter and Eric want to offer snacks and drinks at the party that these friends can enjoy. What can they buy at Supermart?

   a. _____
   b. _____
   c. _____

   What words tell you that people who want to lose weight can eat this snack?

   a. _____
   b. _____
   c. _____

4. Walter wants to have two cans of soft drinks for each person he invited to the party. He wants to have a couple of extra ones too. How many six-packs should he buy? Explain your answer.
   a. Six.
   b. Five.
   c. Three.
   d. Twelve.

   _____
   _____

KOOL & MILD TODAY
POWELL & HYDE Sts.
SAN FRANCISCO MUNICIPAL RAILWAY

TRANSIT
MCI
PA 6299

CHAPTER EIGHT

TRANSPORTATION

PRE-READING QUESTIONS

What types of *public transportation* are there in your country?

___ city/town buses   ___ ferry boats   ___ airplanes
___ subways/metros   ___ taxis   ___ intra-city buses
___ regional trains   ___ commuter trains   ___ other (please specify)

Fill out the following questionnaire about public transportation services in your country. This will help you analyze the service that exists in your country and give you opportunities to compare it to public transportation in the countries of your classmates and in the United States.

1. Where does the service exist?

	BUS	SUBWAY/TRAIN	OTHER
in some small towns	___	___	___
in every small town	___	___	___
in every city	___	___	___
between every major city	___	___	___
from every small village or town to every larger city	___	___	___

2. How often do you use the service?

	BUS	SUBWAY/TRAIN	OTHER
daily	___	___	___
once or twice a week	___	___	___
rarely	___	___	___
never	___	___	___

3. Who uses the service (either buses, subways, or trains)?

   a. Commuters

   ___ people without cars
   ___ people without second cars (i.e., one family member drives)
   ___ people who have to commute a long way
   ___ people who like to read during their commute
   ___ people who have no parking space at their office
   ___ schoolchildren (primary and secondary school)
   ___ university students

b. Shoppers

___ people without cars
___ people without second cars
___ elderly people
___ people who cannot carry heavy bags back from the shop, but can walk there.
___ other (please specify)_____

4. Who pays for the service?

___ the users pay full costs
___ government gives a little financial help
___ government gives a lot of financial help
___ government gives no assistance
___ government gives free passes to elderly during non-rush hours
___ Other (please specify)_____

5. How much is the service?

___ under 50¢
___ 50¢–$1.00
___ $1.00–$1.50
___ $1.50–$2.00
___ over $2.00

6. What percentage of your friends use public transportation? _____

7. What percentage of the people in your town or city use it? _____

8. What types of public transportation exist in your town or city in the United States? Talk to your classmates to make a complete list.

_____
_____
_____
_____

9. Which public transportation services do you think you will use in the United States? If these are different from the types that you use in your own country, say why.

_____
_____

10. In the long reading of this chapter, Sarah Anne is going back to Greenville from a nearby city (four to five hours away). What type of public transportation do you think she will be taking in the story? Why?

_____

A. VOCABULARY IN CONTEXT

Before reading the story "Getting Home," read the following paragraphs. Try to guess the meaning of the underlined words from the context.

1. When I travel by long-distance bus I am as <u>nervous</u> as when I take an exam. For instance, the last time I went to the city, I set out in time to walk from home to the bus <u>terminal</u> and be there an hour early. But then I started to worry that I would have to wait in line a long time to buy my ticket. So I took a <u>cab</u> to the terminal, even though it cost a lot.

   <u>Nervous</u> is

   a. happy and relaxed.
   b. excited and a bit afraid.
   c. very well prepared.
   d. crazy but quite smart.

   A <u>terminal</u> is

   a. a bus stop.
   b. a building where long-distance buses begin and end their trips.
   c. a railway station where only a few passing trains stop.
   d. a place where you can get a cab.

   A <u>cab</u> is

   a. a taxi—a car that takes passengers for pay.
   b. a friend's car.
   c. your own car.
   d. a bus that does not always follow the same route.

2. When Martha is in a nearby city she often takes buses. On the side of each city bus it says:

   FARE $1.00
   EXACT CHANGE

   This means that the driver will not take a five-dollar bill and give a passenger four dollars back in <u>change</u>. The passenger must give the driver exactly $1.00. This way, the driver does not have to think about making change and can watch the traffic on the street. Martha always carries a lot of change—small bills and coins—in her purse when she is visiting the city.

A <u>purse</u> is

a. a pocket in a dress.
b. a credit card.
c. a bank account.
(d.) something to keep money in.

<u>Change</u> means (more than one is possible)

a. something to keep money in.
b. coins.
c. a check for the exact amount.
(d.) money you get back when you pay more than the exact amount.
e. small bills

3. After spending so much money on a new tennis racket, Eric couldn't <u>afford</u> to buy tennis balls. Luckily, his friend brought some to their tennis game.

<u>Can afford</u> means

(a.) remember to bring something.
b. find something in a store.
c. have enough money to buy something.
d. look forward to doing something.

B. LONG READING

GETTING HOME

Sarah Anne visited her friends in a nearby large city for a weekend. On Sunday afternoon they took her to the bus terminal. She felt nervous when she got there. Did she have time to wait in the long line to find out the gate number and catch the bus, too?

"Don't worry," said her friend. "You've got a round-trip ticket, don't you. You don't have to stand in line."

"But I don't know my gate number."

Her friend examined a television screen hanging on a wall and said, "Gate 18."

As they walked toward the gate, Sarah Anne started worrying about something else. On Friday afternoon it had been easy to walk to the bus station in Greenville, but now, after a weekend in the city, she had twice as many things to carry. "It's going to be an awfully long walk from the bus station to my apartment tonight."

"Well, take the city bus," her friend said. "Have you got enough change, in case it's exact change?"

Sarah Anne looked in her purse. "Yeah," she said, "but I don't think the buses run on Sunday in Greenville the way they do here."

Her friend was sure that buses run every day, but Sarah Anne still wasn't certain. She knew she was able to walk the two miles to her home. She just didn't want to.

At the gate she saw Ellen from her statistics class. The two young women decided to sit together on the bus. The driver opened the gate, and they got on the bus. Ten minutes later, the bus left the terminal. First, they looked out the window and talked. Then they studied and fell asleep for a while. As the bus approached Greenville, Sarah Anne began thinking again about the problem of getting home. "When we get in, are you going to take the city bus to your sorority house?" she asked Ellen.

"I'm going to take a taxi," Ellen replied.

"Do you know if the city bus runs on Sunday nights?" said Sarah Anne.

"Gee, I don't think so. But I hardly ever take buses," Ellen explained.

"How much does it cost to take a taxi?" asked Sarah Anne.

"Ummm, I don't remember."

Sarah Anne knew that after spending so much money on a bus ticket to the city, she couldn't afford a taxi. But Ellen also thought the city buses didn't run on Sundays. Sarah Anne was getting quite nervous. She looked around the bus and wondered what the other passengers were going to do. One person looked familiar. She decided to ask him.

"Hello, Luis! How are you?" she said as she turned around. "I have a question. Do you know if the city buses in Greenville run on Sunday nights?"

"I wish they did, but they don't," he told her. "Never on Sundays and not many evenings either. Why?"

"Oh well, I guess I'll have to walk home. Or take a cab."

"Look, Martha's meeting me at the bus station. We can give you a ride — and your friend, too."

"That's great. Thanks a lot!"

"No problem."

C. COMPREHENSION QUESTIONS

Choose the correct answer to the following questions. Do not look back at the reading.

1. Which of the following are implied in the reading "Getting Home"? (Choose one or more.)

   a. Sarah Anne worries about spending too much money.
   b. Ellen worries about spending too much money.
   c. Buses run longer hours in the big city than in a small town like Greenville.
   d. Luis is going to walk home from the bus station.

2. Why was Sarah Anne worried? (More than one is correct.)

   a. She was worried that she would have to wait in line to find the gate number and therefore miss the bus to Greenville.
   b. She was worried that the information on the television screen was incorrect.
   c. She was worried that it would be impossible to carry all her things from the bus station to her apartment.
   d. She was worried that she didn't have exact change for the bus in Greenville.
   e. She was worried that she would fall asleep during the bus ride.
   f. She was worried that Luis didn't want to give her a ride home.
   g. She was worried that she couldn't afford a taxi.
   h. She was worried that the buses didn't run in Greenville on Sundays.

3. Do you think it made sense for Sarah Anne to worry? Give your opinion of each thing she worried about.

   _____
   _____
   _____
   _____
   _____

D. FILL-IN EXERCISE

Fill in the blanks with the correct words from the following list. Each word must be used. No word can be used twice.

gate　　　**examine**　　　**catch**　　　**ride**
line　　　**familiar**　　　**awful**

1. If the class ends very late, my friend will give me a _____. He has a car and can take me home in it.

2. Yesterday was _____. It was a very bad day.

3. When you look over something very carefully, you _____ it.

4. A _____ is a door or entrance through which you go into a place.

5. I thought this book would be _____ to you, because it is well known to almost everybody in our field.

6. Ellen left home late. Fortunately, she arrived at the bus terminal in time to _____ the bus.

7. So many people wanted to see the movie that there was a very long _____ in front of the theater.

E. SCANNING EXERCISE

Scan the story "Getting Home" for any form of the word "get." Each time you find "get", write down the phrase it is used in next to the more formal meaning.

Example:　　　　　　　　**Formal Meaning:**
she got there　　　　　　　arrive

_____　　　　　have
_____　　　　　enter
_____　　　　　arrive
_____　　　　　become

F. WORD FORM CHART

Vocabulary Word	Adjective	Noun	Verb	Adverb
1. She felt <u>nervous</u>.	nervous	nerve nervousness		nervously
2. Her friend... <u>announced</u>, "Gate 18."		announcement	announce	
3. They <u>walked</u> toward the gate.		walk walking	walk	
4. Have you got ... <u>change</u>?	change* changeable	change	change	
5. The bus <u>approached</u> Greenville.		approach	approach	
6. I have a <u>question</u>.	question* questionable	question	question	
7. Give you a <u>ride</u>		ride rider	ride	

Suffixes: ▓▓▓-able changes a noun to a(n) _____ .

*A noun used as an adjective in a compound noun.

G. WORD FORM EXERCISE

Choose the correct word form and fill in the blank. Look at number (1) on the Word Form Chart to choose the correct answer for question (1) in this exercise, and so forth. Name the part of speech in the blank at the right.

1. The little cat walked _____ through the new house.
   Part of speech _____

2. They sat in the terminal and listened for the _____ of their bus.
   Part of speech _____

3. Wear comfortable shoes. We are going for a long _____.

   Part of speech _____

4. Can you _____ a dollar? I need a dime to make a phone call.

   Part of speech _____

5. Try a different _____ to the problem, and maybe it will be easier.

   Part of speech _____

6. When you write a sentence that asks about something, put a _____ mark at the end.

   Part of speech _____

7. Do you _____ the bus to work every day?

   Part of speech _____

H. VOCABULARY IN CONTEXT

Before reading the article "Public Transportation," read the following paragraphs. Try to guess the meaning of the underlined words from the context.

1. There are many different kinds of transportation that help people go from one place to another. Anyone who pays the fare can be a passenger on buses, trains, airplanes, or subways (underground trains in cities), because these are all examples of public transportation. But cars are a type of private transportation. They are only for people who can afford to buy them and for their passengers.

Transportation is

   a. a way of buying something.
   b. a way of making yourself understood.
   c. a way of getting somewhere.
   d. a way of communicating.

Fare is

   a. the price of something.
   b. a dollar coin that looks like a quarter.
   c. a kind of tax.
   d. the amount you pay to ride a bus, taxi, subway, plane, or train.

Public means

a. for everybody.
b. where you always have to pay to get in.
c. for citizens and residents.
d. for government workers.

Private means

a. for everybody.
b. for government workers.
c. only for some people.
d. only for passengers.

Subways run

a. through mountains.
b. between cities.
c. in big cities.
d. in big cities and small towns.

A passenger

a. rides some kind of transportation.
b. always pays.
c. has a car or rents one.
d. has to have enough money to be able to afford a car.

2. A politician has an elected government job or wants to have one. The people elect their government officials. Therefore every politician wants people to like him/her.

Which of the following is certainly a politician?

a. a teacher in high school
b. the President of the United States
c. a biologist at the university
d. a bank teller

When people elect officials, they

a. tax them.
b. pay them.
c. complain about them.
d. choose them.

3. Students complain a lot. When the cafeteria serves the same food three days in a row, they complain about the food. When professors assign books to read and papers to write, students complain about having too much work. When it rains, they complain about the weather.

   People complain about things that they

   a. like.
   b. dislike.
   c. want.
   d. fear.

4. Every government needs money, so governments take money from the people, in other words, they collect taxes. When Americans earn money, part of it goes to the government as income taxes. If you look at your telephone bill, you will see that you pay both the cost of the calls you made and a tax.

   Money that people pay as taxes goes

   a. to the government.
   b. to banks.
   c. to buy a car.
   d. to pay bus fare.

5. Most motors use fuel. They burn coal, oil, or gas. If they run on electricity, then the electricity is usually made by burning fuel.

   Fuel makes a car

   a. stop.
   b. go.
   c. crash.
   d. turn.

6. Tuition at American universities increases every year. Sometimes the increase is as high as 10 percent; other years it is lower. How much tuition goes up depends partly on how much prices go up. The increase also depends on the university. Private universities may need to increase tuition more rapidly than public universities because public universities get more money from the government.

   To increase is

   a. to go up.
   b. to go down.
   c. to stay the same.
   d. to go up, then come down.

I. SHORT READING

Read the following article. Then answer the comprehension questions.

PUBLIC TRANSPORTATION

In many American cities public transportation is a political issue. So many people live in these cities that it is impossible for them all to drive cars. Besides, many of them cannot afford cars. Many people want to ride fast, clean subways and buses, but nobody wants to pay for them. This is a problem for city politicians, who want to be elected and reelected. Some cities pay for part of the cost of public transportation from taxes. However, the costs go up as the price of fuel increases, and the politicians do not want to increase taxes. The rest of the cost has to come from fares that the passengers pay.

The fare system varies from city to city. In some, such as New York, every passenger pays the same amount, whether he or she takes a short ride or a long one. In other cities, such as Washington, there is a system of zones. A passenger who only wants to go a short distance pays one amount. A passenger who goes through more zones pays more.

In all systems, passengers complain that politicians let fares get too high. Other people complain that politicians let taxes get too high. Everybody blames the politicians.

J. COMPREHENSION QUESTIONS

Choose the best way to complete the following sentence. You may look at the article to help you find the correct answers.

1. The main idea of "Public Transportation" is stated in

   a. the first sentence in paragraph one.
   b. the first sentence in paragraph two.
   c. the first sentence in paragraph three.

2. Are the following true or false?

   a. True False   Americans reelect politicians because they help increase taxes.
   b. True False   Subway fares depend partly on the cost of fuel.
   c. True False   Many poor people need to use public transportation.
   d. True False   Both taxes and fares pay for public transportation.
   e. True False   In all American cities there is a system of zones for paying the bus fare.

TRANSPORTATION

K. WORD FORM CHART

Vocabulary Word	Adjective	Noun	Verb	Adverb
1. public <u>transporation</u>		transportation	transport	
2. a <u>political</u> issue city <u>politician</u>	political	politician politics		politically
3. want to be <u>elected</u> and <u>reelected</u>	election*	election reelection	elect reelect	
4. the <u>cost</u> of . . . transportation		cost	cost	
5. <u>differs</u> in <u>different</u> cities	different	difference	differ	

*A noun used as an adjective in a compound noun.

I. WORD FORM EXERCISE

Choose the correct word form and fill in the blank. Look at number (1) on the Word Form Chart to choose the correct answer for question (1) in this exercise, and so forth. Name the part of speech in the blank at the right.

1. You can take small things in a car, but to _____ large things you need a truck.

    Part of speech _____

2. If you want to become president, you have to be good at _____.

    Part of speech _____

3. The television showed the results of the voting on _____ day.

    Part of speech _____

4. This book _____ $10.

    Part of speech _____

5. What is the _____ between ice and snow?

    Part of speech _____

M. SHORT READING

Read the following letter. Then do exercises N, O, and P.

GETTING TO GORDON'S HOUSE

Gordon wrote the following letter to his brother.

Dear Ian,

It's great to hear that you're coming for the weekend.

Your bus gets to Greenville at 5:00, so I won't be able to meet you, since I have a class till 4:45. You'll have to take the Greenville bus and meet me at my place. Leave the bus terminal through the door marked "Front St." Turn right and you'll see a bus stop sign a few yards away. Take the number 6 "Main St." bus. Be sure you have 35 cents ready in exact change. Better yet, give the driver a dollar and get three metal tokens. Put one of them in the fare box. Ask the driver for a free transfer right away when you get on, so that you won't have to pay for the second bus. When the bus approaches Woolworth's, pull the cord to make the driver stop and get off. When a number 2 "Campus Hill" bus comes, get on and give the driver your transfer. The bus will go up a hill and turn left. After it crosses a bridge, get off. My house is right there, and I'll be home by then.

See you soon,

Love,

Gordon

N. VOCABULARY IN CONTEXT

Figure out the meaning of these words from their context in the short reading.

1. A <u>token</u> is

   a. a quarter.
   b. something that looks like a coin but is used only for a special purpose.
   c. 50 cents.
   d. a ticket.

2. A <u>transfer</u>

   a. lets you change from one bus to another without paying again.
   b. is a token.
   c. is a map of the city bus routes.
   d. lets you know where to get off.

3. <u>My place</u> is

   a. a bus stop.
   b. where I live.
   c. where I work.
   d. the square near my house.

O. FILL-IN EXERCISE

Fill in the blanks in the following paragraph. Then look back at Gordon's letter to his brother to check your answers. The answers may be one or two words.

The town library is three miles from here. That is too far to walk. You had better _____ the bus. Go to the corner of Main Street and Elm Street and wait for the number 5 bus. When you _____ it, ask the driver to tell you where to _____ for the library.

P. COMPREHENSION CHECK

You may look back at the reading as you do the following exercises.

1. Choose the best way to end the sentence.

   Gordon will meet his brother

   a. at the bus terminal.
   b. at a city bus stop.
   c. in front of Woolworth's.
   d. at home.

2. Mark all the ways you can pay your fare on a Greenville bus.

   a. With 35 cents exact change.
   b. With a personal check.
   c. With a token.
   d. With a credit card.
   e. With a traveler's check.

3. According to the short reading, are the following statements true or false? Some of these may be implied.

   a. True False Gordon's brother doesn't know Greenville well.
   b. True False Gordon's brother may be trying not to spend a lot of money.
   c. True False If Gordon went directly from class to the bus station, he would get there in time to meet his brother's bus.
   d. True False The Number 6 "Main St." bus stop is very near the bus terminal.
   e. True False The driver on the Greenville bus will give you change for a dollar.
   f. True False A transfer costs 25 cents.

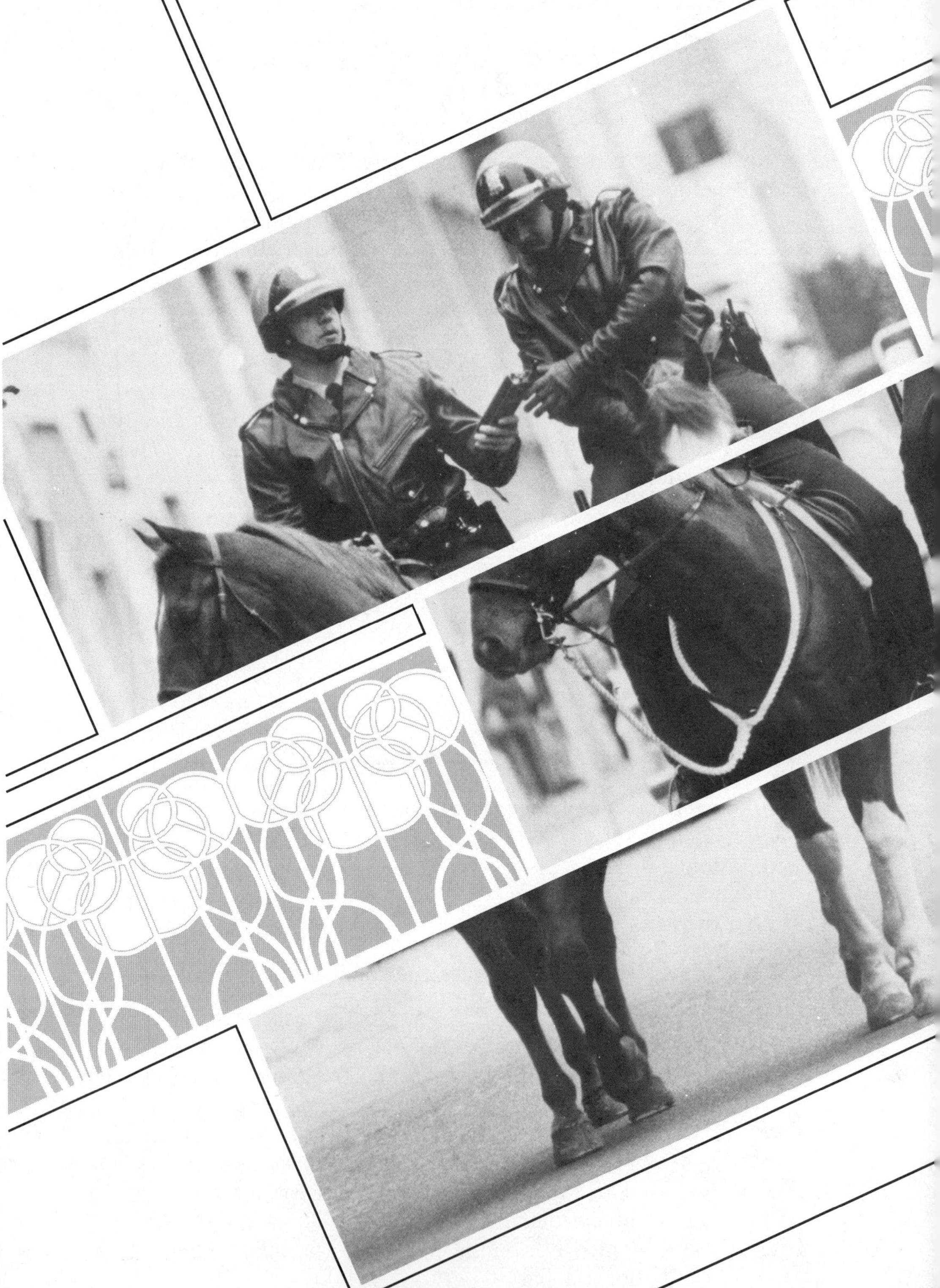

CHAPTER NINE

POLICE

POLICE 183

PRE-READING QUESTIONS

What words come to mind when you hear the word "police"? Write down several words below and share them with the class. Your teacher will write them on the board.

_____ _____

_____ _____

_____ _____

The words that you chose indicate your attitudes, or feelings, about police in your country. Of course, your reactions really depend on what type of police and what type of situation. Look at the following list of the different types of police that exist in the United States. Which type is shown in the photograph? Make sure that you understand the differences among them and whether or not the same types of police exist in your country. As a class or in a group, discuss them. Briefly write down what you think the duties are of each type of police.

TYPES OF POLICE IN AMERICA

1. campus security police _____
2. city and county police
   (uniformed and plainclothesmen) _____
3. state (trooper) police _____
4. security, police at stores,
   office, and apartment buildings _____
5. National guard _____
6. drug enforcement officers
   (undercover detectives) _____
7. FBI _____

Choose two types of police to analyze more closely. Fill out the attitudinal surveys that follow and compare your answers with your classmates'. Remember to write down your feelings about police in your country.

My attitudes about _____

    I have **respect** 1 2 3 4 **disrespect** for them.
    I have **no fear** 1 2 3 4 **fear** of them.
    I am **not suspicious** 1 2 3 4 **suspicious** of them.
    They make me feel **safe** 1 2 3 4 **in danger**.
    I feel they are **effective** 1 2 3 4 **ineffective**.
    I feel their jobs are **dangerous** 1 2 3 4 **safe**.
    I see them in real life **frequently** 1 2 3 4 **infrequently**.
    I see them on TV shows **frequently** 1 2 3 4 **infrequently**.

My attitudes about _____

    I have **respect** 1 2 3 4 **disrespect** for them.
    I have **no fear** 1 2 3 4 **fear** of them.
    I am **not suspicious** 1 2 3 4 **suspicious** of them.
    They make me feel **safe** 1 2 3 4 **in danger**.
    I feel they are **effective** 1 2 3 4 **ineffective**.
    I feel their jobs are **dangerous** 1 2 3 4 **safe**.
    I see them in real life **frequently** 1 2 3 4 **infrequently**.
    I see them on TV shows **frequently** 1 2 3 4 **infrequently**.

1. With what type of police do university students in your country usually deal? _____

2. What type of crime do you think exists on American university campuses? _____

A. VOCABULARY IN CONTEXT

Before reading the story "Call the Police," read the following paragraphs. Try to guess the meaning of the underlined words from the context.

1. Even in very small towns people sometimes take other people's things or get into fights. Even the smallest town needs <u>police</u> for protection.

   <u>Police</u> are people who

   a. put out fires.
   b. keep people safe from crime.
   c. take bus tickets.
   d. fly airplanes.

2. Luis has a bicycle. He plans to ride it to campus and leave it outside a building there, but he is afraid someone will take it. Therefore he needs to buy a lock for it. He can choose a combination lock, which opens when you turn it to the correct numbers, or he can choose a lock that opens with a <u>key</u>. He has decided to buy a lock with a key. He will be careful to keep his keys in his pocket and not lose them.

   A <u>lock</u> can keep a bicycle safe. It can also keep

   a. food cold.
   b. gym clothes and equipment.
   c. a window open.
   d. a door closed.

The right key will

a. move heavy things.
b. start an electric typewriter.
c. open a locked door.
d. let you get on a bus.

3. Lee finished writing a paper. She read it over carefully and crossed out all the mistakes that she found. When she thought it was good enough, she copied it on her typewriter.

That picture is a copy of this one.

a. They both show the same things.
b. They are very different.
c. It's much worse than this one.
d. It's much better than this one.

A typewriter is

a. a special kind of pen.
b. a machine that lets you write more quickly and more neatly.
c. a kind of cassette player.
d. a Xerox copier.

4. Ellen got a new pocketbook for her birthday. It came with a matching wallet and change purse. She put her paper money, credit card, I.D. card, and driver's license in the wallet. She put her small change in the change purse. Then she put them both in the new pocketbook.

A wallet is

a. as big as a pack.
b. big enough to hold money and cards.
c. usually too big to go in a man's pocket.
d. smaller than a change purse.

B. LONG READING

CALL THE POLICE!

Walter was reading the newspaper on Saturday morning in his dormitory room when he saw that a new tape by his favorite singer was on sale at the campus store. He had a small tape recorder but not many cassettes, so he was eager to add the new one to his collection. He grabbed his wallet and ran out, closing the door quickly. He ran to the store, looked over all the tapes, bought the one he wanted, and hurried home.

When he got back to his room the door was open. This was strange, because he thought he had closed it. He reached for the tape recorder, but it wasn't there! Maybe a friend had borrowed it. But a friend would surely leave a note—and close the door. It had probably been stolen.

He opened the telephone directory and found the number for the city police on the inside of the cover. He picked up the phone and dialed. A voice answered.

"City Police. Officer Jones speaking."

"Somebody stole my tape recorder," said Walter.

"Where are you?"

"Rockefeller Hall, Room 420."

"So you're on campus," the officer said.

"Yes."

"Then you should call the campus police, not us."

"Oh, sorry!"

Walter hung up and then noticed that a sticker on his phone gave the campus police number. He dialed the number.

"Campus Police. Officer George Herbert speaking."

"Someone stole my tape recorder."

"Where are you?"

"Rockefeller Hall, Room 420," Walter replied.

"When did it happen?"

"I guess in the last half hour. I just got back from the store and it wasn't there."

"What's your name?"

"Walter Stevenson."

"Can you wait there a few minutes? An officer will be there soon."

"Sure."

In fifteen minutes the campus police officer arrived.

"So your tape recorder's gone," he said. "What kind was it?"

"A portable cassette player."

"How was your door locked?"

"I didn't lock it. I closed it, but it was open when I got back. I was only gone for half an hour."

"Five minutes is enough time for a quick thief to steal something."

"But it's daytime," Walter said in surprise.

"That's when most burglaries happen. You should always lock your door when you leave your room."

This was new to Walter. In the little town where he had grown up his parents had never locked the house door during the day.

"This lock on the doorknob doesn't help much," the officer continued. "Anyone can open it with a credit card. Use the upper lock. By the way, did your tape recorder have a Furnell identification number?"

"No, it didn't."

"That's too bad. If you have a radio or a typewriter or anything else valuable, bring it to our office in Tower Hall. We'll put a number on it and keep a copy of that number. If it gets stolen and left somewhere or just gets lost, someone may bring it to us. We run the campus Lost and Found Office. If something comes to us with a number on it, we can easily return it to you."

"Will you be able to find this tape recorder?"

"Not much chance. There are so many just like it."

"I guess it's a good thing I didn't come back while the burglar was here. I could have been killed."

"That's really not very likely. Most burglars will just make an excuse and then leave."

The officer took down a few notes and left. Walter picked up his keys from the desk and put them in his pocket.

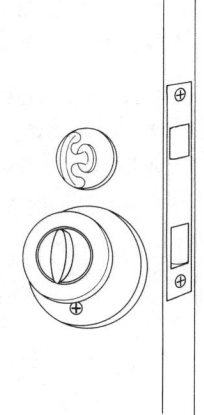

C. COMPREHENSION QUESTIONS

Choose the best way to complete the following sentences first. Then look back at the reading to check your answers.

1. The story doesn't tell us exactly who took Walter's tape recorder. It is implied that the tape recorder was taken by

    a. a friend.
    b. his roommate.
    c. the city police.
    d. a thief or burglar.

2. What is an important lesson that Walter learned from this experience?

    a. To stay away from sales of cassettes.
    b. To take his tape recorder with him when he goes out.
    c. To lock his door well every time he leaves.
    d. Not to come back when a burglar is in his room.

3. Walter wanted to buy the cassette by his favorite singer because

    a. he didn't have any other tapes by this singer.
    b. the tape was new and cheaper than usual.
    c. although the tape was expensive, it was new.
    d. it was hard to get tapes by this singer.

4. The city police did not help Walter because

    a. he was on campus.
    b. a tape recorder is too small for them to worry about.
    c. they only handle violent crimes.
    d. he was from a small town.

5. Walter's tape recorder was

    a. heavy.
    b. easy to carry.
    c. excellent quality.
    d. from his parents.

6. Burglaries are more likely to occur

    a. during the night.
    b. during the day.
    c. when it is dark.
    d. when people have credit cards.

7. To steal something a burglar needs

    a. enough time to plan.
    b. a knife or gun.
    c. a check or credit card.
    d. just five minutes.

8. It is implied that Walter did not lock his door because

   a. he was not used to locking his door at home.
   b. he was in a hurry.
   c. he did not carry his keys with him.
   d. all of the above.

9. The campus police do not have

   a. an office in Tower Hall.
   b. a Lost and Found.
   c. a program for registering property.
   d. Walter's tape recorder.

D. VOCABULARY IN CONTEXT

Before reading the story "Parking," read the following paragraphs. Try to guess the meaning of the underlined words from the context.

1. Martha had to work late at the laboratory. She <u>expected</u> Luis to be home around six as usual. So she called him at 6:15. He wasn't home. She phoned again and again. By 7:30 she <u>suspected</u> that something was wrong. When she phoned at eight o'clock he answered. He explained that his car had had a flat tire.

   Mrs. Shaw's students noticed that she was getting fatter every week. They <u>suspected</u> that she was pregnant. Finally, after several months, she told them that her baby was due in June.

   When you <u>expect</u> something, you

   a. think it will happen.
   b. hope it won't happen.
   c. know all about it.
   d. want it to happen soon.

   When you <u>suspect</u> something, you

   a. know it is true.
   b. know it is false.
   c. think it might be true.
   d. think is bad.

2. Schools in the United States are either public—when the state or local government runs them—or private—when individuals or a group (such as a church) runs them.

   If some land is private, it can belong to

   a. everybody.
   b. one or more people.
   c. the federal government.
   d. the state.

3. "I got a parking ticket. Now what do I do?"
   "Is this the first time you've gotten one?"
   "Yes."
   "Then the easiest thing is to pay it by mail. The fine for a first offense isn't too high."
   "But I didn't do anything wrong!"
   "Then you can go to court and explain to the judge what happened. Maybe the judge will let you off without paying."

   A parking ticket

   a. lets you park free.
   b. lets you park for a fee.
   c. informs you that you have to pay a fine for illegal parking.
   d. gives you the schedule telling when you may park on what side of the street.

   A fine is

   a. money paid as a kind of punishment.
   b. something you find.
   c. a tax.
   d. something excellent.

   When someone commits an offense, he or she is doing something

   a. good.
   b. wrong
   c. aggressive.
   d. ridiculous.

   A judge

   a. writes laws.
   b. writes parking tickets.
   c. decides who is right in some cases.
   d. commits offenses.

   Court is where

   a. all parking tickets must be paid.
   b. you can find a parking space.
   c. you can go and talk.
   d. a judge conducts trials and decides cases.

E. SHORT READING

Read the following and then answer the questions that follow.

PARKING

It was a bad night for Luis. His research in a neighboring town had taken longer than he expected. It was late and he was very tired when he drove home. He turned into his building's parking lot, but all the spaces were full. He drove back out onto the street looking for a parking space. The first block was full. The next block was almost empty. Luis didn't see a No Parking sign, but he suspected that if parking were allowed there, most of the spaces would be filled. Then he saw a small parking lot with two free spaces. He was so glad to see them that he didn't even think to read the sign by the entrance. He drove in, parked, and hurried home to go to bed.

The next morning he went back to the lot to get his car. It was gone!

He ran home and telephoned the city police to say that his car had been stolen. It took the police only a minute to tell him what had happened. His car had been on a private lot. It had been towed away.

Luis had to take a taxi to the city garage far from the center of town. He had to pay a $40 towing fee to get the car back. In addition, he got a parking ticket, his first one ever in Greenville.

Greenville, NY PARKING VIOLATION : INFRACTIONS and FINES		No: 576 342
1 ☐ Overtime, meter 2 ☐ Outside lines 3 ☐ School zone 4 ☐ Prohibited area 5 ☐ Bus stop 6 ☐ Fire hydrant	7 ☐ Crosswalk 8 ☐ Sidewalk 9 ☐ Driveway 10 ☒ Private property 11 ☐ Double-parking 12 ☐ Other	Date _4-20-90_ Time _12:30 AM_ License No. _BQE 144_ State _NY_ Make _VW_ Color _RED_ Location _413 ELM ST._ Officer's signature
Fines: 1-8 9-12	1st offense within year $2.00 $5.00	2nd offense within year $4.00 $10.00	3rd & after within year $6.00 $15.00	*John Smith*

Mail or present this ticket and fine within five days to the Traffic Bureau, 650 Main St. or appear in person before the City Judge at City Court in the Courthouse, Main & Broad Streets. If payment is late the fine will be increased.

F. COMPREHENSION QUESTIONS

Choose the correct answer or the best way to complete the following sentences. You may look back at the story to help you find the answers.

1. It is implied that Luis usually parks

   a. in the city garage.
   b. in his building's lot.
   c. on the street.
   d. in a park for cars.

2. On the night of this story, Luis parked

   a. in a garage.
   b. in the lot belonging to his building.
   c. about three blocks from home.
   d. in a neighboring town.

3. Luis got to the city garage

   a. on foot.
   b. by cab.
   c. by bus.
   d. by riding in a friend's car.

4. It is implied that there was a No Parking sign

   a. on the first block.
   b. in his building's lot.
   c. at the entrance to the lot where he parked.
   d. on almost every corner in town.

5. When Luis didn't find his car in the morning, he first thought that

   a. his wife had taken it.
   b. he had left it in the neighboring town.
   c. it was in the garage.
   d. it had been stolen.

6. Which fine did Luis have to pay? Look at both the story and the ticket, and circle the answer.

   a. $2
   b. $4
   c. $5
   d. $6
   e. $10
   f. $15

G. FILL-IN EXERCISE

Fill in the blanks with the correct words from the following list. Each word must be used. No word can be used twice.

strange	run	infraction
prohibit	fee	favorite
eager	return	

1. Ellen likes tennis best. Tennis is her _____ sport.
2. Please _____ your library books on time. Do not bring them back late.

3. At Furnell students pay a $30 sports _____ . The $30 is for services provided by the Athletics Department when students use the gym.

4. Walter wants to meet you as soon as possible. He is very _____ to meet you.

5. The Student Council decided to _____ smoking in the lounge. Smoking in the lounge will be forbidden from now on.

6. It is odd that such a good student failed an exam. It is really very _____ .

7. Martha will be in charge of the laboratory while the senior technician is on vacation. She will _____ the laboratory during most of July.

8. Driving faster than 65 miles per hour is a violation in every state. However, the _____ may have different penalties in different states.

H. VOCABULARY IN CONTEXT

Before reading the article "Furnell's Finest," read the following paragraphs. Try to guess the meaning of the underlined words from the context.

1. As Don was driving home one snowy evening, he saw an <u>accident</u>. A car had gone off the road and hit a tree. The police were there and so was an ambulance. After that, Don drove very slowly and <u>carefully</u>.

    Some <u>accidents</u> happen when

    a. people want them.
    b. people don't want them.
    c. the police are there.
    d. people don't pay attention.

A <u>careful</u> person will have

a. more accidents.
b. better accidents.
c. fewer accidents.
d. no accidents ever.

2. Martha had an accident in the laboratory. She broke a glass tube and cut her hand quite deeply. It was bleeding hard. Since this was an <u>emergency</u>, the director drove her to the clinic.

In an <u>emergency</u>

a. you have plenty of time.
b. you have to drive a car.
c. you are in a laboratory.
d. you have to act fast.

3. My grandfather told me, "It is foolish and wrong to try to settle an argument by <u>violent</u> means. Don't fight! Talk!"

Using <u>violence</u> means using

a. peaceful methods.
b. illegal methods.
c. force.
d. legal methods.

4. The department needs another secretary. They will <u>hire</u> another secretary as soon as they have the money to do it.

When a department <u>hires</u> somebody, they pay that person in return for his or her

a. parking.
b. food.
c. work.
d. furniture.

5. Ellen likes to dress neatly every day. <u>On the other hand,</u> Don wears blue jeans, dirty boots, and old work shirts.

The words <u>on the other hand</u> express

a. sameness.
b. left and right.
c. right and wrong.
d. a contrast or a difference.

I. SHORT READING

Read the following article and then answer the questions that follow.

THE FURNELL DAILY STAR

25¢

Brrr..., see p. 2   Wednesday, January 17, 1990

Furnell's Finest

Students have been complaining more and more about stolen property. Radios, tape recorders, bicycles, pocket calculators, and books have been reported stolen. Are there enough campus police to do the job?

There are 20 officers (17 men and three women) in the Campus Security Division. Their job is to handle crime, accidents, lost and found items, and traffic problems on campus. More than half of their time is spent directing traffic and writing parking tickets. Responding to accidents and other emergencies is important, but it takes the least amount of their time.

Dealing with crime takes up the rest of their time. Very rarely do any violent crimes occur. In the last five years there have been no murders, seven rapes and about 60 other assaults, most of these involving fights at parties. On the other hand, there have been hundreds of thefts and cases of vandalism. Vandalism here usually involves breaking windows or lights or writing on walls. The thefts are not armed robberies or carefully planned burglaries, such as you see in movies. Things get stolen when it is easy to steal them—when they are left lying around unwatched or in unlocked rooms.

Do we really need more police? Hiring more campus police would cost money, possibly making our tuition go up again. A better way to solve this problem might be for all of us to be more careful with our things.

J. COMPREHENSION QUESTIONS

1. What is the main idea of this reading?
    a. There are not enough campus police.
    b. There are seventeen men and three women on the Furnell Police Force.
    c. Furnell campus police spend most of their time dealing with crime.
    d. There is a crime problem on campus, but hiring more police may not be the answer.
    e. The problem is that the campus police spend more than half their time directing traffic and writing parking tickets.

2. Are these sentences true or false, according to the reading? Write *T* for true or *F* for false in the blank to the left of each sentence.

1. ___ There are at least three women police officers on campus.
2. ___ There haven't been any violent crimes on campus in the past five years.
3. ___ Most crimes on campus are crimes against property, such as robbery and vandalism.
4. ___ Most of the campus robberies that happen are carefully planned crimes.

K. FACT AND OPINION

Decide whether the following sentences state facts or opinions. Write F for fact or O for opinion to the left of each sentence. Be prepared to explain why you chose F or O in each case.

1. ___ The campus police should spend more time on crime and less time on traffic.
2. ___ There are twenty officers on the campus police force.
3. ___ There are not enough women on the campus police force.
4. ___ Hiring more police is not necessary.
5. ___ Hiring more police would cost money.
6. ___ Students have been complaining that things are being stolen.

L. VOCABULARY IN CONTEXT

*Read paragraph 3 of "Furnell's Finest" again, paying close attention to the words **assault** and **vandalism**. Then do the following exercise.*

Which of the following are examples of assault or vandalism? Put **A** in the blank by assaults and **V** in the blank by vandalism. Some cases will be neither.

1. ___ Walter parked his car in a No Parking zone on campus and got a $15 ticket.

2. ___ At Ellen's last sorority party, she and Don saw a student hit another student. Both students were very drunk.

3. ___ A robber who was caught with $57,000 tried to escape from the police. He shot at them three times with a handgun.

4. ___ Over the Thanksgiving vacation someone broke into the Greenville High School and broke thirty-four windows, wrote all over the walls, and overturned the desks and chairs in several classrooms.

5. ___ People have written all over the cars of the New York City subways.

6. ___ My mother's home was burglarized last weekend while she was visiting me in Greenville. They took her television set, stereo, and 35-mm. camera.

M. FILL-IN EXERCISE

Fill in the blanks with the correct words from the following list. Each word must be used. No word can be used twice.

| property | rape | murder | vandalism |
| theft | crimes | violent | |

What kind of _____ are there against people? _____ is the most serious one, since it takes a person's life. Also very serious is _____ , which makes women afraid to go out alone at night.

Other crimes involve people's _____ . In a _____ , a person's possessions are stolen; in _____ , a person's possessions are damaged or destroyed. But in neither of the previous cases is the property owner hurt or threatened. Perhaps that is why robbery, especially armed robbery, is seen as a _____ crime; it is a crime against the person and his or her property at the same time.

N. WORD FORM CHART

Vocabulary Word	Adjective	Noun	Verb	Adverb
1. to add ... to his <u>collection</u>	collected	collection	collect	
2. It had ... been <u>stolen</u>.	stolen	stealing	steal	
3. a <u>sticker</u> on his phone	sticky	sticker	stick	
4. most <u>burglaries</u> happen...		burglar burglary	burglarize	
5. <u>registered</u> it with us	registered	registration register	register	
6. anything else <u>valuable</u>	valuable	value	value	
7. <u>parking</u> lot	parking	parking	park	
8. a <u>neighboring</u> town	neighboring	neighbor neighborhood		
9. The ... block was <u>full</u>.	full		fill	
10. parking <u>violation</u>		violation	violate	
11. The <u>thefts</u> are not ...		thief theft		
12. <u>robberies</u> with guns		robber robbery	rob	
13. <u>violent</u> crimes	violent	violence		violently
14. dealing with <u>crime</u>	criminal	crime		criminally

198   Chapter 9

O. WORD FORM EXERCISE

Choose the correct word form and fill in the blank. Look at number (1) on the Word Form Chart to choose the correct answer for question (1) in this exercise, and so forth. Name the part of speech in the blank at the right.

1. Walter _____ cassettes.
   Part of speech _____

2. Somebody _____ my umbrella while I wasn't looking.
   Part of speech _____

3. Just _____ a stamp on the envelope and mail it.
   Part of speech _____

4. Is there any way that a _____ could enter this house?
   Part of speech _____

5. There are always long lines of students at _____.
   Part of speech _____

6. The _____ of a dollar keeps changing.
   Part of speech _____

7. If we go by car, where are we going to _____ ?
   Part of speech _____

8. This is my _____, John Jones, who lives in the white house next to mine.
   Part of speech _____

9. Some say this glass is half _____ ; others say it is half empty.
   Part of speech _____

10. Those who _____ the law will be fined.
    Part of speech _____

11. A _____ stole my raincoat while I was eating lunch.
    Part of speech _____

12. John Dillinger was a bank _____ .
    Part of speech _____

13. Many people complain that too much _____ is shown on television.
    Part of speech _____

14. Some law students at Furnell work with the _____ at the local city jail.
    Part of speech _____

P. SKIMMING AND SCANNING EXERCISE

First, skim the reading, "The Crime Beat" to get a general idea of what the article is about and how it is organized.

A. What is the reading about?

B. How is it organized? Complete this outline from your skimming.

    1. Introduction—enough police?

    2. _____

    3. _____

    4. Conclusion
       a. no additional police
       b. be more careful

Now, imagine that you are writing a report on crimes on campus and you are interested in what the most common kinds of crime are and how many rapes there are on campuses. Specifically, you want answers to the following questions:

1. How many rapes are there on the Furnell campus in a typical semester?

2. What is the most common kind of crime, and what are some examples?

    In which paragraph would you expect to find the answer to question (1)? To question (2.)?

Find the answers to the scanning questions above.

1. (look for a number) _____

2. _____

Now scan for the answers to the following questions.

3. On what day does Florence report most physical fighting?

4. Are there some kinds of crimes that she does not report?

5. What is a general meaning of "embezzlement"?

Q. VOCABULARY REVIEW READING

THE CRIME BEAT

Florence Hayes is a journalist for the *Greenville Journal*, the daily newspaper in town. Specifically, she covers crime in the Greenville area. This responsibility takes her to many different places every week—the police station, the courts, the university's Public Safety Division, and the hospital. Most of the crimes that she writes about fall into two groups, violent crimes and property crimes.

There isn't much violent crime in a small town like Greenville, or at least not as much as in large urban areas. But assaults often occur on Friday and Saturday nights near the bars downtown. Florence includes short reports of these fights in Monday's newspaper. There are also one or two rapes on the Furnell campus every semester. She is very interested in this type of crime and tries to write a long article about each one. She expects that this will make women more careful when they walk around Greenville alone at night. Fortunately, there are usually no murders in Greenville. (Violence here seems to stop before any killing happens.)

Property crimes make up most of Ms. Hayes' reporting. They range from minor cases of vandalism in schools to much more serious offenses, such as car accidents involving drunk drivers, embezzlement, or bank robberies. But Florence has to report all of these violations, from the thief who took typewriters from every unlocked room in a dormitory to the thief who stole $1 million worth of artwork from the university museum.

Ms. Hayes enjoys working for a newspaper, but she sometimes feels unhappy about all the crimes she has to report. She would prefer to start writing about something more interesting and less unpleasant, such as community events or politics. Maybe next year!

R. COMPREHENSION QUESTIONS

Answer the following questions. Refer to the reading if necessary.

1. Why does she write long articles about the rapes on the Furnell campus?
   a. Because violence in Greenville usually stops before any killing happens.
   b. Because she thinks it will help women be more careful.
   c. Because it helps the police find the rapists.
   d. Because she was raped and wants to help other women.

2. What does Ms. Hayes spend most of her time writing about?
   a. Violations such as theft and assaults.
   b. Local news and politics.
   c. Property crimes.
   d. Violent crime.

3. Where does Ms. Hayes get information about crime?

   a. The police station.
   b. The hospital.
   c. The courts.
   d. The university.
   e. All of the above.

4. Which of the following is implied in this story?

   a. Ms. Hayes has been raped.
   b. Florence Hayes would prefer to report on crime in New York City.
   c. Ms. Hayes thinks that Furnell students read the *Greenville Journal*.

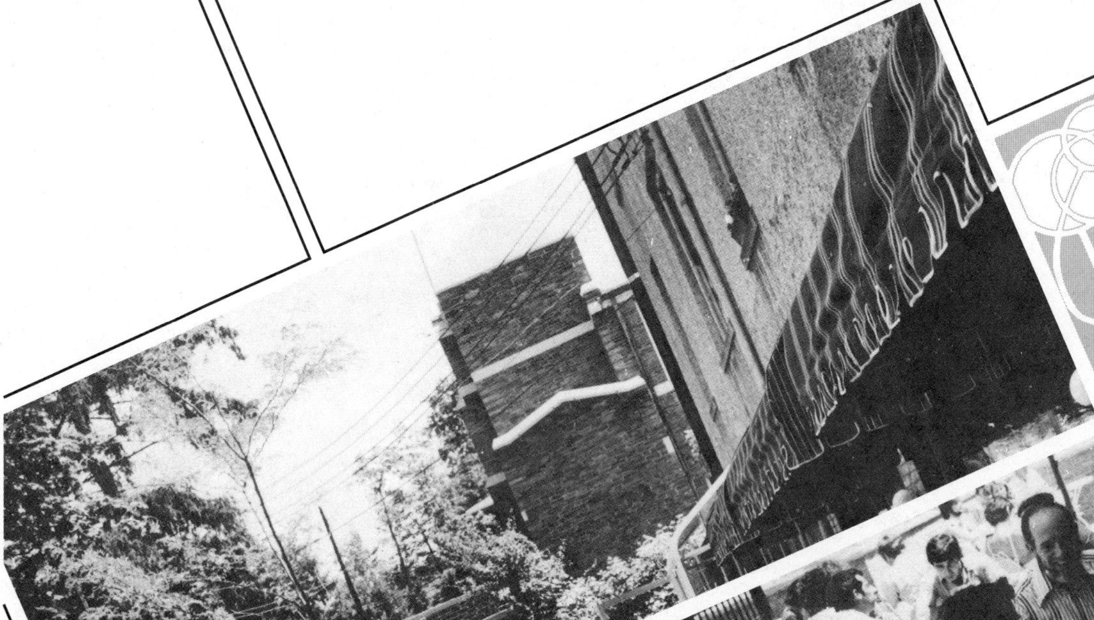
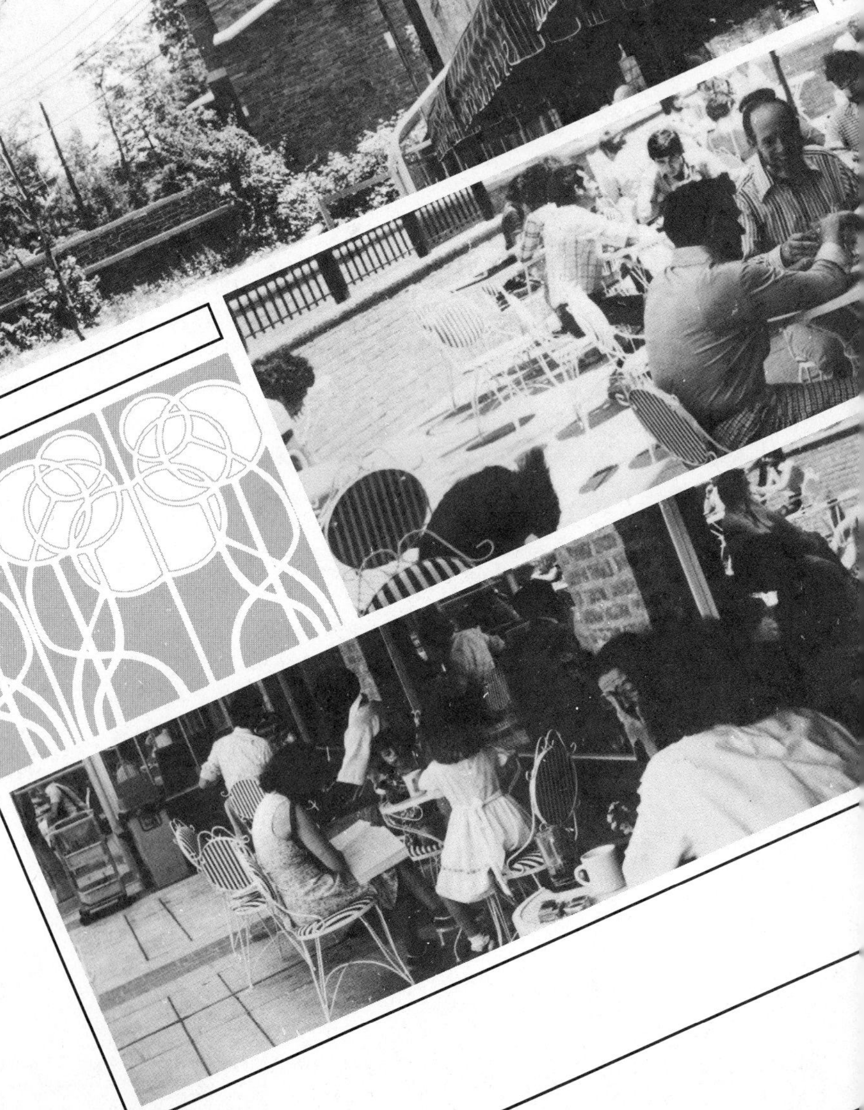

CHAPTER TEN

RESTAURANTS

PRE-READING QUESTIONS

*This chapter is about restaurants. There are many types of restaurants, which we will analyze according to three different criteria. To understand better just what type of restaurants you go to, think about the last five times you ate in a restaurant in **your country**. Put a check underneath each category that applies to each restaurant visit.*

*For example, let's say that you went to an **expensive** restaurant that served **typical** food from your country. For this type of restaurant, in number (1), you should check "formal"; number (2), "typical"; and number (3), "expensive."*

*Perhaps you also went to a **Chinese** restaurant in your country. It was very **informal** and **started by someone in town**, not by a national or regional company. You would check "informal local," "ethnic," and "inexpensive."*

If you cannot remember exactly the last ten times, try to imagine the restaurants you usually go to and describe them.

When you have finished, share your statistics with your classmates, and compare your restaurant habits with theirs.

1. Types of restaurants:

   fast-food   informal local   informal national chain   formal
   _____   _____   _____   _____

2. Types of food:

   typical   ethnic   vegetarian   steak   hamburger   seafood   other
   _____   _____   _____   _____   _____   _____   _____

3. Cost of a meal:

   very inexpensive   inexpensive   moderately expensive   expensive
   _____   _____   _____   _____

   (What is the equivalent in U.S. dollars for each of these four levels of cost?)

   _____   _____   _____   _____

4. What type of restaurant do you think the one in the photograph is?
   _____

DISCUSSION QUESTIONS:

1. What are some special occasions in your country when many people eat out in a restaurant?

2. In what types of restaurants have you eaten in your city or town in the United States? Use the categories above to analyze them. Share your answers with your classmates. You may discover some interesting restaurants in your area! _____

_____

_____

3. How are your eating-out habits here different from in your country?

_____

_____

4. What types of restaurants do you think are the most popular in the United States? _____

_____

A. VOCABULARY IN CONTEXT

Before reading the story "Don's Birthday Dinner," read the following paragraphs. Try to guess the meaning of the underlined words from the context.

1. Ellen planned to take Don to a restaurant for his birthday. Sometimes *he* took *her* out, but he couldn't afford to spend much. This time, because of the special occasion, *she* was treating instead, and she selected an excellent restaurant. She told Don that it was not appropriate to wear blue jeans or other informal clothes. She asked him to dress up for dinner as he does for church on Sundays.

Treating means

a. having a birthday.
b. cooking a special meal.
c. paying for someone else.
d. wearing blue jeans.

Appropriate means

a. suitable or correct for a situation.
b. very formal.
c. too cold.
d. extremely uncomfortable.

To dress up means to

a. put on some clothes.
b. wear good clothes.
c. pay for dinner in a restaurant.
d. buy expensive clothes.

2. Daphne's father visited Greenville and took her out to dinner. After the meal, he asked for the check and paid by credit card.

In this context, check means

a. the bill for a restaurant meal.
b. a paper from a bank.
c. a special kind of mark.
d. a kind of dessert.

B. LONG READING

DON'S BIRTHDAY DINNER

Ellen invited Don out to Greenville's best restaurant for his twenty-first birthday. She made reservations for two people at eight o'clock on Friday night.

Ellen hoped Don wouldn't wear his usual jeans and boots to the restaurant. When she came down the stairs, a half hour late, she was relieved to see he was dressed up. He was wearing a sport jacket and slacks.

"You know, Ellen," Don said, "it's not appropriate to arrive late when you make reservations in advance."

"Nobody at the Lakeview Restaurant will even notice that we are late for our reservations," argued Ellen.

"I hope you're right," said Don as they got into his truck.

As they went into the restaurant, Don said to Ellen, "My parents were surprised that you were taking *me* out to dinner."

"Well, it's your birthday," she grinned.

When the waiter seated them at a table with a view of the lake, he handed them menus. As they looked at the choices, Ellen said, "Have whatever you want, Don. Remember, I'm treating."

"Would you like to order the dinner or à la carte?" the waiter asked. "The dinner includes a choice of appetizer or soup, a baked potato, the vegetable of the day, the salad bar, rolls and butter, dessert, and coffee or tea."

Don ordered a dinner. "I'll take my delmonico steak well done. I'd like stuffed mushrooms as the appetizer."

Because she wasn't very hungry, Ellen ordered her meal à la carte. She paid less and got just chicken marengo with a side order of asparagus and the salad bar. She had a glass of white wine with her dinner. She suggested that Don have a glass of red wine, and he agreed.

As soon as they finished ordering, Don and Ellen got up to go to the salad bar. After twenty minutes, Ellen went back to the salad bar to refill her plate just before the main dish was served.

Don and Ellen enjoyed a leisurely dinner. After Don had dessert and two cups of coffee, Ellen picked up the check, which the waiter had put on the table. She signaled to him quietly with her hand. "I'd like to pay by credit card, please," she said.

"This was a very good meal. Why don't you let me leave the tip for the waiter," said Don.

"Okay. That's really nice of you," Ellen said.

Don looked at the bill and put some cash on the table for the waiter.

"Don't you think that's too much tip to leave?" Ellen said with surprise. "Fifteen percent is enough."

"No, it isn't. The dinner was very good and the service was excellent. I was a waiter one summer, so I know what hard work it is."

The Lakeview Restaurant
fine dining since 1867

Appetizers

Shrimp Cocktail — seven fat bay shrimp on ice	3.50
Chopped Chicken Livers — sauteed with seasonings	3.25
Stuffed Mushrooms — overflowing with cheese and crab	3.25
Oysters on the Half Shell — flown in fresh daily	4.50
Soup du Jour	2.25

Side Orders

Baked Potato — served with butter & sour cream	1.25
Asparagus — with our tangy hollandaise sauce	2.25
Broccoli — and NY state cheddar cheese sauce	2.25
Rice Pilaf — rice tossed with fried scallions, mushrooms and green peppers	1.75

Salad Bar

Served with all dinners or a la carte — 2.75
your selection of our many fine salad greens, marinated vegetables, steamed shrimp, and assorted salads such as potato or macaroni

Check Our Extensive Wine List

Entrees
...each dinner is served with your choice of appetizer or soup, a baked potato, vegetable of the day, the salad bar, rolls and butter, dessert, and coffee or tea

	A La Carte	Dinner
Fresh Filet of Haddock — sauteed in butter, white wine & lemon	9.95	11.95
Delmonico Steak — 9oz. of choice cut beef	12.95	14.95
Chicken Marengo — sauteed in white wine, with tomatoes & mushrooms	9.95	11.95
Shish Kebab — marinated chunks of lamb, skewered with vegetables, then charbroiled	10.95	12.95
Filet Mignon — 9oz of center cut tenderloin	11.95	13.95
Fettucini Alfredo — homemade pasta in white sauce	8.95	10.95
Duck a l'Orange — baked in our tempting Peking orange sauce	10.95	12.95

Desserts

Black Forest Cake	2.25
Strawberry Cheesecake	2.75
Mousse au Chocolat	2.25
Barry's Cherries Jubilee	4.75
Assorted Flavors of Ice Cream	1.25

Beverages

Espresso	1.00	Cappuccino	1.35
Coffee (hawaiian or colombian)	.85	Milk	.65
Tea (darjeeling or jasmine)	.85	Soda	.65

C. COMPREHENSION QUESTIONS

Answer the following true/false questions about the story. Then look back at the text and check your answers.

1. True False Ellen took Don out, but Don picked Ellen up.
2. True False Don didn't dress up.
3. True False The waiter was angry that Don and Ellen were late for their reservations.
4. True False Don and Ellen had to hurry through dinner.
5. True False Ellen made a loud noise with her fingers to get the waiter's attention.
6. True False Don paid for the meal by credit card.
7. True False Ellen left a big tip.
8. True False Ellen ordered her meal a la carte.

Now choose the best answer to the following questions. Try to answer the questions first. Then look back at the story to check your answers.

9. Which of the following was implied in the story?

   a. It is sometimes appropriate in the United States for a woman to pay the bill in a restaurant.
   b. Don didn't enjoy his dinner very much.
   c. You should get a waiter's attention by calling in a loud voice.
   d. You should wear blue jeans to a good restaurant.

10. In which of the following ways are Don and Ellen different? (More than one answer is possible.)

    a. The way they dress.
    b. Their level of education.
    c. Their feelings about lateness.
    d. Their feelings about tipping.

11. Don and Ellen ordered their meals in different ways. Don ordered "the dinner." Ellen ordered "a la carte."

    a. What did Ellen order?

    b. How much did she pay for her meal, not including wine?

    c. How much did she pay for Don's dinner?

    d. If you were very hungry, which way would you order?

D. SCANNING EXERCISE

Scan the menu to find all dishes that use

wine _____

cheese _____

butter _____

What are the least and most expensive items on the menu?

least expensive _____

most expensive _____

What items can you order that will then allow you to make choices?

_____
_____
_____

E. DISCUSSION QUESTIONS

Answer the following questions by looking at the menu from the Lakeview Restaurant.

1. What are the six main sections of the menu?

   _____   _____   _____

   _____   _____   _____

2. How does this differ from the main sections of a typical menu from your country?

   _____
   _____

3. What is the difference in price between an entree a la carte and an entree as part of a dinner?

   _____
   _____

4. Can you order entrees in these two different ways in your country?

   _____

5. Have you been to restaurants in your city in the United States that also offer this choice? If you have, which way did you order?

   _____

   _____

6. Four of the entrees have words with -ed following them (sauteed, char-broiled, baked). What do you think these words tell us?

   a. A way of cutting the meat or fish.
   b. A way of preparing the meat or fish.
   c. Where the meat or fish was bought.
   d. Which country the dish comes from.

E. FACT AND OPINION

Read the following statements. Decide if they are facts or opinion. Write F or O at the left of each statement. Be prepared to explain how you chose your answer.

1. _____ A man, not a woman, should pay for dinner in a restaurant.
2. _____ There are twenty-six restaurants in Greenville.
3. _____ Don ordered a steak at his birthday dinner.
4. _____ You should not wear jeans to a nice restaurant.
5. _____ Well-done steak tastes better than medium-rare steak.
6. _____ Don turned twenty-one on May 11.
7. _____ It is always appropriate to leave a 15 percent tip for the waiter or waitress in an American restaurant.
8. _____ It was impolite for Ellen to be thirty minutes late.
9. _____ The service at the Lakeview Restaurant is excellent.
10. _____ Don saved money by ordering the dinner instead of ordering a la carte.

212   Chapter 10

G. WORD FORM CHART

Vocabulary Word	Adjective	Noun	Verb	Adverb
1. She made <u>reservations</u>.	reserved	reservation(s)	reserve	
2. He was <u>dressed up</u>.	dressed up		dress up	
3. She <u>signaled</u> to him quietly.		signal	signal	
4. leave the <u>tip</u>		tip	tip	
5. enjoyed a <u>leisurely</u> dinner	leisurely	leisure		
6. She <u>grinned</u>.		grin	grin	

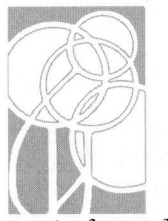

H. WORD FORM EXERCISE

Choose the correct word form and fill in the blank. Look at number (1) on the Word Form Chart to choose the correct answer for question (1) in this exercise, and so forth. Name the part of speech in the blank at the right.

1. She called the restaurant two days before the dinner to _____ a big table for the occasion.

    Part of speech _____

2. When she arrived at the party, she realized that she was the only person who was _____ ; everyone else was wearing blue jeans.

    Part of speech _____

3. Martha stopped at the traffic _____ . When it turned green, she continued along Route 13 for about a mile before turning left at the state park.

    Part of speech _____

4. The service was so bad that Daphne's father didn't _____ the waitress at all.

    Part of speech _____

5. Now that my uncle has retired and left his job, he has a lot of time for _____ . He is beginning to play a lot of golf.

Part of speech _____

6. When Eric received a good grade on his economics exam, there was a big _____ on his face. He had thought he had failed the exam.

Part of speech _____

I. VOCABULARY CHECKLIST

Here are some words that you will need to know when you read the story "A Quick Lunch." Put each word in the correct blank. Use each word only once.

| **cash register** | **nutritious** | **booth** |
| **uniform** | **convenient** | **exhausted** |

1. If you are extremely tired, you are _____ .
2. A _____ is a machine that calculates the cost of items. It is also a place to keep money.
3. A _____ is a table with connected benches in a restaurant.
4. If something is _____ , it is easy and saves work.
5. _____ food is healthful and good for you.
6. A special type of clothing that is worn for work (by mailmen, nurses, etc.) is called a _____ .

J. SHORT READING

A QUICK LUNCH

Sarah Anne and Lee were exhausted after shopping at the mall all morning. They went into a fast-food restaurant for lunch and got in one of the lines. They read the menu on the wall while they waited. Almost immediately, it was their turn to order.

"Can I help you?" asked a young man in a uniform.

"Yes, thanks. I'd like a hamburger, a large order of french fries, a medium cola, and a vanilla shake," said Lee.

The young man turned around and took four items from the shelf behind him. Then he took Lee's money and put it in the cash register.

Sarah Anne ordered only a fried chicken sandwich and a small glass of milk.

"I have a lot of food at home in the refrigerator. I also ate a big breakfast," she explained as they sat down in a booth to eat. In fact, she was thinking that she would much rather have a nutritious lunch.

"This is high-calorie food and not very good for you," she said to Lee.

"I know, Sarah Anne, but it certainly is convenient. We only have twenty minutes left to catch the bus," Lee answered.

K. COMPREHENSION QUESTIONS

Choose the best way to complete the following sentences. Try to answer the questions first. Then look back at the reading, if necessary, to check your answers.

1. Sarah Anne and Lee chose a fast-food restaurant for lunch because
   a. they wanted to have a leisurely lunch.
   b. they wanted to have a nutritious lunch.
   c. it was convenient.
   d. Sarah Anne does not like to eat junk food.

2. It is implied but not stated that
   a. Sarah Anne and Lee did not catch the bus to campus.
   b. Sarah Anne ate a big breakfast before shopping at the mall.
   c. all the food at the fast-food restaurant was nutritious.
   d. the food at this fast-food restaurant was prepared in advance.

L. SCANNING EXERCISE

Scan the following wall menu from the fast-food restaurant in order to answer the following questions.

Delbert's QUICKSTOP Restaurant

Breakfast Menu

Hot Cereal	.45	Home Fries	.50
Cold Cereal	.40	Bacon	.70
Hot Cakes	1.10	Sausage	.75
Waffles	.95		

Breakfast Special   2.10
(Hot cakes, home fries, sausage, and coffee)

Beverages

Soft Drinks	.40	.50	.70
Diet Soft Drinks	.50	.60	.75
Milk	.45	.60	
Coffee	.45	.55	
Tea	.40		

Lunch Menu

Hamburger	.95	
Double-decker Burger	1.45	
Cheeseburger	1.05	
Fried Fish Sandwich	1.25	
Fried Chicken Sandwich	1.35	
French Fries	.55	.75
Onion Rings	.50	.65
Shakes	1.10	
vanilla, chocolate, strawberry		
Sundaes	.80	1.10
chocolate, hot fudge, butterscotch	.50	.65
Hot Cherry Pie	1.05	
à la mode	1.25	
Chocolate Chip Cookies	.50	

Come back again!!!

RESTAURANTS   215

1. How much did Sarah Anne spend on lunch? What about Lee?

   _____

2. What flavor milk shakes are for sale?

   _____

3. Which costs more, cherry pie with a large coffee or a small hot fudge sundae with a large cola?

   _____

4. Does a diet soft drink cost more or less than regular soft drinks?

   _____

5. How much would you save by getting the breakfast special instead of separate orders of hot cakes, home fries, sausage, and a small coffee?

   _____

6. You have $2.50 to spend on a lunch at the Quick Stop. How would you spend it? Choose the most nutritious lunch possible.

   _____

   _____

M. VOCABULARY IN CONTEXT

Before reading "Changing American Eating Habits," read the following paragraphs. Try to guess the meaning of the underlined words.

1. The professor gave a lecture about good study habits. He suggested taking good notes, looking over your notes every day after class, and studying carefully for each quiz. He also suggested sleeping eight hours the night before a quiz.

   A habit is something you do

   a. once in a while.
   b. usually or often.
   c. once.
   d. in school.

2. Daphne wanted to bake a chocolate cake. She checked the recipe to make sure that she had all the necessary ingredients—milk, flour, eggs, sugar, butter, baking powder, and chocolate. After she put these things on the kitchen counter, she began to follow the recipe, step by step. One hour and a half later, she had made a beautiful chocolate cake for the potluck supper.

Ingredients are

a. cookbooks.
b. milk and flour.
c. the food used to prepare a dish.
d. written instructions for preparing a certain dish.

A recipe is

a. a cookbook.
b. a piece of paper you get when you pay money for something.
c. the things you need to make a cake.
d. written instructions for preparing a certain dish.

N. SHORT READING

CHANGING AMERICAN EATING HABITS

There have been a lot of changes in American eating habits in the last twenty years. One is the growing awareness of the nutritional value of food. Another is an increasing interest in a variety of international foods.

Since about 1970, Americans have been more and more concerned about health. They have begun to notice the ingredients in what they eat. When they select food in the supermarket, they turn the packages over to read the labels carefully. They prefer to eat food that is produced without unnecessary chemicals. They often choose fruits and vegetables grown without poisons used to kill insects. A small group of Americans, called vegetarians, has decided not to eat meat. These people choose a complete diet from other kinds of food, because they think that meat products are not healthy.

Also, more and more Americans have become interested in food from other countries. They have been going to international restaurants and eagerly trying unfamiliar dishes. Chinese, Japanese, French, Italian, and Greek cooking, as well as many other recipes, are all popular these days in the United States.

People used to say that Americans ate uninteresting, unhealthy food. This has changed in the last twenty years.

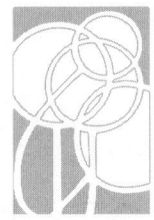

Q. COMPREHENSION QUESTIONS

Choose the best answer to the following questions.

1. The main idea of this article is that

    a. vegetarians are healthier than people who eat meat.
    b. all food products in the United States have labels with ingredients listed.
    c. American eating habits are different from what they were twenty years ago.
    d. Americans are very concerned about health.

2. It is implied that thirty years ago
    a. more Americans ate French and Japanese food.
    b. fewer Americans ate Japanese and French food.
    c. fewer Americans lived abroad.
    d. fewer Americans knew how to cook.

3. It is implied that
    a. most Americans still eat uninteresting, unhealthy food.
    b. Americans are concerned about nutrition because they are eating unfamiliar foods.
    c. Americans are eating unfamiliar foods because they are concerned about nutrition.
    d. insect-killing poisons are not always necessary to grow fruits and vegetables.

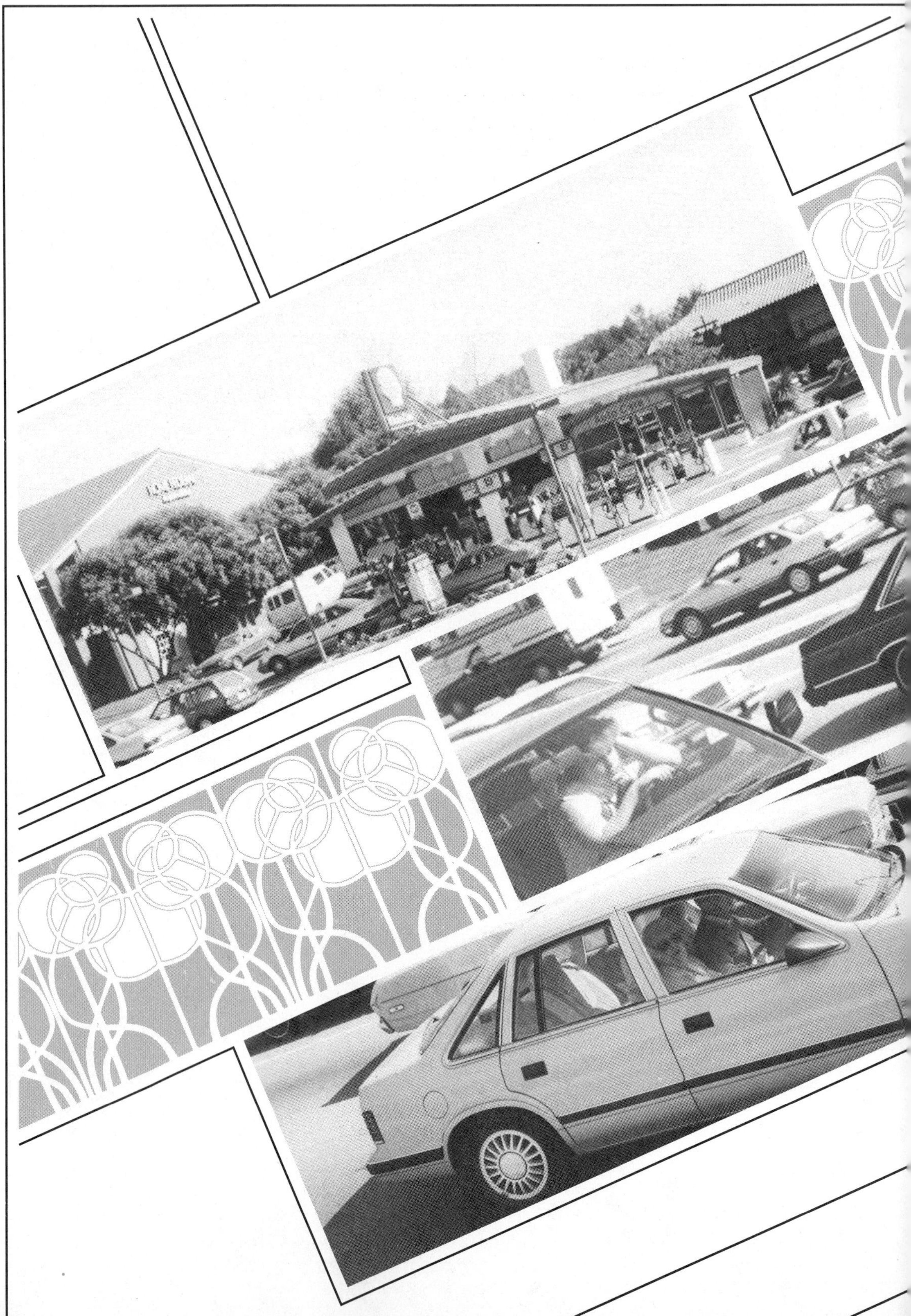
Auto Care

CHAPTER ELEVEN

DRIVING

DRIVING

PRE-READING QUESTIONS

This chapter is about driving cars, the most common form of private transportation in America. Since riding in a car can be dangerous, people must pay attention to automobile safety.

Answer the following questions about driving in your country and compare your answers with your classmates'. Notice that the questions refer to the people you know, not to you.

Do you know anyone who has

1. yes/no   had a parking ticket?
2. yes/no   driven without a driver's license?
3. yes/no   gotten a speeding ticket?
4. yes/no   driven a car while under the influence of alcohol (drunk driving)?
5. yes/no   been caught by the police for driving under the influence of alcohol?
6. yes/no   had a car accident?
7. yes/no   hurt someone or gotten hurt in a car accident?
8. yes/no   had his/her driver's license taken away because of too many tickets or accidents?
9. yes/no   hitchhiked (stood at the side of the road to catch a ride with a stranger)?
10. What is the minimum age that people can drive in your country?

11. Do drivers need to have formal driving lessons in order to get a driver's license?
12. What is included in the driver's license test?

13. Do people have to make an appointment to take this exam? If they do, how long do they have to wait to get one?

14. How much does it cost to get a license?

222   Chapter 11

15. How often do people have to take this exam?
   _____

16. Do you drive in your country? If you don't, how do you get around?
   _____

17. Do you feel more or less safe driving (or riding, if you don't drive) in the United States than in your country? Why?
   _____

A. VOCABULARY IN CONTEXT

Before reading the story "Going Home," read the following paragraphs. Try to guess the meaning of the underlined words from the context.

1. Don's sister Janet has just started working as a secretary at Furnell. There are no buses that go where they live. She wanted to get a ride to work with Don, but his classes start earlier than her job does, and Don often goes home before she finishes work. Therefore, Janet had to buy an old car to drive to work.

    Daphne is trying to get a ride home at the end of the semester. She can help drive and pay for gas. She's sure that it would be much cheaper than the airplane trip to Washington, D.C., and much faster than the bus.

    Which of the following people get a ride with someone? *Write yes or no in the blanks.*

    a. _____ Mr. Hatch   Mr. Hatch commutes to his office in Washington, D.C., from the Maryland suburb, Silver Spring, every day in his small car.

    b. _____ John   John and Mary both work in New York City, but they live on Long Island. They ride the Long Island Railway to work every morning at 7:45 and return at 5:30 in the afternoon.
    c. _____ Mary

    d. _____ Mary Jane   Mary Jane works at a hospital in Tabasco, Oregon. Her co-worker Judy lives two miles from her house. Every morning Mary Jane picks her up and then drives to the hospital twenty miles away.
    e. _____ Judy

    f. _____ Prof. Silverman   Professor Silverman lives in downtown Greenville. He takes the bus up the hill to Furnell on Tuesdays and Thursdays when he teaches.

g. _____ John lives in a suburb in Philadelphia, and so does
   John   Kathy. Every vacation, John travels home to
h. _____ Philadelphia from Furnell in Kathy's car. He drives
   Kathy   half of the way and gives her $5 to help pay for the
              gas.

2. "Look out!" she said, as she watched a car coming toward them on the wrong side of the road. Just in time to avoid an accident, the driver of the car went back onto his own side. "Even when we drive carefully, reckless drivers like that one make it dangerous."

   The speed limit in Greenville is 30 miles per hour (mph), as it is in most cities and towns in New York State. Last year, more than forty people were stopped by the police for driving more than 20 mph over the speed limit. Several of these drivers hit pedestrians or animals, others ran into other cars or property, and the rest almost had accidents of some kind. The city police are always watching for reckless drivers such as these.

   Reckless drivers are those who

   a. go 55 mph on the highway.
   b. go 30 mph in Greenville.
   c. drive on their side of the road.
   d. are very careless when driving.

   What does speed limit mean?

   a. The maximum speed permitted by the police.
   b. The maximum speed the car can go.
   c. How long it takes to drive downtown in rush hour.
   d. Where you can drive fast.

3. John had been driving for one year. He was 17 years old and in his last year of high school. When his father found out that the police had stopped him for driving 25 miles over the speed limit, he called John a reckless driver. "I'm going to teach you a lesson, son. You cannot drive our car for one month."

   What does teach someone a lesson mean?

   a. Give someone a ticket for driving too fast.
   b. Teach someone the last year of high school.
   c. Punish someone for breaking the rules.
   d. Call someone a reckless driver.

   What did John's father want him to learn?

   a. To stay away from the police.
   b. To study hard during his last year of school.
   c. To be a reckless driver.
   d. Not to exceed the speed limit.

224   Chapter 11

4. Because the government wants to keep a record of people in business, they require people in certain businesses to have a <u>license</u>. In New York State, every bar and restaurant that sells alcohol must get a liquor <u>license</u>. Anyone selling something on the sidewalk has to have a <u>license</u> from the city to do so. And of course, driver's <u>licenses</u> are necessary in order to drive a car.

A <u>license</u>

a. permits you to do something.
b. trains you to do something.
c. prohibits you from doing something.

B. SCANNING

Read the first paragraph of the long reading "Going Home" and then scan for the answers to the following questions.

1. List all the people who have received tickets and what kind of ticket each person has received.

   a. _____
   b. _____
   c. _____
   d. _____
   e. _____

2. How much was Gordon fined?
3. How old was Eric when he went off to college?
4. How many DWI arrests had the *Greenville Journal* reported in a recent month?
5. How many of those arrested for DWI were involved in accidents?

C. LONG READING

GOING HOME

Walter, Gordon, and Daphne were having coffee after the last class in Chemistry 102. They were talking about going home at the end of the semester. Gordon and Walter were making plans to drive to the Midwest together. Daphne was looking for a ride to Washington. "I need to get a ride to D.C. Have you heard of anyone going there?" she asked Walter and Gordon.

"Nick lives there," Walter said. "He's a really reckless driver—makes the trip to Washington in six hours and that kind of thing."

"It takes at least eight hours to get to Washington. I don't think it would be safe to ride with him," Daphne said.

"Well, he's trying to find someone to drive his car home for him," Walter explained. "He lost his license on his last trip to Washington. The police caught him going 78 miles per hour on the highway and gave him his third ticket in 18 months. He got a $100 fine. On top of that, he can't drive for a year. They really want to teach him a lesson."

"I guess that's bad luck for him and good luck for me," Daphne said. "I'll give him a call. Thanks."

Gordon had to admit that he once got a speeding ticket. "You know, when I lived in Quebec Province, the speed limit was higher, and I used to forget to slow down to 55 when I crossed the border. When the police stopped me, I was going 65. But it only took one speeding ticket and the $25 fine to help me remember to go 55. Besides, I don't want to lose my license."

Walter laughed. "I sure hope you've learned your lesson, Gordon, if I'm traveling all the way to Iowa with you after exams."

"Haven't you ever been stopped by the cops, Walter?" Gordon asked.

"Only once, when I didn't stop at a stop sign, and the policeman was right in back of me," Walter replied. "I didn't have my registration or insurance card with me. I spent ten minutes looking for them, and the cop finally got tired of waiting. Luckily, he was really nice. He gave me a ticket for going through the stop sign, but he gave me only a warning ticket for not having the papers in the car. He could have taken me to the police station."

He added that Eric was once arrested for driving without a driver's license. Eric had passed his driving test and gotten his license at age sixteen. At eighteen, he went off to college, where he had no car. He forgot to renew his license. That summer he went back home and drove the family car. One light was missing, so the police stopped him, and naturally they asked for his license first.

"He was probably really upset," said Gordon. "Remember how upset Luis was when he got his parking ticket? But parking in the wrong place is very different from going 78 in a 55 miles per hour zone. And driving while intoxicated is a lot worse than that."

He had just read in the *Greenville Journal* that the police made forty arrests for driving while intoxicated (DWI) just last month, most of them on Friday and Saturday nights after the bars closed. Twenty of the drunk drivers were involved in accidents. "It seems as if all the accidents I see reported in the *Journal* are caused by drunk drivers," Gordon added.

"You don't really have to be drunk to be considered intoxicated for legal purposes," Walter reminded them.

"So you'll have to live without beer all the way from here to Iowa," said Daphne.

226   Chapter 11

D. COMPREHENSION QUESTIONS

Answer the following questions based on the Long Reading "Going Home."

1. Make another list of the tickets each person has gotten starting with the least serious infraction and ending with the most serious. Compare your order of tickets to that of your classmates.

   _____

   _____

Now choose the best answer to the following questions.

2. Which of the following are implied in the reading? (More than one answer is possible.)

   a. A driver should always have his/her registration and insurance card in the car.
   b. The police arrested Eric because his light was missing.
   c. Walter is a reckless driver.
   d. It is possible to lose your license after a few speeding tickets.

3. Daphne said to Walter, "I guess that's bad luck for him and good luck for me." What is the good luck?

   a. She can get to Washington in six hours with Nick.
   b. She can travel to Iowa with Gordon, but Walter can't.
   c. She can get a ride with Nick and still be safe.
   d. She can go 78 mph without getting stopped by the police.

4. How many speeding tickets has Gordon received?

   a. One.
   b. Two.
   c. Three.
   d. Not enough information.

E. FILL-IN EXERCISE

Fill in the blanks with the correct words from the following list. Each word must be used. No word can be used twice.

warning   **border**   **cops**

intoxicated   **reminded**

1. Before a train crosses a highway, it always give a loud _____ signal. This is to tell drivers to stop.

2. Most Americans speak only one language—English. But on the U.S. _____ with Mexico many people speak Spanish. Parts of cities in these areas are all Spanish-speaking. There are Spanish-language newspapers, Mexican restaurants, and other Latin businesses there.

3. A game that many children play is called "_____ and robbers." The "good guys" are the policemen, and the "bad guys" are the criminals.

4. Some drivers who are stopped by the police for driving while _____ do not think they are really drunk. But a chemical analysis of their breath shows that their alcohol level is above the legal limit.

5. On Monday, Gordon announced a quiz for Friday. Daphne forgot about it until Ellen _____ her on Thursday. "Don't forget the quiz tomorrow, Daphne," she said.

F. WORD FORM CHART

Vocabulary Word	Adjective	Noun	Verb	Adverb
1. I didn't have my <u>registration</u>...	registered	registration	register	
2. ...or my <u>insurance</u> card with me.	insured	insurance	insure	
3. He only gave me a <u>warning</u> ticket.	warning*	warning	warn	
4. Eric was <u>arrested</u>.	arrested	arrest	arrest	
5. He forgot to <u>renew</u> his license.	renewable	renewal	renew	
6. <u>Drunk</u> drivers were involved.	drunk	drunk	drink	drunkenly

*A noun used as an adjective in a compound noun.

228   Chapter 11

G. WORD FORM EXERCISE

Choose the correct word form and fill in the blank. Look at number (1) on the Word Form Chart to choose the correct answer for question (1) in this exercise, and so forth. Name the part of speech in the blank at the right.

1. Before every election both the Democratic and Republican parties try to convince as many people as possible to _____, so that they will be on the list of those who can vote.

    Part of speech _____

2. A reckless driver in Greenville who had had five accidents and seven speeding tickets in five years had trouble finding a company that was willing to _____ him.

    Part of speech _____

3. The robber _____ the bank teller, "Give me all your money, or I'll shoot you."

    Part of speech _____

4. An average Greenville policeman might make two or three _____ each week.

    Part of speech _____

5. That magazine subscription cost $18 the first year, but the _____ for the second year was only $15.

    Part of speech _____

6. We had to stop the car suddenly to avoid hitting a _____ who was walking carelessly across the street.

    Part of speech _____

H. VOCABULARY IN CONTEXT

Read the following paragraphs. Try to guess the meaning of the underlined words from the context. Find two expressions in the following paragraph that mean the same as take trips.

1. Ellen and Daphne travel abroad in the summertime. Their parents take them to Italy, England, and other European countries. Lee, Eric, and Walter travel with their parents in the United States, going on vacation for two or three weeks in nearby states. Don and Sarah Anne take trips only on weekends to see their college friends during the summer. They can't take longer vacations because of their summer jobs.

DRIVING 229

2. Don's parents are trying to save enough money to buy a new car. Right now they have a 1982 car with a powerful engine. It uses a lot of gasoline. It gets only 12 miles per gallon (mpg) of gas. With gas prices so high, Don's mother is sure they can save money if they buy a smaller car. Those cars have much better gas mileage, at least two or three times better than their 1982 car. Some cars get 40 mpg.

> Buy the newest model car from Detroit! It has fantastic gas mileage—32 in the city and 40 on the highway. Forget your old car that gets under 20 miles per gallon. Come see us today at Ralph Atkins Buick!

   a. True False   A car with good gas mileage does not get many miles per gallon.
   b. True False   It is more expensive to buy gasoline for a car with good gas mileage.
   c. True False   An example of a car with good gas mileage is one that gets 17 mpg.
   d. True False   A car with good gas mileage will use less gas than a car with bad gas mileage.

3. Fifteen or twenty years ago, most American cars were very powerful, with six- or eight-cylinder engines. But their gas mileage was very low. On the other hand, most European and Japanese cars have always had small, four-cylinder engines that get many more miles to the gallon. Nowadays, Detroit is making a new type of four-cylinder car to compete with foreign cars.

   Match the characteristics on the right with the types of cars on the left. Put the numbers that apply in the blank.

   a. Six- or eight-cylinder engines.   1. Good gas mileage.
   _____   2. Bad gas mileage.
                                         3. Powerful engine.
   b. Four-cylinder engines.   4. Most foreign cars.
   _____   5. American cars before 1973.
                                         6. A new type of American car.

4. "Can't you hurry up, Lee?" Daphne asked. "We have to leave for Washington in half an hour. I haven't packed the car yet because I'm waiting for your things."
   "I'm almost finished packing my suitcase, Daphne," Lee answered. "I promise I'll help you put all these things in the car. I know that packing a small car can be hard."

   George has a Honda Civic, a small four-cylinder car from Japan. When he leaves Furnell for the summer, he always has trouble packing his car. He has many boxes of books, records, clothes, skis, and

230   Chapter 11

pictures. Usually, he puts some of the boxes and suitcases on top of his car, because there isn't enough room for everything in his trunk and back seat.

Don's mother called up to his bedroom one morning. "Donny, I'm <u>packing your lunch</u>. I've already put in a tuna fish sandwich and some cookies. Would you like an orange or an apple?" she asked.

"I'll take an orange, Mom. Thanks," he replied.

Fill in the blanks with the following words:

books	**clothing**	**boxes**
trunk	**suitcases**	**food**

a. We pack _____ in a bag for lunch.
b. We pack _____ in a suitcase before traveling.
c. We pack _____ in boxes when we move.
d. We pack _____ and _____ in the car when we take a trip.
e. We pack them in the _____ of the car to leave room for the passengers inside.

5. Buying books for school can be expensive. Follow this <u>cost-saving suggestion</u> and buy used books at the Greenville Book Store, where most Furnell students and faculty shop.

   Gordon and his housemates wanted to <u>save</u> money when they bought groceries this year. Their friends suggested that they buy their food at the local food cooperative, where it <u>costs</u> 15 to 20 percent less than at most supermarkets. That was a wonderful <u>suggestion</u>. They <u>save</u> $75 each month on their food bills.

   Which of the following are <u>cost-saving suggestions</u>? Put yes or no in the blank.

   ____ a. Buy your clothes during sales, when prices are reduced from 20 to 50 percent.
   ____ b. Burkue brand chicken is more expensive, but it is much better quality.
   ____ c. Buy self-serve gas at the gas station. It is at least 5 cents per gallon cheaper than full-service gas.
   ____ d. A round-trip ticket can be 10 to 50 percent cheaper than buying separate tickets to and from your destination.
   ____ e. Buy "Le Moulin" French bread. We bake it right here in Greenville with only the best-quality flour, butter, and eggs.
   ____ f. Greg's Discount Store has a canoe on sale for $325. That's $50 lower than at the Rapid River Outdoor Store at the mall.
   ____ g. The SAT preparation course at the high school costs $45, and the one at the private school downtown costs only $30. But I've heard that the high school course prepares you better. I suggest going there, if you have the extra $15.

I. SHORT READING

Read the following and then answer the Comprehension Questions.

TRAVELING BY CAR

The last week of the semester is always busy. Everyone is studying for exams, saying goodbye to friends, and making travel plans. Gordon is going to get a ride to Minnesota with Walter. Gordon lives in Montreal, Canada, only eight hours from Greenville, but he has been planning to take a trip to Minneapolis, Minnesota, to visit his cousins before going home. Minneapolis isn't far from the part of Iowa where Walter lives. It's always much nicer to have someone in the car to talk to, help drive, and share the travel costs.

Both Walter and Gordon want to travel as cheaply as possible. Since they don't have any camping equipment, they want to find out where the cheapest motels are. They also want to save money on food and gas. Walter's car is an old eight-cylinder American car that he bought for $200 last year. It has a lot of room in the trunk and back seat for packing suitcases and boxes of books. However, it doesn't get many miles per gallon, so Gordon and Walter have to think of ways to get better gas mileage. Gordon has found a brochure called "Cost-Saving Suggestions for Vacation Driving," which both of them are going to read.

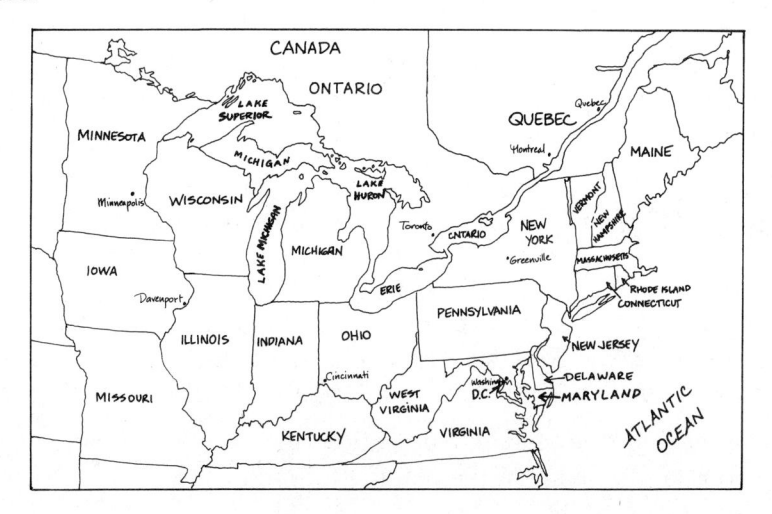

J. COMPREHENSION QUESTIONS

Choose the best answer to the following questions.

1. Why is Gordon getting a ride to Minnesota with Walter?

   a. Because Iowa is only four hours away from Montreal.
   b. Because Walter is going home to a nearby state.
   c. Because Walter wants to do a favor for Gordon.
   d. Because Gordon doesn't like to ride in airplanes.

2. Where are they going to sleep at night on their way out to Iowa?
   a. In a campground.
   b. In the best motel in Columbus, Ohio.
   c. In inexpensive motels.
   d. They are going to drive straight through, without stopping.

3. Which is true about Walter's car? (The answer may be implied.)
   a. The trunk and back seat are both small, so they are packing some things on top of the car.
   b. When Walter bought the car last year, he paid a lot of money for it.
   c. Walter has probably already spent as much, if not more, money on gasoline traveling to and from Iowa during vacations than he paid for the car a year ago.
   d. The car has trouble going up the hills in Greenville.

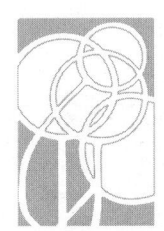

K. SCANNING EXERCISE

1. Scan the list of eight rules at the end of the following reading. Then, circle the correct answers in the following true/false questions. Write the number of the rule that helped you in the blank on the right.

   Rule

   a. True False   Packing the car well does not improve   _____
                    gas mileage.
   b. True False   Good tires help save gas.   _____
   c. True False   Going 65 miles per hour saves money.   _____
   d. True False   Speeding up quickly saves gas.   _____
   e. True False   Traffic jams can use a lot of gas.   _____

2. Before reading "Cost-Saving Suggestions for Vacation Driving," scan the chart on the first page of the reading to find answers to these questions as quickly as possible.

   a. What is the difference in gas costs per 100 miles in a low-cost area between a 4-cylinder and an 8-cylinder car? _____

   b. If you are taking a 300-mile trip in a high-cost area, what will the difference be between going in a 4- and an 8-cylinder car? _____

   c. If you have a small 6-cylinder car, how much will your gas, oil, repair, and tire costs be for a 500-mile trip through the Midwest (low-cost area)? _____

   d. How much more expensive (per hundred miles) are the costs in question c for a 6-cylinder car in a high-cost area than in a low-cost area? _____

L. SHORT READING

Read "Cost-Saving Suggestions for Vacation Driving" thoroughly. Then do the comprehension questions that follow.
There are some words here that you will not know. Many of them are words about taking care of your car. If you are interested in this, you can use your vocabulary-in-context skills to guess their meaning and/or look them up in a dictionary.

COST-SAVING SUGGESTIONS FOR VACATION DRIVING

Vacationing by car can be very satisfying. With no bus, train, plane schedule, or route to follow, you can decide when and where to go. You can reduce your food and motel costs more easily than when you travel by plane or train. Let's see how.

The average daily cost for three meals in restaurants is $48 for two people, plus $10 for each child. Motel or hotel rooms also average $48 daily, adding $5 per child. In small towns and in the country, these costs could be 25 percent lower, but they could increase up to 75 percent in large cities. When traveling by car, you can cut your costs by following these suggestions:

1. Have some picnic lunches or dinners along the road in roadside rest and picnic areas.
2. Get information from tourist bureaus or automobile clubs. They can tell you about motel and restaurant prices and services.
3. Schedule your daily trip so that you arrive early. This will give you a chance to choose the best motel for the least money.

Another large expense will be gasoline for your car. The following chart shows average gasoline, oil, repair, and tire costs for every hundred miles traveled. Much of the cost is for gasoline.

COST PER 100 MILES

Type of Engine/Car	Low Cost Area	High Cost Area
4-cylinder	$7.00	$7.25
6-cylinder, small body	$8.00	$8.29
6-cylinder, large body	$8.90	$9.22
8-cylinder	$10.20	$10.56

The best way to save money on gas is to travel in a small car, either a four-cylinder or a small six-cylinder car. But there are many other ways to save gas money, no matter what kind of car you have:

1. *Give your car engine a tune-up before you leave.* Good maintenance increases gas mileage. This includes such things as clean oil, a new air filter and spark plugs, a well-timed distributor, and so on.
2. *Pack well to avoid carrying unnecessary weight.* Gas mileage is reduced by 1–2 percent for every extra 100 pounds that you carry.
3. *Use radial tires for the best gas mileage.* You can save up to 10 percent in gas with radials. Be sure to inflate them properly to reduce tire wear, too.
4. *Follow the 55 mph speed limit.* For every 5 miles an hour over 50 that you go, you lose 1 mile per gallon of gas.
5. *Start your traveling early in the day to use your air conditioner less.* This allows you to stay cool naturally, with the cool morning air. Air conditioners can decrease gas mileage by 9–20 percent, depending on driving conditions.
6. *Keep away from busy roads to reduce idling time.* If you cannot avoid rush hour or busy traffic, turn the car engine off when sitting in one place for more than a minute. This saves gas and prevents the car from overheating.
7. *Speed up and slow down gradually.* Fast acceleration and hard braking use about 15 percent more gas than gradual, easy starts and stops. Looking down the road to where you are going will help you stop slowly. This will save you money and make the trip more comfortable for your passengers.

234   Chapter 11

M. COMPREHENSION QUESTIONS

Answer the following Comprehension Questions based on the "Cost-Saving Suggestions for Vacation Driving."

1. How much are the average motel and food costs per day for a family of four? _____

2. To cut these costs, a family can

   a. eat in one of the restaurants in the hotel where they are staying.
   b. stay with friends or family instead of in a motel.
   c. make sandwiches for lunch and have a picnic in one of the rest stops along the road.
   d. stay in the first motel that they see when they enter a city.
   e. leave late in the morning and arrive after dinner.

   Can you think of any other ways to reduce traveling costs?

   _____
   _____

3. Which of the seven suggestions listed for saving gas can be followed in everyday driving, not only driving on a long trip? _____

   _____

N. VOCABULARY IN CONTEXT

Read the following paragraph and answer the question that follows.

Don's mother grew up in the country in Pennsylvania. She has been a farmer all her life, living in <u>rural</u> areas in Pennsylvania and New York. Her favorite part of the day is after dinner, when she takes a long walk with her dog in the woods. She could never live in a city. She hates the noise and smell of traffic. Unfortunately, her daughter Ethel has just moved to a big <u>metropolitan</u> area—Chicago. Ethel is worried that her mother will never come to visit her there.

There are many differences between rural and metropolitan areas. Look at the list on this page and the top of the next page and decide if each item is usually found in <u>rural</u> or <u>metropolitan</u> areas. Write *R* or *M* in the blanks at the left.

_____ Farms   _____ Air pollution

_____ State and national parks   _____ Pickup trucks

_____ Big department stores   _____ Traffic jams

____ Subways   ____ Tall buildings
____ Big gardens   ____ Forests
____ Pigs, cows, and horses   ____ A lot of entertainment choices

O. FILL-IN EXERCISE

Read the following paragraphs and notice how the underlined words are used. Then, do the fill-in exercise that follows.

Sarah Anne's rent is going to <u>increase</u> from $225 per month to $275. She's thinking of changing apartments. If she doesn't, she'll have to <u>decrease</u> her spending on other things such as movies and clothes. But she's not sure that she can cut $50 from the money she spends every month, so she'll probably have to move.

My new car <u>accelerates</u> much more quickly than my old car. It used to be difficult to pass slow cars on a two-lane country road. Now, I can <u>speed up</u> very quickly. My car can <u>increase</u> its speed from 50 to 70 mph in 6 seconds, making it easier to pass other cars.

Driving in Greenville is like driving in San Francisco because of all the hills, so good <u>brakes</u> are very important. The New York State government inspects each car yearly to make sure that the <u>brakes</u> are in good condition. Going down a big hill, most drivers begin to <u>slow down</u> at the top of the hill. They continue to <u>brake</u> the whole way down, so that it is easier to stop at the bottom.

Use the following words to fill in the blanks in the following sentences. Use each word only once. Do not change the form of the word.

increase	**decreased**	**speed up**
accelerate	**brakes**	**slow down**

1. The interest rate on bank loans at The First National Bank of Greenville has _____ from 18 percent to 15 percent in the past fifteen months.

2. Don was driving from his house to Furnell one snowy morning last winter. The road conditions were so bad that he had to _____ to 20 mph on Route 13 near Freeville. He usually goes 55 on that road.

3. Martha found out yesterday that her boss is going to _____ her salary next month by 8 percent. That won't beat inflation, but it will help pay the bills while Luis is still in graduate school.

4. The National Aeronautics and Space Administration (NASA) would like to _____ its space shuttle program. It wants to have three different space shuttles operating at the same time. It needs to get more money from the U.S. Congress to do this, however.

5. What is a typical bad dream that people who live in San Francisco have? Coming down a big hill in a car and discovering that the _____ don't work!

6. A businessman was eating lunch at the Neopolitan restaurant in Greenville. He was in a big hurry and shouted to the waiter, "Can you _____ the service? I don't have all day, you know." The waiter had never seen such an impolite customer.

P. VOCABULARY REVIEW READING

POPULATION CHANGES AND THEIR EFFECTS

In the last 100 years, there has been a great change in where people live in the United States, which has several effects on American society. The population has migrated from the rural areas of the United States to the metropolitan areas—cities and their suburbs (the surrounding areas). This migration is mostly a result of the large decrease in the number of small farms. Farms have turned into "agribusinesses," with one huge farm replacing 100 small farms.

This change in population distrubution means that cities have had to speed up the building of facilities such as housing and roads, as well as services such as schools and hospitals, to take care of the new people. Some local governments would like to slow down this change, because it is very expensive to provide and maintain these facilities and services. Some citizens are also worried about the damaging effect that too many people can have on the environment. On the other hand, metropolitan businesses such as construction companies want to see this increase in population accelerate, because it means better business, with more jobs and profits for them.

We therefore have two opposing groups in the growing metropolitan areas. One group, including environmentalists and local governments, wishes to put the brake on this increase, to protect the land and decrease costs. The other group, including construction companies, wants to see the change in population continue, or preferably see it speed up, to make more money.

Q. COMPREHENSION QUESTIONS

Choose the best answer of the following questions.

1. What is the main idea of this reading? (Only one is correct.)

    a. There has been a change in where people live as very large farms replace small ones.

    b. Local governments have to provide and maintain facilities and services for new people.

    c. There is disagreement about how big metropolitan areas should become.

DRIVING   237

    d. Construction companies want to make profits.
    e. Businesses usually want more people to move to a metropolitan area.

2. Which of the following are implied but not stated in this passage? (More than one is possible.)
    a. Agribusinesses have replaced small farms, with one huge farm taking the place of 100 small farms.
    b. It is difficult for small farms to make a profit.
    c. Owners of businesses in shopping centers and malls usually want to see an increase in population.
    d. Environmentalists are too idealistic and are wrong to be against increasing population.

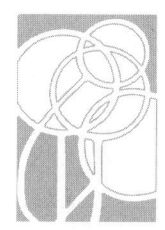

R. WORD FORM CHART

Vocabulary Word	Adjective	Noun	Verb	Adverb
1. plane <u>schedule</u>	scheduled	schedule	schedule	
2. <u>average</u> daily costs	average	average	average	
3. hard <u>braking</u>		brake(s) braking	brake	
4. another large <u>expense</u>	expensive	expense expenditures	expend	
5. good <u>maintenance</u>		maintenance	maintain	
6. be sure to <u>inflate</u> them	inflationary inflated	inflation	inflate	
7. The gas <u>expands</u>.	expansive	expansion	expand	
8. <u>Avoid</u> rush hour.		avoidance	avoid	
9. <u>Prevent</u> it from overheating.	preventive	prevention	prevent	
10. fast <u>acceleration</u>		acceleration	accelerate	

S. WORD FORM EXERCISE

Choose the correct word form and fill in the blank. Look at number (1) on the Word Form Chart to choose the correct answer for question (1) in this exercise, and so forth. Name the part of speech in the blank at the right.

1. "When does the next bus to Dallas leave?"
   "Look at the _____ . Here it is. It leaves at 7:15 p.m."

   Part of speech _____

2. What is the _____ TOEFL score of a student in the Intensive English Program?

   Part of speech _____

3. One of my _____ is in bad condition. I can smell it burning every time I drive.

   Part of speech _____

4. Let's eat at that new restaurant tonight. I have heard it's not very _____ .

   Part of speech _____

5. When you buy a used car, it is usually cheaper than a new one. But, you have to spend more money to _____ it because things usually start to break quickly.

   Part of speech _____

6. _____ has increased greatly in the world. In some countries, prices are 75 percent more each year.

   Part of speech _____

7. Boulder, Colorado, is an example of a city that voted against _____ in the 1970s. There is a maximum limit to how many new houses or apartments can be built there.

   Part of speech _____

8. "Uh oh! There's Dr. Williams," Eric told Walter. "Let's turn around and go the other way. I skipped his class this morning, so I want to _____ seeing him."

   Part of speech _____

9. _____ should be an important part of health care. Many lives can be saved if people stop smoking cigarettes and start doing exercises every day.

   Part of speech _____

10. Walter's old eight-cylinder car can _____ much more quickly than a small new American car, but it also uses a lot more gas.

    Part of speech _____

STRATEGIES

INTRODUCTION

SURVEYING SKILLS: *WHAT ARE THEY?*

Surveying means systematically looking over written material *before* reading it carefully. When university students survey new material, they prepare themselves to read it more effectively. In other words, they take steps to help themselves learn more and remember more of what they read. In the first part of this book you practiced these surveying skills individually, reading the organizational tools built into a textbook and other written information you need to read in a university. In order to get the main idea of the reading before actually reading every word, you looked at such things as a table of contents, an outline, and titles of information sheets.

In this mini-unit, you will do a college history course assignment designed to help you review these surveying skills. The students in Dr. Klammer's American history class were given the following assignment:

> Read Chapter 10, "Antebellum* America," p. 202–227 in your textbook. Prepare for a lecture at our next class to be presented by Dr. Angela Wentworth of the University of California at Berkeley. Dr. Wentworth, a well-known historian and author of a recent book on this period, will speak on "The Slave South in Antebellum America." Students are responsible for the information presented in the chapter and in Dr. Wentworth's lecture. A short-answer quiz on the subject of the Slave South will be given in class on November 15th.

These are the surveying skills that you will practice in this mini-unit:

1. Getting information from the **table of contents** of the American history textbook.
2. Surveying the **whole chapter** section by section by reading:
   a. the **introduction** for an overview,
   b. the **section headings**,
   c. the **first paragraph** of each section,
   d. the **subheadings** in each section, and
   e. the **summary** at the end of the chapter.
3. Studying nonprose material such as **graphs, charts, and photographs**.

VOCABULARY IN CONTEXT

ante = before, coming before; **bellum** = war

*With the other information in Dr. Wentworth's lecture title, you can assume that antebellum means *before the war*, the American Civil War, in the 1860s.

PRE-READING QUESTIONS

1. What is a civil war? What are some examples of civil wars that you know about?

2. Do you know any of the social or economic causes of the American Civil War?

3. What do you already know about slavery in America before the Civil War?

4. Name some other countries where slavery has existed.

5. List five words that you predict the authors of Chapter 10 will use in this chapter.

PART ONE: GETTING INFORMATION FROM THE TABLE OF CONTENTS

Surveying the table of contents of this textbook will give you some information about how this pre–Civil War period fits into the rest of the course on American history. *For the following questions, try to predict in which chapter the specific information asked for is found. Write down the **key words** in each statement that helped you make your choice.*

1. The Declaration of Rights and Sentiments was adopted at one of the first women's rights conventions, in Seneca Falls, New York, in 1828.

   Chapter ____ Key words _____

2. While tensions between Mexico and the Union increased, Davy Crockett and Jim Bowie died defending the Alamo from the troops of General Santa Ana, the Mexican president.

   Chapter ____ Key words _____

3. Abraham Lincoln won the election of 1860, causing the leaders of the South to separate from the Union.

   Chapter ____ Key words _____

4. By 1820, some states in the Union allowed all taxpayers to vote. Until then, only landowners had the right to vote.

   Chapter ____ Key words _____

5. The Louisiana Purchase of 1803, during Thomas Jefferson's administration, added a vast new territory to the Union.

   Chapter ____ Key words _____

6. General Lee's surrender at Appomattox on April 9, 1865, ended the Civil War.

   Chapter ____ Key words _____

7. Harriet Tubman, known as the Moses of her people, helped more than 300 slaves escape to the North.

   Chapter ____ Key words _____

PART TWO: SURVEYING THE WHOLE CHAPTER

In this section you will survey the chapter to get an overview before you read it thoroughly. You will read:

a. the title page, with illustration and outline;

b. the introduction to the chapter;

c. the section headings;

d. the first paragraph of each section;

e. the subheadings in each section; and

f. the summary at the end of the chapter.

The original chapter in the textbook is more than twenty pages long. All of the material listed above was taken from the chapter and printed in this mini-unit for you*. You should read every word that follows. It includes only the parts of the chapter in a–f listed above.

Survey the chapter by reading the following pages and answer the general comprehension questions that follow on page 247.

*From *The American Tradition: A History of the United States*, by R. Green, L. Becker, and R. Coviello. Copyright 1984, Merrill Publishing Company. All text in this mini-unit on pre-Civil War America is reprinted by permission of the publisher.

UNIT 3

NATIONALISM AND SECTIONALISM — 142

CHAPTER 7 The Jeffersonian Republicans — 144
Jefferson in Power — 145
Trials of a Neutral Nation — 150
The War of 1812 — 153
American Nationalism — 157
The Rise of Sectionalism — 161

CHAPTER 8 The Age of Jackson — 166
Political Events in the 1820's — 167
The Era of the Common People — 170
States' Rights and Union — 172
The Bank War — 176
Economics and Politics After Jackson — 179

CHAPTER 9 Westward Expansion — 184
Significance of the Frontier — 185
Indian Relations — 188
Moving Westward — 190
War With Mexico — 197

CHAPTER 10 Antebellum America — 202
Transportation and Communication — 203
Industrialization — 205
Cultural Trends — 210
The Spirit of Reform — 213
Women's Rights — 217
The Antislavery Movement — 219
The Slave South — 222
Unit Review — 227

UNIT 4

THE NATION DIVIDED — 230

CHAPTER 11 Toward Civil War — 232
Sectional Politics — 233
Temporary Reprieve — 235
The Kansas Question — 237
On the Brink of War — 240
The Union Divides — 243

CHAPTER 12 The Civil War — 248
North Versus South — 249
Early Stages of the War — 251
A Step Toward Freedom — 256
The Home Front — 257
Union Victory — 262

vi

CHAPTER

13 Reconstruction   270

Presidential Reconstruction ___ 271
Restoration Under Johnson ___ 274
Radical Reconstruction ___ 278
The Radical Regimes ___ 282
Redemption ___ 284
Unit Review ___ 289

UNIT

5

THE AGE OF INDUSTRIALIZATION   292

CHAPTER

14 Industrial Growth   294

Foundations for Growth ___ 295
The Railroads ___ 297
The Giants of Industry ___ 301
Philosophy for an Era ___ 305
Attempts at Regulation ___ 306

CHAPTER

15 The Rise of Labor   310

Workers and Their Problems ___ 311
The Union Movement ___ 314
Problems of the Labor Movement ___ 318
Labor Clashes ___ 320

CHAPTER

16 The Last Frontier   326

Opening the West ___ 327
The Farming Frontier ___ 331
Conflict With the Indians ___ 335

CHAPTER

17 The Gilded Age   344

Postwar Politics ___ 345
The Presidential Procession ___ 349
Populism ___ 352
The New South ___ 356

CHAPTER

18 An Urban Society   362

Urbanization ___ 363
Impact of Immigration ___ 365
Urban Life and Culture ___ 369
Urban Reform ___ 377

CHAPTER

19 The Progressive Era   382

The Progressives ___ 383
Progressive Goals ___ 386
Theodore Roosevelt ___ 390
William Howard Taft ___ 394
Woodrow Wilson ___ 397
Unit Review ___ 402

UNIT

6

CHAPTER 10

1	Transportation and Communication	203
2	Industrialization	205
3	Cultural Trends	210
4	The Spirit of Reform	213
5	Women's Rights	217
6	The Antislavery Movement	219
7	The Slave South	222

Chapter 10

Antebellum America

America in the years before the Civil War, the antebellum years, was a nation in ferment. While the West was rapidly expanding, the North was going through major changes due to industrialization and immigration.

The antebellum period was a time of great nationalism and optimism. Americans had shown the world that a republican form of government could work, and material progress was bringing many added comforts to daily life. Although society was not yet perfect, no evil seemed impossible to remedy. Reformers attacked every kind of social injustice, including the one issue that threatened to break up the Union: slavery. Slavery was essential to the culture and economy of the South, which had changed little compared to the North and West. In defense of their "peculiar institution," southerners became more and more determined to maintain their own way of life.

1. Transportation and Communication

Westward expansion during the years 1820 through 1860 had created an urgent need for better connections between the West and the East. Because the federal government repeatedly refused to finance internal improvements, individual states undertook the funding for such projects.

Roads and Canals

The Steamboat

The Railroad

Overseas Transportation

Communication

2. Industrialization

Improved transportation and communication increased the importance of northern cities as centers of trade. As city merchants grew wealthier, they sought investments that would further increase their business. Much of their **capital**, or investment money, went into manufacturing industries.

Early Factories

New Technology

The Corporation

Immigration

Industrial Change

Social Conflict

Growth of Cities

Material Progress

3. Cultural Trends

The optimism of the antebellum years was well-suited to a cultural movement called **romanticism**, which took place in both Europe and America during the first half of the 1800's. Romanticism was a revolt against the logic, order, and reason of the Enlightenment.

Romanticism valued emotion and imagination over reason, nature over civilization, and the wisdom of the common people over the sophistication of the upper classes. Romantics were interested in folklore and legend; in exotic, faraway places; and in the supernatural. The romantic hero was an individualist who rebelled against unjust rules. This stress on individualism and the virtues of the common people fitted the democratic spirit of the Age of Jackson.

Transcendentalism

Literature and Art

Popular Culture

Religion

4. The Spirit of Reform

During the first half of the 1800's, many Americans were interested in perfecting their society. The result was an age of social reform, which was strengthened by the religious revivals of the Second Great Awakening. Reformers banded together in voluntary organizations to work for their goals. Voluntary organizations provided social ties that were missing in a rapidly changing industrial society.

Utopias

Prison Reform

Mental Hospitals

Temperance

Educational Reform

Labor Reform

The Peace Movement

continued . . .

5. Women's Rights

Many women were active in various reform movements. In working for the rights of others, they were often made aware of their own lack of rights. For example, they were forbidden by custom from speaking in front of mixed groups. When antislavery reformers Sarah and Angelina Grimke tried to speak to mixed groups, they found themselves booed by the men. In 1840 the World Antislavery Convention in London refused to seat women delegates. Experiences such as these propelled women into a fight for their own cause.

Different Regions, Different Treatment

Women's Rights Convention

6. The Antislavery Movement

Of all the reform movements that took place in the early 1800's, the one with most far-reaching consequences was the antislavery movement. The movement for **abolition** (putting an end to slavery) had begun even before the American Revolution. The first antislavery society was formed by Quakers in 1775. It was not until the 1830's, however, that abolition became a major cause.

Early Efforts

Radical Abolition

Black Support

Reaction

7. The Slave South

The culture and economy of the South depended on cotton production for export. Demand for cotton soared as textile factories in the northern states and Europe found faster, cheaper ways to make cloth.

Southern planters rushed to meet the demand with the help of slave labor and the cotton gin. Cotton production went from 200,000 bales a year in 1800 to 2 million bales by the 1830's and 3 million by the 1850's. In the 30 years before the Civil War, cotton accounted for more than one-half of the total value of American exports. The increase was due mainly to the spread of the plantation system into new areas. The plantation was the basis of southern society.

Southern Society

The Peculiar Institution

Cavalier and Yankee

Chapter 10 Summary

Review

1. Improved communication and transportation systems contributed to major economic and social changes in the United States.
2. The factory system, stimulated by new technology and the development of the corporation, began to take over the process of manufacturing.
3. A wave of immigration from Europe provided a new labor force for the factories.
4. Rapid industrialization and growth of the cities created new social problems.
5. In spite of problems, many Americans came to believe that they were living in an age of progress that would eventually result in an ideal society.
6. A cultural movement called romanticism was reflected in American literature, arts, and philosophy.
7. A widespread religious revival provided support for various reform movements.
8. Women began a concerted effort to gain equality in all fields of endeavor.
9. The antislavery movement gained force, but abolitionists aroused hostility in the North as well as the South.
10. Southerners began a more vigorous defense of slavery to combat the arguments of radical abolitionists.

Mini-Unit 1: Surveying   247

COMPREHENSION QUESTIONS—AFTER SURVEYING

Answer these comprehension questions by looking back at the chapter on page 244–246. Look for the key words in each topic, and try to find them in the part that you surveyed. When you find the words, or related words, write the section number after the statement. If you think the topic is not discussed in Chapter 10, explain why.

A. Put a check by the topics below that are likely to be covered in this chapter on antebellum America.

____ The Election of 1848
____ The Married Women's Property Act of 1848
____ The American Antislavery Society, started in 1933
____ The effect of the railroad on the northern economy
____ The result of the Civil War
____ The Waltham System, an early factory production system
____ Life on the western frontier in the 1840s

2. After Dr. Klammer's students read and study Chapter 10, which of the following will they be able to do? Put a check by them.

____ list some of the American romantic writers and their works
____ describe the socio-economic system of Southern society
____ explain how religious thought developed during the antebellum period
____ compare life in England and America during the 1850s
____ explain why slavery is a social and economic evil
____ list the various types of reform attempted during the antebellum period

PART THREE: FINDING INFORMATION FROM NON-PROSE MATERIAL

An important part of the surveying process is looking at the pictures, charts, and graphs in the chapter.

A. *Look at the picture on page 244.* What does this tell you about

transportation?
dress?
housing?
farming methods?

Discuss these with a partner and share your ideas with your classmates. Does the picture give any other information about life in the pre–Civil War South?

B. *Look at the pie chart below called "Immigration, 1821–1860." Work with a partner. Mark the following statements **true** or **false**.*

1. ____ Irish immigration reached its highest level between 1841 and 1850.

2. ____ German immigration continued to grow from 1821–1850.

3. ____ Immigration to America from England, Scotland, and Wales did not change much during this period.

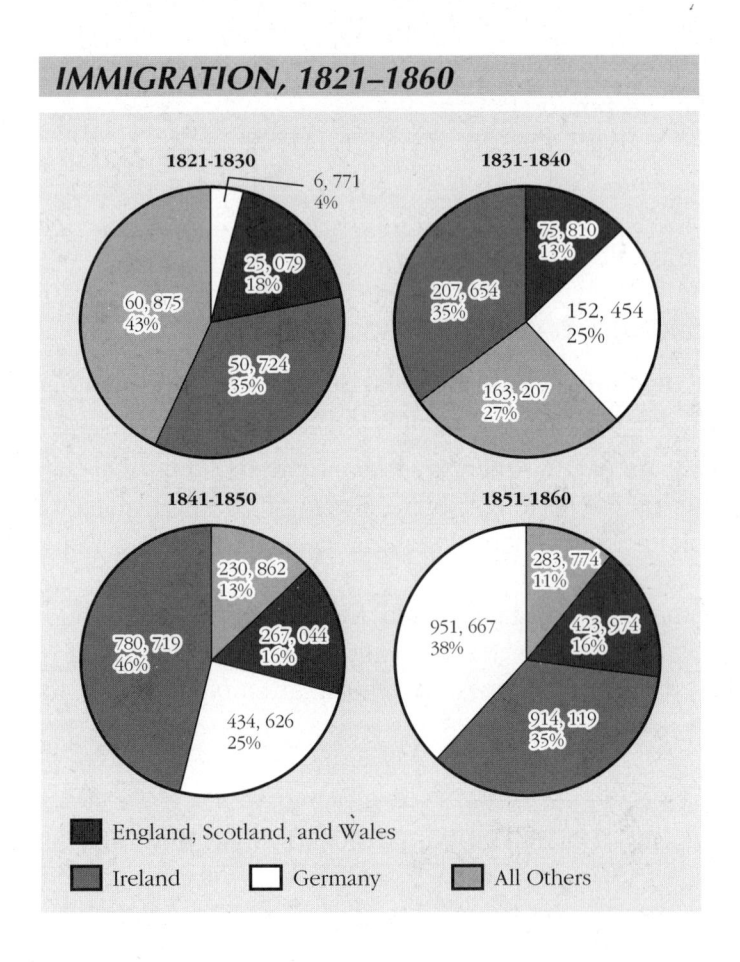

IMMIGRATION, 1821–1860

1821-1830
- 6,771 — 4%
- 25,079 — 18%
- 60,875 — 43%
- 50,724 — 35%

1831-1840
- 75,810 — 13%
- 207,654 — 35%
- 152,454 — 25%
- 163,207 — 27%

1841-1850
- 230,862 — 13%
- 780,719 — 46%
- 267,044 — 16%
- 434,626 — 25%

1851-1860
- 283,774 — 11%
- 423,974 — 16%
- 951,667 — 38%
- 914,119 — 35%

■ England, Scotland, and Wales
■ Ireland   □ Germany   ■ All Others

C. *Look at the bar graph at the top of the next page called "Slave Owners." Mark the following statements **true** or **false**.*

1. ____ A very small percentage of southern whites owned 50 or more slaves.

2. ____ Most southern whites owned no slaves.

3. ____ 50 percent of southern whites owned between ten and fifty slaves.

4. ____ About 17 percent of southern whites owned between one and nine slaves.

SLAVE OWNERS

(Bar chart: Southern Whites vs. Slaves owned)
- 0 slaves: ~75%
- 1–9 slaves: ~19%
- 10–50 slaves: ~8%
- 50 or more: ~3%

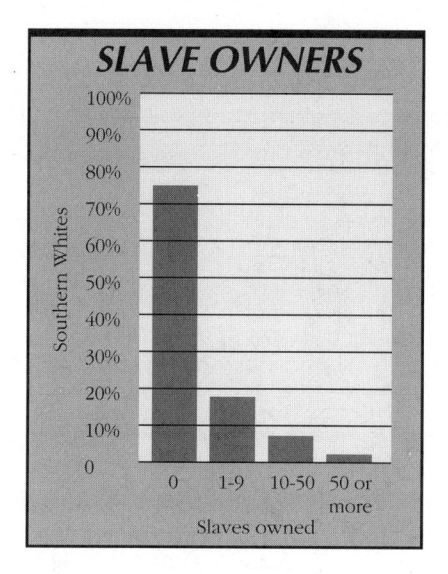

PART FOUR: SURVEYING SECTION 7, "THE SLAVE SOUTH"

Now use your surveying skills to take a quick look at Section 7 on pages 250 and 251. Notice that no parts of Section 7 are missing. This is because you will need to read it carefully after you survey it.

A. *Read the introduction (the first two paragraphs) to the section.*

Which of the following will probably be covered in Section 7?

1. ____ The Civil War in the South.
2. ____ Southern cooking in the antebellum period.
3. ____ The role of the plantation in the cotton industry.
4. ____ Black Americans in the 1930s.
5. ____ The socio-economic system in the Slave South.
6. ____ Products produced from cotton.

B. *Read the subheadings, first paragraphs of each subsection, and the first and last sentences of all other paragraphs.*

Which of the following will probably be covered in Section 7?

1. ____ The details of a slave's life in antebellum America.
2. ____ The differences between a slave owner in America and a slave owner in other cultures.
3. ____ Similarities and differences between the North and the South.
4. ____ Religious groups in the North and the South.
5. ____ The characteristics of the dangerous trip from Africa to America.
6. ____ Ways that slaves rebelled against their masters.

7. The Slave South

The culture and economy of the South depended on cotton production for export. Demand for cotton soared as textile factories in the northern states and Europe found faster, cheaper ways to make cloth.

Southern planters rushed to meet the demand with the help of slave labor and the cotton gin. Cotton production went from 200,000 bales a year in 1800 to 2 million bales by the 1830's and 3 million by the 1850's. In the 30 years before the Civil War, cotton accounted for more than one-half of the total value of American exports. The increase was due mainly to the spread of the plantation system into new areas. The plantation was the basis of southern society.

Southern Society

Society and politics in most of the South were dominated by the large plantation owners. The census of 1860 showed that there were 46,274 planters in the South who owned 20 or more slaves. However, fewer than 3000 planters owned over 100 slaves. About 10,000 planters owned from 50 to 100 slaves.

The large plantation owners, however, set the tone for southern society. An imposing mansion, complete with veranda and columns, was an indication of wealth and prestige. Many well-to-do planters, however, lived in plain farmhouses. In either case, they were the natural leaders of an agricultural society. In much of the South, this class supplied county and state officials and members of Congress.

Beneath the planter class were the typical southern farmers, who owned fewer than 200 acres of land and 10 or fewer slaves. Many owned no slaves at all. These farmers produced crops primarily for subsistence. Cash crops like cotton or tobacco were grown to sell for necessities and small luxuries that the farmers could not produce for themselves. Their standard of living was generally low. These families, along with the overseers of large plantations and the mechanics, professionals, and business people of the cities, made up the southern middle class.

The lower class was known as "poor white trash." They were poverty-stricken people who lived on the poorest lands. They made up less than 10 percent of the white population. Also in the lower class were white farm workers and tenant farmers.

Lower than whites on the southern scale were the free blacks. By 1860 about 250,000 free blacks lived in the South, mostly in the towns and cities. They were severely discriminated against, more so than free blacks in the North. In some places they were even forbidden to learn to read or write.

At the very bottom of southern society were the slaves. Although most southern whites did not own slaves, it was the presence of slavery, the "peculiar institution," that made the South so different from the rest of the nation.

The Peculiar Institution

Slavery was called "peculiar" because it existed in only one part of the country. Actually, slavery had existed in many different cultures throughout history. But slavery in America was different from the slavery of ancient Egypt or Rome. In those societies, almost anyone might become a slave if taken as a captive in war. In America, slavery was based on race.

The Europeans had tried to make slaves of the Indians, but they either became sick and died or escaped. Attempts to enslave poor whites were also unsuccessful, because whites could escape and blend into the general population. Black slaves also died, but they seemed to be stronger than the Indians. And if they escaped, they found themselves in an unknown country where their dark skins made them obvious.

Roots

The slaves with which western European nations populated their American colonies were from the Guinea Coast of West Africa. This area encompassed the West African coast from the Seneca and Gambia Rivers to Angola. The tribes and kingdoms of the Guinea Coast had largely agricultural economies. Political institutions ranged from extended-family groups to village states, kingdoms, and empires with armies, courts, and tax collectors. Religion, art and music were important parts of African culture.

Although slavery existed in West African society, slaves had certain rights. The various tribes or kingdoms followed somewhat different customs, but generally slaves could own property, marry free people, or purchase their freedom. They frequently gained freedom through adoption into the families of their captors.

The Slave Trade

The first European country to trade in slaves was Portugal. During the first half of the 1700's, the French, English, and Dutch began to challenge the Portuguese monopoly. By the 1780's, the British and the American colonists controlled roughly one half of the European slave traffic. The British colonial merchants who most profited from the slave trade were those from Massachusetts and Rhode Island.

European and American slave traders rarely took part in the raids to capture slaves. They usually traded with African rulers or merchants who sold their war captives. Among those captured were priests, princes, warriors, and merchants. Because of the slave trade, raiding for slaves became the primary cause of war among West African kingdoms. Many Africans, however, refused to take part in the slave trade.

Once sold to a slave trader, the new slaves were branded with red-hot irons and chained. They were then packed into ships for what was called the "Middle Passage"—the voyage across the Atlantic, which lasted from 40 to 60 days. The slaves were forced to lie between decks which were less than four feet apart. Unable to move, suffering from a lack of fresh air, many suffocated or died from epidemics of smallpox and other diseases. The dead were thrown overboard. William E. B. DuBois, historian and early leader of the civil rights movement, described the slave trade eloquently:

> For four hundred years, the dark captives wound to the sea amid the bleaching bones of the dead; for four hundred years the sharks followed the scurrying ships; for four hundred years America was strewn with the living and dying millions of a transported race...

Of the hundreds of thousands who survived the trip, the greatest number were taken to the West Indies or Brazil. Many of those who went first to the West Indies were later shipped to the North American colonies. Others were taken directly to North American ports, where they were sold from the ships or shown in markets and taverns.

The Life of a Slave

Most slaves in the North American colonies worked in the cotton fields. Other slaves were house servants, artisans, or factory hands.

All of the Southern states had **slave codes**—laws which defined slaves as property, with few if any legal rights. Slaves could not sue, testify against whites in court, make contracts, buy or sell goods, or—with minor exceptions—own property. The marriages of slaves had no legal standing. Husbands, wives, and children could be sold separately. Slaves were encouraged to have as many children as possible, because the children of slaves belonged to the slaveowners. Some slaveowners actually bred slaves for sale. In spite of this treatment, family life was highly important to most slaves.

Field hands usually lived in crudely-built, one-room cabins with little furniture. The slave's diet was mostly hominy and fatback, with some cornmeal and saltpork. Some planters allowed their slaves to have their own gardens.

Discipline was often severe. The most common punishment was whipping. A slave's crime might be oversleeping or using a less than humble tone of voice. Masters also did their best to convince slaves that they were truly inferior beings who deserved to be slaves.

Slave Resistance

Many slaves rebelled against their masters in any way they could. One of the major slave revolts was Nat Turner's rebellion in Virginia in 1831. Turner, a black preacher, felt divinely inspired to lead his people to freedom. He and his followers killed about 60 whites before they were caught. Violence such as this was a source of great fear to southern whites. The slave codes forbade slaves to leave their plantations or to gather in large groups, so that the organization of a widespread revolt was impossible.

Slaves also rebelled in more subtle ways such as working as slowly as possible or breaking tools on purpose. Another method of revenge was setting fire to barns, houses, and crops.

Perhaps the most effective form of slave resistance was running away. Although most runaways were caught and punished, some made it to the northern states or to Canada. Ex-slaves spoke at abolitionist meetings and had a great influence on the opinions of northern whites.

Cavalier and Yankee

From the 1820's through the 1860's, the differences between northern and southern societies grew. The industrial North was symbolized by the aggressive, money-minded "Yankee." In contrast, the more agrarian South was symbolized by the old-fashioned aristocrat, the "Cavalier."

In fact, the North and the South had much in common. Both had experienced the political upheavals of the age of Jackson. Both had experienced the Second Great Awakening. Yet there were also great differences. The spirit of democracy had less impact in the South. Wealth remained more concentrated in the upper class. The economy of the South remained agricultural, with fewer than 8 percent of people in the South living in cities with populations over 4000. But the existence of slavery was the most striking difference of all.

As attacks against slavery increased, many southerners began to see it as the basis for their different—and they felt, superior—society. They saw slavery as good for both the slave and the South. John C. Calhoun argued that slavery improved the slave "so much so, that it had attained a degree of civilization never before attained by the black race in any age or country." In a speech to Congress in 1838, Calhoun spoke of the South's changing views on slavery:

> Many in the South once believed that it was a moral and political evil; that folly and delusion are gone; we see it now in its true light, and regard it as the most safe and stable basis for free institutions in the world. It is impossible with us that the conflict can take place between labor and capital, which make it so difficult to establish and maintain free institutions in all wealthy and highly civilized nations where such institutions as ours do not exist.

George Fitzhugh, in his *Sociology for the South* (1854), argued that slaves were better off than the free workers of the North because slaves did not have to compete for jobs. Fitzhugh wrote, "The slaves are all well fed, well clad, have plenty of food and are happy."

These attempts of southerners to justify slavery hardened the views of abolitionists. By the mid-1800's the slavery issue was approaching a crisis. Tension was reaching a peak that threatened to split the nation in two. These tensions were increasingly apparent in national politics.

Section Review

1. Identify the following: Middle Passage, Nat Turner, Cavalier, Yankee.
2. What influence did plantation owners have on southern society?
3. How did slavery in America differ from slavery in other societies?
4. How did blacks rebel against slavery?
5. In what ways did southern society differ from northern society?

PART FIVE: CAREFUL READING OF SECTION 7

Now read the complete section. After you finish, answer the following questions. Then look back at the section to check your answers.

A. True or False

1. ____ Cotton production increased in the antebellum period.
2. ____ The growth of the plantation system slowed down the exportation of cotton.
3. ____ During the antebellum period, the South and the North became more and more alike in attitude toward slavery.
4. ____ Although many northern whites spoke out against slavery, the slaves themselves did nothing to protest.
5. ____ Many slaves escaped from the South to reach freedom in the North or Canada.
6. ____ Slave families were always sold together as a unit.
7. ____ Slaves could not buy or sell anything.
8. ____ The slaves in antebellum America had originated in West Africa.
9. ____ Many Southerners began to think that slavery was the best economic and social arrangement for black people.
10. ____ Slaves were often punished physically and mentally.

B. Matching

Match the following adjectives with the region they describe.

Cavalier	**agrarian**	**aggressive**
Yankee	**old-fashioned**	**money-minded**
industrial	**democratic**	**antislavery**
cotton-producing		**aristocratic**

The North

_____
_____
_____
_____
_____

The South

_____
_____
_____
_____
_____

Mini-Unit 2: Research 253

STRATEGIES

DOING RESEARCH WITH PERIODICAL INDEXES (FOR ARTICLES IN MAGAZINES) AND NEWSPAPER INDEXES

To complete his research paper on "The Effects of Acid Rain on Trees and Related Industries in the United States and Canada," Don needed up-to-date information from recent magazines and journals (periodicals) and newspapers. He had to use **indexes** to periodicals and newspapers to find articles about his research topic.

PART ONE: USING PERIODICAL INDEXES (FOR MAGAZINES AND JOURNALS)

First, Don looked at the *Reader's Guide to Periodical Literature*. In this index, subject headings for topics like acid rain are arranged alphabetically. *Look at one example from the* **Reader's Guide** *below. Find the* ***fourth*** *entry under acid rain and write down the important information below.*

Readers' Guide to Periodical Literature
SEPTEMBER 10, 1983

Acetates
  Urinary phenyl acetate: a diagnostic test for depression? H. C. Sabelli and others. bibl f il *Science* 220:1187-8 Je 10 '83
Achievement *See* Success
Achievement tests *See* Educational tests and measurements
Achyla *See* Molds (Botany)
Acid precipitation (Meteorology) *See* Acid rain
Acid rain
  Acid rain, il *UN Mon Chron* 20:38-42 My '83
  Acid rain costs U.S. $5 billion annually. D. Kaufman, *Natl Parks* 57:42 Jl/Ag '83
  Acid rain report blames man-made pollution [report by the Interagency Task Force on Acid Precipitation] I. Peterson, *Ser News* 123-390 Je 18 '83
  Acid rain researchers issue joint report [report by the Interagency Task Force on Acid Precipitation] E. Marshall, *Science* 220:1359 Je 24 '83
  Catastrophe on Camels Hump, continued [Vermont tree deaths'] E. Eckholm, il *Nat Hist* 92:4 Ag '83
  How dangerous is acid rain? M. Hornblower, il map *Natl Wildl* 214-11 Je/Jl '83
  Washington wakes up to acid rain. P. Ohlendorf, il *Macleans* 96:40-1 Jl 18 '83
    Laws and regulations
  Confronting the acid test. il *Time* 122:19 Jl 11 '83

---

1. Title of article: _____
2. Author of article: _____
3. Name of periodical: _____
   (these are abbreviated; at the beginning of each volume there is an abbreviation key)
4. Volume and page numbers: _____
5. Month and year: _____

There are many other periodical indexes. Most of them are more specific because they keep track of academic and industry journals in a specific field. However, they are all organized in a way similar to the *Reader's Guide*.

PART TWO: USING NEWSPAPER INDEXES

Don also wanted to look at the *Wall Street Journal Index*, which covers the most well-known daily business newspaper in the United States. The organization of the information about the articles differs in *three ways* from the *Reader's Guide*.

1. Information about the *Journal's* articles is in the order of the newspaper articles' dates of publication (**chronological order**).

2. Articles about acid rain are found under a **different subject heading** from the one found in the *Reader's Guide*. In the *Journal*, acid rain is found under "Environmental Issues," combined with articles about other issues relating to the environment.

3. For each entry there is a **short summary** of the information in the news article. These summaries can save the researcher time by helping him or her decide more easily whether an article is related to the term paper topic.

In your groups, use a pencil and scan the entries under "Environmental Issues" from the 1986 Wall Street Journal at the top of the next page. Underline the words "acid rain" each time you see them. How many are there?

After the summary, you will find out *when* and *where* each article was published in the newspaper. For example, at the end of the first entry about acid rain:

"1/8–56.3" = *January 8th (remember the month comes before the day), page 56, column 3.*

In the same way, explain when and where the two other articles about acid rain were published.

1. 1/8–56.3   Jan. 8, p. 56, column 3.
2. _____   _____
3. _____   _____

Look at the summaries for these three articles. Which of these three might be important for Don to read for his paper? Why or why not?

1. _____
2. _____
3. _____

The Wall Street Journal Index
Environmental Issues
(*see also* **Pollution, Toxic Substances, Waste Materials, Wildlife**)

U.S. and Canadian envoys on acid rain plan to recommend to President Reagan that the U.S. spend $5 billion over five years to demonstrate cleaner ways to burn coal 1/8-56:3

Special U.S. and Canadian envoys proposed that the U.S. government and industry spend $5 billion over five years to reduce acid rain by finding cleaner technologies for burning coal—the proposal drew complaints from environmentalists. Reagan administration officials and lawmakers. 1/9-48:1

Seeds of Revolution: New perennial crops are urged as way to save U.S. farmers. Wes Jackson, others involved in 'alternative' or ecological agriculture see a reduction in pollution, erosion and bankruptcies, but it could take a century. 1/10-4:1

All Wet on Acid Rain. Editorial criticizes a report issued by a U.S.-Canadian 'acid rain' panel headed by Drew Lewis, which recommended a five-year, $5 billion program to develop new coal technologies 1/10-16:1

The Natural Resources Defense Council Inc.'s influence on U.S. environmental laws and policies has earned it a reputation as a shadow EPA. 1/13-50:1

A U.S. court judge in Anchorage issued an injunction blocking the Interior Department from offering 5.6 million acres of offshore on leases in Alaska's salmon-rich Bristol Bay: federal government planned to appeal the order Jan. 14. 1/14-64:1

Greenpeace U.S.A., an environmental activist group, turned out to be the most prolific bidder at a controversial sale of oil leases in Alaska's Bristol Bay, the group made 990 bids—one for each tract. 1/16-26:1

GenCorp Inc.'s Acropet General Corp. did agree to clean up extensive toxic contamination at a plant site in Rancho Cordova, Calif. GenCorp will reserve $45 million for the job. 1/16-12:2

Regulatory Efficiency: Editorial 'Asides' about a group of firms which just petitioned the EPA to use mobile treatment units to deal with hazardous wastes without having to get a permit for each site. 1/16-28:1

States with lax pollution standards have had a 'very slight tendency' to make gains in employment relative to environmentally tougher states in industries where pollution control is a major expense, but these same states made bigger job gains in manufacturing, suggesting other factors have been major site location drawing cards (Regions) 1/28-33:1

Jobs & Values: Editorial page article illustrating the advantage of environmental spending as a major profit-making, job-creating industry 1/29-30:1

An EPA official describes a one-in-a-million chance of death from environmental hazards as 'a micromort.' (Washington Wire) 1/31-1:5

Reagan's Budget: How Reagan fiscal '87 budget treats major programs spending plans would cut many federal services by substantial amounts; looks at some of the major proposals and how they affect government programs; includes chart. 2/6-9:1

Blackbirds and starlings have gone south in their usual multitudes this winter; by one estimate, 260 large roosts, most comprising at least a million birds, have been established in Southern states; despite attacks with noise, balloons and lethal spray, the fowl keep fouling land. 2/7-1:4

For Equity's Sake, Raise Federal Grazing Fees: Editorial-page article by Gaylord Nelson which says the federal government should raise the fees charged ranchers who graze cattle on public rangelands in the West; the ranchers now pay much less than that charged for comparable private land, causing overgrazing on public lands. 2/14-20:4

Rollins Environmental Services is being investigated by Louisiana authorities for possible tampering of emergency shutdown gear at its Baton Rouge hazardous-waste plant. 2/18-8:1

Under strong pressure from environmentalists and lawmakers, utilities are stepping up efforts to burn coal cleanly: the federal government will spend some $750 million for a clean-coal technology program 2/21-6:1

Nuclear Mess Uranium null wastes piled high in West, pose complex cleanup issues: debate is raging over who should pay burial costs and when 'ecological bombshell' is seen. 2/25-1:1

Federal Power Sale Makes Environmental Sense: Editorial page article by David Campbell supports the administration's proposed sale of the five regional federal Power Marketing Administrations 3/4-30:3

Finally, Don consulted the *New York Times Index*. This index is organized very much like the *Wall Street Journal Index*. The abbreviations for the publishing information are different, however. This index also gives you information about how long the article is. Look under "acid rain," at the eleventh entry in the third column (on pages 256 and 257 you will need to turn the book clockwise 90° in order to read the index columns from right to left):

(S), D 7, I, 69: 1 = (Short), December 7th, Section 1, Page 69, column 1.

The *New York Times Index* has many more articles on acid rain than the two other indexes. Don has to decide which of the articles will be useful to him for his topic.

- 7 -

Jay G Baris Op-Ed article contends that concern of lawyers and accountants that much-heralded tax overhaul will result in unemployment among their ranks is unfounded; says what seems to have been overlooked in all hoopla over new tax bill is that it leaves much of cumbersome tax code intact (M), S 2,I,19:1

Peat Marwick International and Klynveld Main Goerdeler announce plan to merge, move that would create world's largest accounting firm; based on combined 1986 revenues, new firm, to be known as Peat Marwick in US and Klynveld Peat Marwick Goerdeler internationally, would amount to $2.7 billion organization; analysts say that despite merger plan such tie is not likely to precipitate wave of mergers in industry (M), S 4,IV,1:6

Talking Business column, in form of interview with Arthur Young & Company chairman William L Gladstone, notes that new mergers in accounting industry are not imminent despite recent announcement by Peat Marwick and KMG; photo (M), S 9,IV,2:1

Many companies are facing difficulty in justifying an investment in advanced production technology; benefits of such technology are widely acknowledged, yet they often fail to show up when particular investment is held to yardstick of traditional financial formulas, which tend to focus on direct labor; proponents of advanced technology complain that companies are holding tomorrow's technology hostage to yesterday's financial techniques; say that result is shortcomings in management accounting systems are slowing introduction of new technology vitally needed to meet competition from abroad; photo (M), O 14,IV,1:3

American Institute of Certified Public Accountants proposes new membership criteria under which new CPA's would have to have master's degree, existing CPA's would have to return to school for one week a year and all CPA firms would have to undergo peer review (S), N 24,IV,2:3

Accuracy in Media Inc. See also
Television—Television's Vietnam: The Impact of Media (TV Program), O 1

Accuracy Corp
Combustion Engineering Inc plans to begin $147 million tender offer for Accuracy Corp (S), D 16,IV,4:6
Accuracy Corp to be acquired by Hercules Inc for $40 a share (S), D 30,IV,4:6

Accuride Corp. See also
Firestone Tire & Rubber Co, D 4

Aceh, Special Territory of (Indonesia). See also
Indonesia, Republic of, Mr 12

Acetaminophen (Drug). See also
Alcoholism, Mr 5
Aspirin, Ap 10
Pain-Relieving Drugs, F 14

Acetone. See also
Drug Traffic, Ag 7

ACF Industries Inc. See also
Carter Automotive Corp, Ja 25

Acheikh Ibn Oumar. See also
Chad, Republic of, N 20

Achenbaum, W Andrew. See also
Book Reviews—Social Security (Book), Je 15

Acheson, David C. See also
Astronautics, F 4, Je 10

Acid Rain – Cont

reducing acid rain sources, but calls for five-year $5 billion program by US to develop cleaner ways of burning coal (M), Mr 13,I,1:1

National Academy of Sciences, in report on acid rain, says that it has found conclusive evidence that burning of coal and other fossil fuels causes environmental damage (M), Mr 15,I,8:1

Canadian Prime Min Brian Mulroney says problem of acid rain will top his agenda at upcoming meeting in Washington with Pres Reagan (M), Mr 16,I,5:1

Maple sugaring season officially opens in Vermont with undercurrent of concern for industry's future; syrup producers say air pollution and acid rain are killing state's maple groves, announcement that Pres Reagan will endorse report calling for action to curb acid rain has not mollified industry; photos (S), Mr 16,I,46:4

Editorial urges Pres Reagan to accept that acid rain in Canada and northeastern US is caused by polluting power plants of Ohio River valley and to take immediate steps to reduce this pollution, Mr 16,IV,24:1

Experts from Maple Syrup Institute, Sierra Club and National Clean Air Coalition are to address National Press Club breakfast on subject of acid rain; drawing (S), Mr 17,I,16:2

Senate Environment and Public Works Committee chairman Sen Robert T Stafford and other committee members announce sweeping new legislative initiative to curb acid rain at estimated cost of $6 billion a year (M), Mr 18,I,25:3

Op-Ed column by Tom Wicker holds that Canadian Prime Min Brian Mulroney, if he takes firm enough stand in meetings in Washington with Pres Reagan, could top off series of events that have put US and Canada on verge of useful program to reduce industrial and automotive emissions that turn to acid rain, snow and fog; notes issue has become major political question in Canada and should be one in US (M), Mr 18,I,27:1

Pres Reagan formally acknowledges that acid rain is serious environmental problem that crosses border between US and Canada; Reagan, meeting with Canadian Prime Min Brian Mulroney in Washington, fully endorses joint Canadian-US report calling for curbs on airborne pollutants; report, prepared by Reagan special envoy Drew Lewis and William Davis of Canada, was made public in January and has already been endorsed by Mulroney; photo (M), Mr 20,I,1:4

Editorial welcomes Pres Reagan's acceptance of need for immediate efforts to reduce acid rain, saying it should help break Congressional impasse on acid rain control, Mr 23, IV,22:1

General Accounting Office is investigating work of Michael K Deaver, former White House deputy chief of staff, as consultant for Canadian Government on issue of acid rain; inquiry focuses on whether there was connection between Deaver's work on issue while at White House, his obtaining consulting job and his role in influencing Administration to change its position and reach agreement with Canada on acid rain (M), Ap 3,I,2:1

Nonpartisan coalition of House members plans to introduce legislation to impose strict curbs on pollution that causes acid rain; legislation would seek to resolve regional conflicts by splitting cost between areas that are heavy

---

Acid Rain – Cont

Investigators in United States Congress and Canadian Parliament join to examine lobbying activities of Michael K Deaver; joint effort involves exchange of information and suggestions of leads, witnesses and lines of questioning; Canadian investigators are focusing on propriety of Canada's hiring Deaver to seek agreement with United States on acid rain; photo (M), My 23,I,11:1

Acid rain bill that was vigorously opposed by White House is re-introduced and supported by many Congressional Republicans, reportedly out of desire to change image of Republicans as anti-environment party; drawing (M), Je 5,II,8:6

US appeals court panel has ruled that the Justice Dept may label as 'political propaganda,' three Canadian films dealing with the subjects of nuclear war and acid rain (S), Je 21,I,7:6

Bob Narus column on the environment notes that the Environmental Protection Agency has proposed stricter standards for sulfur dioxide emissions from industrial boilers, move designed to address the problem of acid rain (M), Je 29,XI,22:1

Dr Kenneth Rahn and Dr Douglas Lowenthal of University of Rhode Island, who have patented technique for analyzing acid rain, report that 'signatures' of air polluters in Middle West are on acid rain damaging lakes and forests in Northeast; say Middle West is also probably source of good share of Canada's acid rain (M), Ag 31,I, 27:1

Britain announces $900 million program to begin limited controls of sulfur emissions, which have contributed to acid rain that has damaged forests, lakes and rivers in Scandinavia (M), S 12,I,3:3

US District Court Judge Antonin Scalia, along with two other judges on three-judge panel, dismisses lawsuit by seven Northeastern states seeking to cut air pollution coming from Middle West; ruling is setback for environmentalists who have argued that pollution from Middle West comes to earth as acidic rain; Reagan Administration maintains more study is needed to determine if acid rain in Northeast and Canada is caused by Middle Western sources (M), S 19,IV,16:6

Researchers report in journal Nature that recently opened giant smelter in Nacozari, Mexico, when it reaches full capacity, will send aloft enough sulfur to raise regional total back to its 1981 high (Science Watch) (S), O 7,III,3:4

Merritt Clifton Op-Ed article on effect of acid rain on farm in Brigham, Quebec, within region that Canadians say is receiving most acid rain anywhere in North America; drawing (M), N 1,I,31:1

Patent is granted to Prof Wayne L Worrell of University of Pennsylvania and Q G Liu for device to measure two main pollutants that cause acid rain; University Patents will make invention commercially available (Patents column) (S), N 15,I,40:6

Forestry experts in Northeast say sugar maple tree is faced with extinction in Northeast unless dramatic environmental protection measures are taken; prediction follows rapid decline in tree population caused reportedly by acid rain and other pollution (S), D 7,I,69:1

New regulations being considered by EPA in effort to benefit asthmatics living near electric utility smokestacks would impose limits on concentrations of sulfur dioxide

Snips and Snipping, F 1,10,11,13, Mr 23, Ap 7,18, My 7,9, 11,12,24, Ag 1,2, O 30, D 6
Achucarro, Joaquin. See also
Music, N 24

ACI Holdings Inc
American Airlines obtains Transportation Department approval to acquire ACI Holdings, parent of AirCal Inc. through creation of voting trust (S), D 6,I.38:3
ACI International (Australian Co). See also
Binswanger Glass, S 6

Acid Rain
Drew Lewis, Pres Reagan's representative on acid rain, will report to Reagan that acid rain is causing serious economic and social problems in US and requires immediate action; concedes acid rain from US is causing damage in Canada; proposes accelerated five-year $50-billion effort to develop clean ways to burn coal (M), Ja 8, II,6:3

American and Canadian officials say Pres Reagan's special representative on acid rain, Drew Lewis, transmitted report to White House that stresses that acid rain need not be 'researched to death' before acting to reduce it; Lewis says his recommendation could be beginning of the process of joint Government-industry effort to reduce pollution that leads to acid rain; chief recommendation of report calls for five-year, $5 billion program to develop ways to burn coal more cleanly, with costs shared by Federal Government and industry; photo (M), Ja 9,II,6:1

Canada's special envoy on acid rain, William Davis, defends report on airborne pollutants, saying it is best that he could achieve for now with Reagan Administration; Canadian environmentalists have expressed disappointment with report (M), Ja 9,II,6:4

Editorial welcomes report Drew Lewis report on acid rain and urges Pres Reagan to accept his solution for solving problem, Ja 12,IV,26:1

Outdoors column discusses growing concern in Western states over acid rain (M), Ja 12,V,10:1

Op-Ed article by John B Oakes holds that recommendations of Drew Lewis, Pres Reagan's special representative on acid rain, indicate that acid rain pollution is likely to continue as usual in eastern North America (M), Ja 21,I,31:1

Editorial, noting that copper smelter at Nacozari, Mexico, will soon start emitting sulfur dioxide gases into air, deplores fact that Reagan Administration, in five years, has developed no national policy on acid rain; holds Environmental Protection Agency should deny new license to Phelps-Dodge copper smelter at Douglas, Ariz, which is exempt from Clean Air Act, F 13,I,30:1

National Coal Assn report contends that sulfur dioxide in air, source of acid rain and other pollution, is diminishing and will continue to do so despite increased use of coal by power plants; Environmental Protection Agency and environmentalists challenge projections (M), Mr 12,I,13:1

Pres Reagan is to endorse report calling for action to curb acid rain; report says acid rain is crossing border between US and Canada and causing environmental, economic and social damage; endorsement is to come when Pres Reagan meets in Washington on March 18 with Canadian Prime Min Brian Mulroney; report proposes no specific targets for

Hudson River Fishermen's Association, which has been monitoring Hudson for two decades, warns acid rain is endangering lakes within 50 miles of Manhattan and threatening lower Hudson Valley; photo (M), Ap 20,IV,6:1

Experiments at University of New Hampshire suggest acid rain may threaten Atlantic salmon by confusing their sense of smell and thus interfering with their ability to find home streams for spawning; diagram (S), Ap 22,III,3:1

General Accounting Office asks to continue investigation of Michael K Deaver, while deputy chief of staff in White House, was closely involved in meeting in March 1985 between Pres Reagan and Prime Min Brian Mulroney of Canada, in which commission to study acid rain was planned; two month later, Deaver left Government and was retained to help Canada deal with Reagan Administration on acid rain and other issues (M), Ap 24,I,18:4

White House officials say in report given to Congress that when Michael K Deaver was deputy White House chief of staff he adamantly urged that special envoy on acid rain issue be appointed, as was sought by Canada, and that two months later he left White House and signed $105,000 contract to lobby for Canada; report has been given to General Accounting Office, which is investigating possibility that Deaver violated Federal law on conflicts of interest; Deaver denies any wrongdoing (M), Ap 27,I,1:2

Environmental Protection Admr Lee M Thomas and Energy Secretary John S Herrington, testifying before House Health and Environment Subcommittee, oppose legislation to control acid rain, citing high cost in view of what they say are continuing uncertainties about causes and effects of acid rain (M), Ap 30,I,16:4

Allan E Gotlieb, Canadian Ambassador to United States, says in letter to Rep John D Dingell that unidentified Canadian official told Michael K Deaver, while Deaver was still senior White House aide but after he had announced intention to set up lobbying business, that Government of Canada could use man of his talents; although Gotlieb claims remark was 'light-hearted' and did not constitute offer, Deaver held talks with Canadians that led to $105,000 lobbying contract first two weeks after he left White House; at issue is role played by Deaver in moving United States toward agreement with Canada on acid rain before he left White House (M), My 11,I,1:5

Tall smokestacks installed at many coal-fired power stations in Middle Wes and Southwest have succeeded in bringing atmosphere around these plants withing air quality standards, but, according to many environmental groups, at cost of acid rain in Northeast and Canada; photo of 1,000-foot smokestack in Kyger Creek power plant near Gallipolis, Ohio (M), My 11,IV,5:5

General Accounting Office tells Congress that Michael Deaver apparently violated conflict-of-interest laws during and after his service as White House deputy chief of staff in moving Reagan Administration toward agreement on acid rain with Canada; agency sends findings to Justice Department for use in considering whether Deaver should be prosecuted (M), My 13,I,1:4

Joe Clark, Canadian External Affairs Minister, says Canada did not knowingly break United States laws by hiring Michael K Deaver as lobbyist in dispute over acid (S), My 15,II,17:1

Drs Robert A Perry and Dennis L Siebers at Sandia National Laboratories have discovered simple chemical method by which nitrogen oxides can be removed from engine exhaust gases, thereby reducing smog and acid rain (S), D 30,III,3:3

Acids. See also
Teeth and Dentistry, Mr 30
Acker, C Edward. See also
Airlines and Airplanes, S 30
Acker, Jack. See also
Mexico, Je 15
Acker, Kathy. See also
Book Reviews—Don Quixote (Book), N 30
Acker, Luc Van. See also
Belgium, Ja 22
Ackerley, J R. See also
Book Reviews—My Dog Tulip (Book), D 20
Ackerman, Alan R. See also
Dynalectron Corp, Ap 6
Ackerman, Diane. See also
Book Reviews—Three-Pound Universe, The (Book), Mr 23
Ackerman, Gary (Repr). See also
Afghanistan, Ja 11
New York City—Politics and Government, Mr 15
New York State—Elections—Senate (US), Jl 23
United States—Government Employees, Mr 18,19
Ackerman, Harold A (Judge). See also
Crime and Criminals, Jl 24
Teamsters, International Brotherhood of, Je 24
Ackerman, Karen. See also
Book Reviews—Flannery Row (Book), Jl 13
Ackerman, Robert S. See also
Housing, N 16
Ackerman, Thomas P. See also
Weather, D 9
Ackerman, William. See also
Music, My 4
Ackland, Valentine. See also
Book Reviews—For Sylvia (Book), Jl 13
Ackland Art Museum
Dr Charles Warren Millard 3d, chief curator at Hirshhorn Museum, will leave post to become director of Ackland Art Museum at University of North Carolina at Chapel Hill (S), Je 15,I,53:2
Ackoff, Russell L (Prof). See also
Executives and Management, Ag 31
Ackroyd, Dan. See also
Restaurants, My 28
Ackroyd, Peter. See also
Book Reviews - Hawksmoor (Book), Ja 19
Acland, Anthony (Sir) (Amb). See also
Great Britain, Ag 27, N 24
ACLU. Use Civil Liberties Union, American (ACLU)
Acme Electric Corp
Acme Electric Corp says G Wayne Hawk will assume additional post of chief executive (S), O 22,IV,2:5
Acme Inc. See also
Executives and Management, F 16
Acme Reporting Co. See also
United States, Ja 15,24, Mr 14
Acorn Stakes. See also
Horse Racing, My 25

258   STRATEGIES

PART THREE: CHOOSING RELEVANT ARTICLES

*Divide into three groups. First, discuss which key words Don should look for when he reads the summaries in the **New York Times Index**. Remember that Don's term paper topic is "The Effects of Acid Rain on Trees and Related Industries in the United States and Canada."*

1. Possible key words _____   _____   _____   _____
   _____   _____   _____   _____

2. Now use these key words while you scan the list of entries. Group 1 should scan column 1; group 2, column 2; and group 3, column 3. Choose the articles about acid rain suitable for Don's topic. Discuss which key words helped you choose.

   _____
   _____
   _____

   Share your choices with the other two groups. Add to your list in number (1) any key words that you found to be helpful.

3. Look at the sixth entry in column 3. Why is this article *not* related to Don's topic? _____

4. Look at the eleventh entry in column 3. The words "forestry" and "maple trees" are related to trees, and maple trees are also part of an important food industry in the United States and Canada. To help you become familiar with the maple syrup industry, please read the following explanation from an encyclopedia and discuss it with your classmates.

> **MAPLE SYRUP.** Maple syrup is produced from the sap or juice of North American maple trees, especially the sugar maple (*Acer saccharum*), which is native to the eastern half of the U.S.A. In late winter and early spring, between January and April, the sap starts to "run." Tapholes are drilled through the bark of the tree. Spouts are inserted in the holes and buckets are hung to collect the dripping sap, which contains up to 10% sugar. This sap is reduced to syrup by boiling and used to sweeten pancakes and in cooking. Some of the syrup is reduced further to a solid candy.

5. Look again at the eleventh entry in column 3. Read the summary in the entry for this article. As in the pre-reading exercise that you did before discussing acid rain in Chapter 6, try to decide which parts of the summary refer to the causes, effects, or possible solutions to the problem. Write down some phrases that support your answer.

Cause(s) _____

Effects _____

Solutions _____

Which of the preceding is specifically related to Don's topic?

_____

PART FOUR: SURVEYING THE ARTICLE

Don chose several articles that he thought would be related to his topic. He found the magazines and newspapers in which the articles had been published (mostly on microfilm). Before he photocopied them, he surveyed each article to make sure that his prediction was right. If he found that there was not any good information about his term paper topic, he did not photocopy it. This saved him time and money.

In your group, survey the article on the next page from the **New York Times** *about acid rain and the maple syrup industry.*

1. Read the title and subtitle. Write them down and then try to put them in your own words.

   a. TITLE: _____

   b. SUBTITLE: _____

2. Do the same with each of the subheadings. You may need to skim the section quickly if the vocabulary in the subheading is unclear.

   a. _____

   b. _____

   c. _____

3. Discuss with your group which section of this article will probably be the most useful to Don. Why?

You have just finished the process of finding an article from the library for Don's research paper. If you were Don, the next step would be to read the specific section very carefully while taking notes. You would also go back to the periodical and newspaper indexes for more articles if necessary.

Sugar Maple Faces Extinction Threat

Experts say acid rain poses grave danger to trees in Vermont and Canada

BOSTON, Dec. 6—The sugar maple tree is threatened with extinction in the Northeast unless drastic environmental protection measures are taken, according to forestry experts here.

The prediction follows a rapid decline in the tree population caused, according to environmental researchers, by acid rain and other pollution.

One forestry researcher, Archibald R.C. Jones of McGill University in Canada, said that unless industrial pollution was controlled and forests were safeguarded, "the delightful taste of maple syrup will remain but a memory."

Nelson Clark, a syrup producer from Wells, Vt., who serves as president of the Vermont Maple Sugar Makers Association, said that the decline in maple sugar production had been acute, with a 26 percent drop from 1985 to 1986 in New York, a 38 percent drop in Vermont, and well over a 50 percent drop in parts of Canada.

"There have been sugar makers up in Quebec that were just plain wiped out," he said. "We're seeing something on the scale that I've never seen in the 40 years that I've been sugaring."

32% of Trees in Decline

In Quebec, where 90 percent of Canada's maple sugar is produced, scientists began to conduct serial surveys of the groves of sugar maples in 1982. That year, 32 percent of the trees were dead or showed such signs of decline as defoliation and tapholes that failed to heal. The most recent aerial survey, carried out in the summer, covered far more territory than the first and showed that 82 percent of trees were in decline.

Environmental experts say the evidence linking the decline to acid rain is the most recent documentation of the pollutant's effect on plant and animal life. Acid rain, the product of sulfur dioxide emissions from Middle Western plants and factories that have been swept north and east by prevailing winds, has come under wide scrutiny since it was first pinned to damage in aquatic systems. Bert Hague, an acid rain expert with the Environmental Protection Agency, predicted that the continued deterioration of forestry and fishing operations would prompt governments to adopt comprehensive protective measures.

"Once the forest influence has been nailed down solidly, I think the nation will take more action on control systems," he said. "A miniscule decline in the rate of growth will affect a lot of people in a lot of industries."

Legislation Blocked

Researchers say that the only way to slow the decline of trees and waterways would be to legislate strict environmental limits on the amount of emissions a factory is allowed and require industries to install cleaning equipment in their smokestacks. All recent efforts on the part of Northeast legislators to impose such standards have failed because of strong opposition from the coal-producing states that generate the emissions and the Reagan Administration, which has consistently questioned the link between the emissions and environmental damage.

David Marvin, a syrup producer from Fairfield, Vt., who traveled to Washington last spring to lobby for clean air legislation, said that sugar makers were feeling increasingly bitter about the issue as their livelihood was threatened. "While all the debate rages on about what to do, nothing is being done," he said. "If the circumstantial evidence were as strong for a human health issue as it is for the problems faced by the forest, then we would have stopped the air pollution long since."

Fears of a mass sugar maple extinction surfaced last month at an international maple syrup producer's conference in Rutland, Vt. Botanists from Vermont and Canada presented environmental evidence to support their dire forecasts and sugar makers confirmed their findings with reports of extensive deaths and serious production losses.

Outlook is Very Gloomy

According to Mr. Jones, a professor of woodland resources at McGill University, pollution-related diseases have caused 15 percent of Quebec's tapholes to dry up since 1982, accounting for an $87.6 million loss to the maple sugar industry last year alone. On top of that, Mr. Jones cited a 35 percent reduction in the growth rate of all sugar maples, and said that all figures seemed to point to a decline that could end in extinction.

The average decline in the United States is reflected in the losses at Acorn Sugar House in Almstead, Vt., which taps New England's largest sugar grove. Typically, Bascom Hill produces 12,000 of the state's 100,000 gallons from its 35,000 trees. This year, it tapped more trees than ever, but produced only 7,800 gallons of syrup.

Forestry experts say that acid rain weakens the leaves' waxy protective layers that help them fight disease and hurts root systems by leaching sugars and amino acids, nutrients that trees require for growth, out of the soil.

Hubert Vogelman, a professor of botany at the University of Vermont who has researched the problem extensively, said that the leaves at the top of the trees are the first to die because they are youngest and most vulnerable.

"Ten years ago," he said, "you would look up in the forest and couldn't see any sky. Now, you look up at the forest crown and all you see is blue sky everywhere and dead trees. They're dropping like flies."

VOCABULARY INDEX

A

abroad, 69
accelerate, 235, 237
accidents, 192
admitted, 74
advantage, 38, 41
advice, 46, 52, 98
aggressive, 252
agrarian, 252
agreed, 74
amazed, 74
and also, 72
announced, 171
announcement, 52
antislavery, 252
appointment, 49
approached, 125, 172
appropriate, 206, 207
are supposed to, 52
aristocratic, 252
arrested, 227
assignment, 52, 54
assorted, 159
average, 237
avoid, 38, 237
awful, 171

B

balance, 31
bank teller, 27

bargain, 148
basic, 52
big, 12
bill, 38
booth, 213
border, 226
borrow, 38
bought, 151
boy, 80
brakes, 235, 237
browse, 147, 151
building, 10
burglaries, 197

C

cab, 267
campus, 10
can afford, 168
canceled, 134
canoe, 126
capsule, 94, 95, 98
careful, 192, 193
cash, 28, 32
cash register, 213
casserole, 69
catch, 171
Cavalier, 252
century, 134
challenge, 52
chance, 128
change, 168, 172

check (noun), 28, 207
check (verb), 27
checked, 98, 100
checking account, 28
cheerfully, 74
chill, 126, 130
chilly, 122, 130
choice, 151
chose, 153
class, 48
clear, 128
clear up, 100
clinic, 94, 95
clouds, 126
cloudy, 128, 130
cold, 98
collect, 31, 32, 36
collection, 197
College of Liberal Arts, 45
come down, 98
company, 157
complain, 175
compliment, 69
concluded, 52
conditions, 134
confessed, 72
consumer, 39, 157
convenience, 39
convenient, 213
cops, 226
copy, 185
correctly, 52, 54
cost, 12, 151, 177
cost-saving suggestion, 230
cotton-producing, 252
course, 48
court, 189
crimes, 196, 197
crowded, 151, 153

D

daily, 54
damp, 122, 126
data, 157
decided, 52

decrease, 235
degrees, 128
delay, 31, 32
democratic, 252
department store, 39
depends, 52
deposited, 31, 36
deposit slip, 29, 31, 32
different, 177
differs, 177
disadvantage, 38, 41
discount, 147
double room, 5, 18
downstairs, 6
dress up, 206, 207, 212
drugstore, 151
drunk, 227

E

eager, 191
easy, 52
eight-cylinder engine, 227
elect, 174
elected, 177
embarrassed, 79
emergencies, 41, 193
endorse, 29, 31, 36
errands, 147
examine, 171
exceeding, 102
exhausted, 213
expands, 237
expect, 188
expense, 237
extremely hungry, 72

F

fact, 155
familiar, 171
fare, 173
favorite, 191
fee, 191
fever, 98
filled out, 36

fine, 189
flock, 125
floor, 6
forecast, 128
forecaster, 130
for sale, 152
four-cylinder engine, 229
four-year colleges, 45
fraternity, 15
freshman, 4, 5, 52
fuel, 175
full, 197
full of people, 151

G

gas mileage, 229
gate, 171
get a ride, 222
get ready, 123
going out with, 72
got there, 171
grinned, 212
ground, 125

H

habit, 215
head resident, 18
high, 52, 128
high school, 52
hires, 193
housing, 3
humanities, 45
hurriedly, 153

I

identification, 32
important, 54
impossible, 52, 54
in advance, 134
income, 156
increase, 175, 235

industrial, 252
inflate, 237
inflation, 41
infraction, 191
ingredients, 215, 216
instructions, 32
instructors, 47
insurance, 227
intended, 72
in that case, 47
in the high 50s, 128
in the low 50s, 128
in time, 73
intoxicated, 226
island, 125

J

judge, 189

K

key, 184, 185
kit, 31

L

lab, 52
late, 73
leisurely, 212
liberal arts education, 45
license, 224
lightning, 125
line, 171
loan, 39
lock, 184
lose, 184
loud, 12

M

maintenance, 237
major, 45

make a profit, 156
mall, 147, 151, 153
marked down, 151
match, 156
medicine, 100
metropolitan area, 234
miles per gallon, 229
missed, 49
moderately, 153
money-minded, 252
move in, 5
much, 12
murder, 196
my place, 178

N

nasal, 102
neighboring, 197
nervous, 167, 172
normal, 98, 100
notes, 54
noticed, 10
nutritious, 213

O

offense, 189
office hours, 49
oh my goodness, 79
old-fashioned, 252
once in a while, 48
on sale, 152
on the other hand, 193
on time, 67
opinion, 155
order form, 32
overcast, 128
owe, 39

P

pack, 123
package, 108
packing, 229, 230

parking, 197
pass, 56
passenger, 173, 174
perfect, 54
personalized checks, 29, 32
pharmacy, 154
picnic, 126
pill, 151
poison, 102
police, 184
political, 177
politician, 174, 177
possibility, 128
potluck dinner, 68
precipitation, 128
predict, 134
prepared, 54, 72
prescribe, 94, 95
prescription, 100
prevent, 237
price, 151
private, 173, 174, 189
product, 157
prohibit, 191
property, 196
provides, 72
public, 173, 174
purchase, 151, 153
purse, 168

Q

question, 172
questionnaires, 157

R

R.A., 18
rain, 128
raindrops, 125
rape, 196
reach for, 123
receipt, 28
recipe, 215, 216
reckless drivers, 223
reduced, 151, 152, 153

reelected, 177
refund, 153
registered, 197
registration, 227
reluctantly, 74
reminded, 226
renew, 227
rent, 125
repeat, 52, 54
report, 128
require attendance, 48
research, 60
research paper, 60
reservations, 212
residence, 18
residence hall, 18
resident, 18
resident aide (R.A.), 18
residential, 18
return, 191
returned, 151
ride, 171, 172
right, 52
robberies, 197
roommates, 5
run, 191
rural area, 234

S

save, 39
schedule, 237
sciences, 45
seal, 108, 109
selection, 151, 153
semester, 31
shining, 126
shop, 151
shopping center, 151
shore, 125, 130
signaled, 212
signature card, 29, 32
single room, 18
situation, 52
six-cylinder engine, 229
skip, 48
slow down, 235

snack, 159
snowstorm, 130
social sciences, 45
soft drinks, 158
sophomore, 27
sore throat, 98, 100
sorority, 16
special, 159
speed limit, 223
speed up, 235
spending money, 36
starving, 74
sticker, 197
stolen, 197
store, 151
strange, 191
studied, 52
subways, 173, 174
suddenly, 126
sunny, 128
sunshine, 130
surprised, 74
suspect, 188
swollen, 94, 95, 100
symptoms, 94, 95, 100

T

tablet, 151
take trips, 228
tamper, 108
taxes, 175
teach someone a lesson, 223
terminal, 167
term paper, 60
theft, 196, 197
think, 54
thunder, 122, 126
ticket, 189
token, 178
took back, 151
transfer, 178
transportation, 173, 177
treating, 206
triple room, 18
tuition, 31
turned over, 125
typewriter, 185

U

unfortunately, 74, 130
uniform, 213
upper, 128
used to, 11

V

valuable, 197
vandalism, 196
violation, 197
violent, 193, 196, 197

W

walked, 172
wallet, 185
warning, 226, 227
was looking around, 151
wholeheartedly, 74
withdraw, 31, 32, 36
worried, 6

Y

yankee, 252

SUBJECT INDEX

A

Adjectives, 15
Adverbs, 15

C

Chapter outline, 111–115
Chapter titles, 40
Charts, 239, 247
Chronological order, 254
Comprehension questions
   on driving, 226, 231–232, 234, 236–237
   on health, 97, 105, 107, 110, 113
   on housing, 8, 11–12, 13–14, 21
   on money, 30, 34, 36, 41
   on the police, 187–188, 190–191, 194–195, 200–201
   on public transportation, 170, 176, 179
   on restaurants, 209, 214, 216–217
   on shopping, 150, 158
   on studying, 51, 57, 59, 63
   after surveying, 247
   on time, 71, 80, 82, 86
   on the weather, 124–125, 129, 132, 135
Context, 4
Credit cards, 38

D

Different subject heading, 254
Discussion questions, 210–211

E

Editorial Research Reports, 137–140

F

Fact and opinion, vii, 155, 195, 211
Fill-in exercises
   on health, 125–126, 130
   on housing, 31, 36–37
   on money, 52–53, 72
   on restaurants, 226–227, 235–236
   on shopping, 171
   on time, 98
   on transportation, 179, 191–192, 196
   on the weather, 151
First paragraph, 239

G

Graphs, 239, 247

H

Homonym exercise, 99
Homonyms, 98–99
Housing, 3
Housing chart, 20
Housing office, 19

I

Implications, vii, 71–72
Indexes, 253
Introduction, 239
Introductory paragraph, 112

K

Key words, 76, 240, 247

L

Library research, 60–62

M

Main idea, vii, 105–106
Main idea exercise, 106–107

N

Newspaper indexes, 254–257
New York Times Index, 255, 258, 259
Nouns, 14

O

Official academic calendar, 84
Opinion, 155
Organization, 106

P

Paragraph, 8
Periodical indexes, 253–254
Photographs, 239, 247
Prefixes, 54, 74, 104
Pre-reading exercises
   on driving, 221–222
   on health, 93–94, 111–113, 115–117
   on housing, 18
   on money, 25–26, 38
   on the police, 183
   on restaurants, 205–206
   on shopping, 145–146
   on studying, 45–47, 60
   and surveying, 240
   on time, 67–68, 84–85, 86
   on transportation, 165–166
   on the weather, 121–122, 136
Public transportation, 165

Q

Questions words, 76

R

Reader's Guide to Periodical Literature, 253
Reading a chart, 115–117
Reading a course outline, 86
Research, 60–62
   choosing relevant articles, 258–259
   preliminary steps in, 136–137
   surveying the article, 259–260
   using newspaper indexes, 254–257
   using periodical indexes, 253–254
Research Paper Assistance Program (RAP), 62

S

Scanning, vii, 76, 81, 87–88, 224
Scanning exercise, 78–79, 129, 160, 171, 210, 214–215, 232
Section headings, 239
Short summary, 254
Skimming, vii, 106
Skimming and scanning exercise, 132–133, 148, 199
Stressful situations, 111
Studying, 45
Subheadings, 239
Suffixes, 32–33, 54, 100, 126, 172
Summary, 239
Surveying, 239–252
  a chapter section, 249–251
  the whole chapter, 241–246
Synonyms, 12, 128, 151

T

Table of contents, 39, 239
Time, 67
Title, 112
Title page, 140
Topic, 106

V

Verbs, 15
Vocabulary checklist, 157, 213

Vocabulary in context
  on driving, 222–224, 228–230, 234–235
  on health, 94–95, 102, 108–109
  on housing, 4–6, 10–11, 15–16
  on money, 27, 41
  on the police, 184–185, 188–189, 192–193, 195–196
  on public transportation, 167–168, 173–175, 178
  restaurants, 206–207, 215–216
  on shopping, 147–148, 156, 158–159
  on studying, 47–49, 56
  and surveying, 239
  on time, 68–69, 79–80
  on the weather, 122–123, 134

W

Wall Street Journal Index, 254
Weather, 121
Weekly class schedule, 83–84
What question, 77
When question, 76
Where question, 76
Whole chapter, 239
Who question, 77
Word association, 53, 73, 152
Word form chart, 32–33, 54, 74, 100, 126, 153, 172, 177, 197, 212, 227, 237–238
Word form exercise, 33, 55, 75, 101, 127, 154, 172, 177, 198, 212, 227
Word forms, 14–15